FILMMAKERS SERIES

edited by
ANTHONY SLIDE

1. *James Whale,* by James Curtis. 1982
2. *Cinema Stylists,* by John Belton. 1983
3. *Harry Langdon,* by William Schelly. 1982
4. *William A. Wellman,* by Frank Thompson. 1983
5. *Stanley Donen,* by Joseph Casper. 1983
6. *Brian DePalma,* by Michael Bliss. 1983
7. *J. Stuart Blackton,* by Marian Blackton Trimble. 1985
8. *Martin Scorsese and Michael Cimino,* by Michael Bliss. 1985
9. *Franklin J. Schaffner,* by Erwin Kim. 1985
10. *D. W. Griffith at Biograph,* by Cooper C. Graham et al. 1985
11. *Some Day We'll Laugh: An Autobiography,* by Esther Ralston. 1985
12. *The Memoirs of Alice Guy Blaché,* trans. by Roberta and Simone Blaché. 1986
13. *Leni Riefenstahl and Olympia,* by Cooper C. Graham. 1986
14. *Robert Florey,* by Brian Taves. 1987
15. *Henry King's America,* by Walter Coppedge. 1986
16. *Aldous Huxley and Film,* by Virginia M. Clark. 1987
17. *Five American Cinematographers,* by Scott Eyman. 1987
18. *Cinematographers on the Art and Craft of Cinematography,* by Anna Kate Sterling. 1987
19. *Stars of the Silents,* by Edward Wagenknecht. 1987
20. *Twentieth Century-Fox,* by Aubrey Solomon. 1988
21. *Highlights and Shadows: The Memoirs of a Hollywood Cameraman,* by Charles G. Clarke. 1989
22. *I Went That-a-Way: The Memoirs of a Western Film Director,* by Harry L. Fraser; edited by Wheeler Winston Dixon and Audrey Brown Fraser. 1990
23. *Order in the Universe: The Films of John Carpenter,* by Robert C. Cumbow. 1990
24. *The Films of Freddie Francis,* by Wheeler Winston Dixon. 1991
25. *Hollywood Be Thy Name,* by William Bakewell. 1991
26. *The Charm of Evil: The Life and Films of Terence Fisher,* by Wheeler Winston Dixon. 1991
27. *Lionheart in Hollywood: The Autobiography of Henry Wilcoxon,* with Katherine Orrison. 1991
28. *William Desmond Taylor: A Dossier,* by Bruce Long. 1991
29. *The Films of Leni Riefenstahl,* 2nd ed., by David B. Hinton. 1991
30. *Hollywood Holyland: The Filming and Scoring of "The Greatest Story Ever Told,"* by Ken Darby. 1992
31. *The Films of Reginald LeBorg: Interviews, Essays, and Filmography,* by Wheeler Winston Dixon. 1992
32. *Memoirs of a Professional Cad,* by George Sanders, with Tony Thomas. 1992
33. *The Holocaust in French Film,* by André Pierre Colombat. 1993
34. *Robert Goldstein and "The Spirit of '76,"* edited and compiled by Anthony Slide, 1993

35. *Those Were the Days, My Friend: My Life in Hollywood with David O. Selznick and Others,* by Paul Macnamara. 1993
36. *The Creative Producer,* by David Lewis; edited by James Curtis. 1993
37. *Reinventing Reality: The Art and Life of Rouben Mamoulian,* by Mark Spergel. 1993
38. *Malcolm St. Clair: His Films, 1915–1948,* by Ruth Anne Dwyer. 1995
39. *Beyond Hollywood's Grasp: American Filmmakers Abroad, 1914–1945,* by Harry Waldman. 1994
40. *A Steady Digression to a Fixed Point,* by Rose Hobart. 1994
41. *Radical Juxtaposition: The Films of Yvonne Rainer,* by Shelley Green. 1994
42. *Company of Heroes: My Life as an Actor in the John Ford Stock Company,* by Harry Carey, Jr. 1994
43. *Strangers in Hollywood: A History of Scandinavian Actors in American Films from 1910 to World War II,* by Hans J. Wollstein. 1994
44. Charlie Chaplin: Intimate Close-Ups, by Georgia Hale, edited with an introduction and notes by Heather Kiernan. 1995
45. *Music from the House of Hammer: Music in the Hammer Horror Films, 1950–1980,* by Randall D. Larson. 1995
46. *The Word Made Flesh: Catholicism and Conflict in the Films of Martin Scorsese,* by Michael Bliss. 1995

Charlie Chaplin

Intimate Close-Ups

Georgia Hale
Edited with an Introduction and Notes by
Heather Kiernan

The Scarecrow Press, Inc.
Lanham, Maryland, and London
1999

SCARECROW PRESS, INC.

Published in the United States of America
by Scarecrow Press, Inc.
4720 Boston Way, Lanham, Maryland 20706
http://www.scarecrowpress.com

4 Pleydell Gardens, Folkestone
Kent CT20 2DN, England

British Library Cataloguing in Publication Information Available
Library of Congress Cataloging-in-Publication Data
Hale, Georgia, d. 1985
Charlie Chaplin : intimate close-ups. / by Georgia Hale; edited with an introduction and notes by Heather Kiernan.
p. cm.
Filmography: p.
Includes bibliographical references and index.
ISBN 1-57886-004-0 (pbk : alk. paper)
1. Hale, Georgia, d. 1985. 2. Motion picture actors and actresses—United States—Biography. 3. Chaplin, Charlie, 1889-1977.
I. Kiernan, Heather. II. Title.
PN2287.H174A3 1995
791.43'028'092—dc20
[B] 95-5002
CIP

The paper used in this publication meets the minimum requirements of American National Standard for Information Sciences—Permanence of Paper for Printed Library Materials, ANSI/NISO Z39.48–1992.
Manufactured in the United States of America.

For Papa and Mama Bessler
and in memory of
Ivor and Hell
with love

Contents

Editor's Introduction

What is not original is of no importance, and what is original is bound to be fraught with the weakness of the individual.

GOETHE

In 1925 when Charlie Chaplin's *Gold Rush*, in his own estimation the finest of all his films, was released, it made an immediate Hollywood star out of a pretty young actress named Georgia Hale. Sixty years later, in the year she died, Georgia was still receiving a trickle of fan mail from admirers round the world, who remembered the performance that earned her a permanent place in film history. Georgia's appearance in *The Gold Rush* was her first major role, and although she continued to act in films until 1931, she would never again have a triumph of the kind she had initially enjoyed. In many ways her experience in Hollywood was typical of that of many young women attracted to the glamour of the silent film world, and then faced with premature oblivion.

The story of how Georgia Hale, the dress extra of Poverty Row, became for a while the leading lady to Charles Chaplin, is a classic example of the American success myth, though in her case success did not last for long. As Daniel Boorstin has written, "the film star legend of the accidentally discovered soda-fountain girl who was quickly elevated to stardom soon took its place alongside the log-cabin-to-White-House legend as a leitmotif of American democratic folk-lore."[1]

It is impossible to write about Georgia except as someone who believed that her fate, desires, aspirations were linked to Charles Chaplin. That she was profoundly affected by her love for him will be obvious to anyone who reads this memoir. Through periods of close and intimate friendship, her devotion to him, next to that of Edna Purviance, was until his marriage to Oona O'Neill the sincerest in Chaplin's experience. Through that fragmented, shifting, and often lonely life, Georgia's attachment persisted unchanged. In spite of waverings and withdrawals, Chaplin for his part seems to have felt a genuine affection for her. Like Edna Purviance, Georgia never married, clinging instead to a belief that there could never be anyone for her but him. "He asked if I had married?" she wrote in a letter after Chaplin's return to Hollywood in 1972, "and I told him, no . . . because everyone else seemed so impossible after knowing him."[2]

After some bitter disappointment both with her career and with the romance, she turned eventually to Christian Science, which comforted her in her middle and later years. In the calm of those years she worked out for herself an explanation that left the object of her infatuation, "Charlie," essentially undisturbed, and put the responsibility for the cruel disappointment on "Mr. Chaplin," a very different person. Charlie, sweet, charming, and innocent, she had loved from adolescence; a love that endured. His opposite, Mr. Chaplin, the cold, self-absorbed, producer-actor-director and socialite, was the source of much pain, as her story makes clear. If Charles Chaplin carried within him many contradictions, was tender-hearted, cruel, sensitive, child-like, a poseur, all of these qualities were parts of his creative spirit.

1 *The Image* (New York: Vintage Books, 1992), pp.156-57.

2 GH (Georgia Hale) to IM (Ivor Montagu), Los Angeles, May 1972: MP (Montagu Papers).

Georgia wrote two versions of *Intimate Close-Ups*. The second, the one that appears here, is considerably longer, denser, and more complex; it lacks the single-threadedness of the first version. Perhaps she looked at her first effort and cast it aside as too one-dimensional a picture of Chaplin. Both were written during the 1960s, long after the events they describe. Both failed to find a publisher. "I've written down all the little incidents I knew with him but it isn't commercial. They want the lurid."[3]

Much has been written about Charles Chaplin. His life has been analysed, annotated, and probed by his biographers, but it is remarkable that so little of this has been by those closest to him. As a source of intimate knowledge relating to Chaplin, Georgia occupies an almost unique place. For apart from Lita Grey's account, *My Life with Chaplin* (see p. 46, fn. 1), and that of May Reeves, *Charles Chaplin Intime* (see p. 152, fn. 1), not one of the women who found a place in Chaplin's life chose to write about her relationship with him. Some may wish to challenge some of Georgia's assertions. Many writers have deemed it necessary to mix fiction with fact in any memorable testimony, very often inventing life rather than recapturing it. Then the question of what happened and how people thought and felt remains open. Apart from the impossibility of seeing into people's hearts and heads, time darkens some things and reveals others. Chaplin as he appeared to the people who knew him was different for each of them.

Looking back into childhood is like turning a telescope the wrong way round. Everything appears in miniature, but with a clarity it probably does not deserve; moreover, it often becomes concentrated and stylised. Happiness and sorrow, love and friendship, hostility, must all find a place somewhere. Some memories are preserved, while others are sealed off behind a curtain.

3 GH to IM, Los Angeles, 1966: MP.

Georgia Theodora was born on June 25, 1900, at St. Joseph, Missouri, the youngest daughter of George Washington Hale and his wife Laura Imbrie. There has been much confusion about the date of her birth, chiefly because she herself gave different dates. Georgia kept among her papers a copy of a birth certificate with the date 1909. In the late 1920s Paramount gave the date as 1904, and Chaplin's biographer David Robinson has given it as 1906. While the 25th of June is the date she consistently gave as her birthday, Georgia's school record makes it clear that the year was 1900.

The Hale family moved in late 1902 or early 1903 to Englewood, Illinois, a then middle-class suburb of Chicago. Following her two older sisters, Eugenia and Helen, Georgia attended the Beale Elementary School, entering in 1906. The early chapters of her memoir depict a family full of the usual jealousies and sibling rivalries; it was, by her account, not a happy or loving one. There is a likeness between some words of Chaplin's about his childhood—"I was aware of the social stigma of our poverty . . ."—and Georgia's "ashamed and dismayed" by the poverty of her surroundings. In her case however, this seems to have made her from a very early age, sensitive to the injustices of the world: "my urgent need for the answer to the tragedies I saw around me was not silenced." Though a "poetic soul," her hard-worked mother was of little help as a counsellor. Still less was her unsympathetic father, whose frequent absences—another resemblance to Chaplin's experience—made him seem more like a boarder. The answer did not come through Nature or religion as Georgia hoped, but "that blessed day" when she first saw Charlie Chaplin.

The Tramp's philosophy, or personality, must have appealed to many individuals like Georgia. Chaplin, as one who had escaped from the slums of Victorian London, was well suited to carry a message across the ocean—that life, however wretched, is always worth living; the same lesson of faith in life so prominent in *Limelight*. With the Tramp as a kind of Redeemer figure, this revelation came to her with something like an Evangelical fervour of conversion, for she was transformed from a sad and despondent young woman into one "changing for the better . . . changing within."

Known affectionately to her family as "Dixie," Georgia entered Englewood High School in 1914. The school yearbook states that she "assisted on a great many school occasions with her singing and expects to go on with her music after leaving school." Following graduation in June 1918, Georgia attended one of Chicago's musical colleges, but it is uncertain whether she completed the course of study. Her only known professional theatrical engagement at this time was at the Chicago Winter Follies during the autumn of 1920, and for some reason, she seems to have appeared under the name of Olive West.

Between the Winter Follies and a beauty contest in 1922 nothing is known of her life. Like much else in Georgia's memoir, her account of the contest is reliable, if a little vague. A scrapbook of newspaper clippings she proudly compiled of the event survives.[4] Chosen from twenty contestants as Queen of the Pageant in August 1922, she was "crowned" by U.S. Post Master General Hubert Work. Jack Dempsey, who had arrived in Chicago to train for his next fight with Bill Brennan, paid the occasion the honour of appearing. After receiving the double honour of being chosen "Miss Chicago" and then "Miss America Pageant Queen of the United States," Georgia stepped into another beauty competition in Atlantic City. Following the lead of the *Chicago Evening American* in establishing an annual Pageant of Progress, Atlantic City inaugurated its own national beauty contest in September 1922. Unsuccessful in her attempt to capture another title, Georgia went to New York.

Contrary to what has been supposed, Georgia's film career did not begin in Hollywood, but in New York. Along with prize money totalling $2,500, she had been offered two movie contracts. Travelling there in the autumn of 1922, she was,

[4] The scrapbook, along with Georgia's personal papers, letters, photographs and so on, are now in the possession of the editor.

according to a newspaper clipping, employed in upwards of ten pictures.[5] Only one however has been identified, *Enemies of Women.* A story of a modern Babylon, the lavish production, directed by Alan Crosland, featured the Broadway veteran Lionel Barrymore as a libertine Russian prince. She was recalled to Chicago by the illness of her mother in April 1923. Deciding against returning to New York, Georgia left the following month for the West coast, and arrived in Los Angeles on May 19, 1923.

Soon after her arrival she was again competing in a beauty contest. Goldwyn studios, together with Hearst's *Los Angeles Examiner*, announced a Motion Picture Exposition to be held in July. Among the committee of judges asked to select the most beautiful blonde and brunette in Southern California were two Goldwyn stars, Claire Windsor and Mae Busch, the author and director Rupert Hughes, and the British novelist Elinor Glyn, one of whose own stories was to be filmed. Supervising the screen tests was the actor Frank Mayo.[6] Georgia, who according to the *L.A. Examiner* had "a striking resemblance to Helene Chadwick, the Goldwyn beauty," and one Lillian Collier, were awarded contracts, each for four weeks, to appear respectively in Rupert Hughes' *Law Against Law*, and what became the hugely successful *Three Weeks.*

"I've been watching Rupert Hughes' productions for a long time," Georgia told the *Examiner*, "and it seems a peculiar twist of fate that this man's pictures that I have always liked so much should now prove a vehicle in which I will make a bow myself."[7] Though production did not begin for several months, Hughes' film was completed and released in December 1923, under its new title, *Reno.* Curiously, it featured Helene Chadwick.

5 *The Chicago Herald and Examiner*, 25 March 1923.

6 Frank Mayo (b. New York 1896) signed a long term contract with the Goldwyn Picture Corporation, but by 1929 he had ceased to be a leading man.

7 *Los Angeles Examiner*, 23 July 1923.

Over the next few months, Georgia found work as one of the "splash me" bathing beauties in pictures like *The Temple of Venus* and *The Goof*.[8] Following the success of Mack Sennett and Al Christie, producers during the early 1920s resumed making clean comedies, which reopened a great opportunity for screen-struck girls to get into movies. Many stars of the silent era, like Gloria Swanson, Phyllis Haver, Bebe Daniels and Betty Compson disported themselves before the camera like daughters of Neptune, on their way to becoming featured players. "For if you are sufficiently pleasing to the eye to land a berth of this kind in a comedy company, your success is assured."[9]

Georgia's recollections of how she came to star in Josef von Sternberg's *The Salvation Hunters* have charm, and in many of their details are consistent with Sternberg's own, though sometimes rather caustic account.[10] They met in the autumn of 1923 when both were working, he as assistant director, she as an extra, on the film *By Divine Right*. A few months later, they worked together again on another that neither refers to: *Vanity's Price*, a Film Booking Office production, with a screenplay by Paul Bern. Georgia was given a part in the chorus, but an unlucky accident to her ankle prevented her from taking it up.

In his memoirs Sternberg said that when he first noticed "this Galatea" she was reading "a book of mine, a translation of a Viennese novel, and the page she was perusing was splashed with a mascara tear."[11] Skeptical readers of this story will feel doubtful about it. Their skepticism may be too cynical; but it

8 This film was released in June 1924 as *A Self-Made Failure*. Georgia was among the beauties known as Spike Malone's diving-girls; the role of Spike was played by "Chuck" Reisner. An actor in three of Chaplin's films made for First National, Reisner was an assistant-director of *The Gold Rush*.

9 *Los Angeles Sunday Times*, 26 August 1923, p. 37.

10 *Fun in a Chinese Laundry* (New York: Macmillan, 1965).

11 Josef von Sternberg, *op. cit.*, p. 153.

is quite easy to suppose that he thought of Georgia when planning his own first film, *The Salvation Hunters*, simply because they had already worked together. She displayed what Sternberg described as a "sullen charm." But no matter what the story, Georgia owed much to *The Salvation Hunters*, as did Sternberg. United Artists agreed to distribute the film, and this provided each of them with a crucial opportunity to advance their careers. For Georgia it meant that rescue had come a second time from her "miracle man," Charles Chaplin.

When *The Salvation Hunters* was completed in November 1924, Chaplin was ten months into production on his epic film, *The Gold Rush*. That month he married Lita Grey, and when it became clear that her pregnancy would keep her from continuing in the role of the dance-hall girl, Chaplin sought a new leading lady. Before Christmas, and after a screen test of Georgia had been completed, it was announced that the heroine would be portrayed by her. Georgia was twenty-four, and compared with many other featured actresses of the time was, by Hollywood standards, almost middle-aged.

Many of the earlier sequences had already been shot, and the appearance of the dance-hall girl in the second half of the film made it easier for Chaplin to re-work the story. It is not certain how the character of the dance-hall girl was originally to have evolved. She is one of Chaplin's few demimondaine heroines—clearly a significant departure from his usual on-screen partnership with a leading lady. Gone are the playful teasing and flirting so characteristic of the love scenes with Edna Purviance. *The Gold Rush* was his first major attempt at portraying a romance between the Tramp and a heroine, a love on his side at first unrequited, but in the end fulfilled. Unrequited love reappears in *The Circus* and *City Lights*, but there ends in disappointment. While Georgia tells us little that is altogether new about the making of *The Gold Rush*, or about Chaplin's directorial methods, she does provide some corroborative detail. His passion for perfection, often requiring numerous retakes, his days absent from the set, are all consistent with what others have told us.

After a colourful and elaborate prologue entitled "Charlie Chaplin's Dream," *The Gold Rush* had its world premiere in Hollywood at Grauman's Egyptian Theatre on June 26, 1925. As part of the publicity campaign, Chaplin and Sid Grauman, in co-operation with the *Los Angeles Examiner*, scheduled a "gold rush" for Sunday, September 27. Chaplin, who had left Los Angeles for New York in July, sent Georgia a wire delegating her to plant the treasure in the sands along Santa Monica. In addition to money, each bag was to contain a pass for that night's showing of *The Gold Rush*. "Fortified with the latest tips furnished daily on the screen at the theater [Grauman's Egyptian] and from the columns of the *Examiner*," thousands of "prospectors" planned visits to the beach in order "to size up the situation as to the possible locations where the $500 in twenty small bags will be planted."[12]

Chaplin began preparations for *The Circus* in the autumn of 1925, and had considered employing Georgia again, as her name in his original outline indicates. The contract that she had signed with him the year before ended on the last day of December 1925. The reason for its not being renewed is unknown. Perhaps it was at the urging of Lita Grey, who wanted Chaplin to cast her childhood friend, Merna Kennedy, in the role of the equestrienne. Whatever the reason, Georgia signed instead a contract with Famous Players-Lasky. From 1926 until *The Circus* was released in January 1928, she appeared in eight films.

One film Georgia appeared in during this time, *The Last Moment*, is worth mentioning if only because of the curious parallels between it and her earlier film, *The Salvation Hunters*. Both were experimental in their technique, and featured the same star actor, Otto Matiesen, and both were made on a modest budget of $5,000. Each was highly acclaimed by the

[12] *Los Angeles Examiner*, 17 September 1925.

Hollywood intelligentsia; and in each case Chaplin's warm interest helped their success.

Shortly after Chaplin's divorce from Lita Grey in August 1928, Georgia became his constant companion. He had been working for more than a year on *City Lights* when he decided that Virginia Cherrill was unsuitable for the role of the blind girl. Naturally perhaps, Georgia was considered for the part. She was tested, and put on the payroll on November 11, 1929. Georgia's screen-test survives, and shows that she would have made a splendid blind girl. Chaplin, however, decided against her. This seems hard to explain, and Georgia leaves the reason in doubt. The only other witness is Chaplin's publicist Carlyle Robinson, whose statement that his own unfavourable opinion of Georgia was what influenced Chaplin has perhaps been too uncritically accepted. She was removed from the payroll at the end of November. Georgia's account of why Chaplin decided to drop her, and of his cruel and inflexible behaviour, is one of the most painful and revealing stories in her memoir. Surprisingly, they continued to be inseparable until his departure for Europe in 1931; but Georgia would cite this bitter disappointment, among other matters, in her attempt to bring suit against the Charles Chaplin Film Corporation in the late 1950s.

Except for the *City Lights* episode, these were the "happiest days" of Georgia's life. Chaplin introduced her to Ivor Montagu and his wife Eileen Hellstern. Known to her friends as "Hell," she and Ivor arrived in Hollywood in the spring of 1930, in part "to play John the Baptist," as he jokingly said, "and put in a word here and there in the right quarters, singing the praises of Eisenstein." [13] He had several letters of introduction, including one from H.G. Wells. A great admirer of Wells, Chaplin had spent several weekends with him and his family during his visit to England in 1921. Ivor was soon joined by his old friends, Sergei Eisenstein, and fellow-Soviet

[13] *With Eisenstein in Hollywood* (Berlin: Seven Seas, 1968), p. 34.

director, Grigory Alexandrov. Given a six months' contract, the three were employed by B. P. Schulberg, then head of Paramount's West Coast studio, to collaborate on two scenarios, including an adaptation of Dreiser's *An American Tragedy.*[14]

By July 1930 Chaplin was nearing completion of *City Lights*, and could now afford to spend a little more time in leisure. He would take the five visitors (Eisenstein's cameraman Eduard Tisse had also come) on his yacht to Catalina. The other who was often with them was Georgia. The Montagu's became for Georgia both allies and confidants. "They understood the relationship between Charlie and me . . . why it had extended over so many years . . . even before and after his marriages" (Memoir, p. 130). When they departed for England in December 1930, she and the Montagu's kept up a close but irregular epistolary friendship that lasted until "Hell," and then Ivor, died in 1984.

Georgia frequently refers to the Bible and to religion. Although this is not the place to discuss her religious development to its culmination, Georgia gropingly came to believe that only through a spiritual rebirth could she effect an emotional liberation from Chaplin. "I was commencing to realize that my teacher was becoming more my idol" (Memoir, p. 131). It was not long after that she discovered "a scientific religion." It is doubtful whether Georgia's adoption of Christian Science came as early as Sternberg suggests, whether or not one accepts his conclusion that religion was for her, as for many others in the film industry, "a spiritual crutch."

Following the premiere of *City Lights* in January 1931, Chaplin departed from Los Angeles with plans to attend the New York and London premieres. However, once in Europe, Chaplin stayed for more than a year. During his absence Georgia seems to have had an active enough social life—

14 Paramount Pictures rejected Eisenstein's treatment as being too incomprehensible and invited Sternberg to replace him. An admirer of Eisenstein, Dreiser brought suit against Paramount, and lost.

> I had dinner the other evening with Dr. Reynolds . . . Poor man is still raring to act . . . What do you think of Charlie's refusing the King and Queen? They have made so much of it here in the papers. Oh I've been playing tennis up at Charlie's and the other day we found a huge snake. It seems to be a rendez-vous for reptiles, animals and insects since Charlie let the Gardeners go . . . I went to the opening of Sid Grauman's *Street Scene* here with big fat Henry [Bergman] and I had the best time. He's a dear and he was so proud to take me to his restaurant afterwards . . . By the way I've been playing quite a bit of table tennis or ping-pong. I like it so much & have improved since I played with you. Thank goodness! I do hope some day we can all see each other again. Why don't you come back with Charlie.[15]

She returned to the screen in a light serial for Mascot, but her film career, such as it had been, was in effect over. She continued to be listed as a leading lady in *The Standard Casting Directory* to July 1933, but there is no evidence of her having been contracted to appear in another film until the re-issue of *The Gold Rush* in 1942. From various sources, we have diverse explanations of why Georgia's career faded. David Robinson's is that "her voice and diction were not as pleasing as her looks and her career was doomed by talking pictures."[16] Sternberg says that

> After her stint with Chaplin she joined the star roster at Paramount . . . and there her talents, such as they were, were exploited by two or three top directors who must have been shocked to find that the attributes she had been credited with were not hers.[17]

[15] GH to IM, Hollywood, 1931: MP.

[16] *Chaplin: His Life and Art* (London: William Collins Sons & Co. Ltd., 1985), p. 366.

[17] Josef von Sternberg, *op. cit.*, p. 157.

Ivor Montagu felt that "the career she should have had . . . failed to materialise. A Studio quarrel which her independence and uprightness forbade her to compromise had brought about her blacklisting."[18] A newspaper article of 1927 described her as a former favourite "now striving to make ends meet."

> Georgia Hale seems to be sinking from sight inasmuch as Famous Players did not take up its option on her contract . . . for some reason [she] failed to click.[19]

But how much weight is to be given to any of these opinions must depend to a certain extent on how true it is that all talented performers become stars, or that all stars are talented. Perhaps there is more truth in the old adage about "the right type in the right place at the right time."

In the letter to Ivor quoted on the previous page, Georgia mentioned having received a telegram from Chaplin; he was writing her no letters however, and she felt neglected. Clearly he was relying on gifts to convince her of his continued affection. This neglect resulted, when he returned to the United States in the summer of 1932, in an almost ten-year rift between them. They did not see one another again until the summer of 1941.

> You & Hell loved Charlie and how badly he needed that love—of course you were close to us and knew how deeply I loved him and still do. I am under contract again with him because of the release of *The Gold Rush* & hope to work in his next picture which is *Substance & Shadow* [*sic*]. I have had for two years a radio program. Singing & doing skits. It was fun but dull compared to pictures . . . You can always reach me at Charlie's studios now . . . Maybe some day we

[18] Ivor Montagu, *op. cit.*, p. 91.
[19] *Boston Advertiser*, 18 March 1927.

> can all work on a picture with Chaplin. He looks just exactly the same as when you were here; he hasn't aged at all and has worlds of pep. In fact the other nite [*sic*] he made all his 2nd Front speeches to me. Then read his script thru, acting and jumping around. At three oclock in the morning I was exhausted just watching him.[20]

Georgia signed a contract with the Charles Chaplin Film Corporation on 1 October 1941, and although it was to have concluded after a year, Chaplin continued to pay her $25 a week, the sum agreed to in her contract, until the end of March 1953.[21]

Georgia's memoir ends with Chaplin's marriage to Oona O'Neill in June 1943, and a very long fictional "dream." His perceived abandonment of her, it is worth pointing out, provided the basis for a novelette she wrote during the early 1950s entitled *The Edge of Life*. Like the memoir, it never found a publisher. The Roy Mack Agency considered it "unsuitable for today's market";[22] Warner Brothers said that it was the "type of story which does not fit into our current production plans."[23] The plot begins with the heroine waiting impatiently for her childhood sweetheart, now a soldier in the Union army, to return from the Civil War so that they can be married. A day or two before the wedding, she receives news that he has been killed. Losing all account of time, much like the jilted Miss Haversham in Dickens' *Great Expectations*, she is condemned to a life of mental paralysis. Years pass, and she now mistakes a young man for her long-lost lover. Though this youth is terminally ill, he too falls in love; and the pair end happily in the belief that Love, the great healer, will cure all. Perhaps as a consequence of having been in movies, Georgia often resorted to dialogue in the florid language so characteristic of late

[20] GH to IM, Los Angeles, 23 April 1943: MP.
[21] Georgia's copy of the contract in KP (Kiernan Papers).
[22] Roy Mack to GH, Hollywood, 2 May 1955: KP.
[23] Wesley Haynes to GH, Burbank, 19 April 1951: KP.

Victorian novels. Melodramatic though it is, the story is full of naïve disclosures about its author and her own romance. Like many writers who have saved their "autotherapy" for their books, Georgia kept the pain of her loss hidden until she could find expression for it in the novelette, and then in the memoir. Both of these served, no doubt, a cathartic function after her deep disappointment.

The information that can be gleaned from Georgia's letters to the Montagu's, however sketchy, is almost all that can be added to the story of her later years. After hearing of Chaplin's marriage she wrote—

> It has been ages since I received your note and my excuse is that I was too low to stay around here, so I took a trip. Charlie as you know is married again & of course you know why. The same reason he has always married. It's so funny the way he detests marriage & then is obliged to marry. He told me all about the Joan episode and also the latest. We have a deep love for one another but I would never play that game. I will always love him, almost as if he were my child but I will never swerve one inch from what I think is right . . . Charlie spoke for the "Second front" again and he stepped on the toes of some of our big shots, that's why the papers have been so mean to him about the latest affairs, but he is fearless and really a great sweet person.[24]

Not surprisingly she doubted his motive for marrying. In her memoir Georgia never mentions Joan Barry. The reference in this letter suggests that she believed her to have been a factor in Chaplin's sudden decision to marry; this perhaps lends some little corroboration to Georgia's claim that he had asked her to run away with him. Joan Barry was a young aspiring actress, who had been introduced to Chaplin early in June 1941, and had signed a six months' contract with him later that month.

[24] GH to IM, Los Angeles, 1943: KP.

Chaplin in his autobiography, and Joan Barry in her testimony to the FBI, gave contradictory versions of their relationship. They had an affair, which continued intermittently through much of 1941 and into 1942, when he brusquely attempted to put an end to it. After an interlude in New York, she returned to Los Angeles, pregnant, in May 1943. When it became clear that Chaplin would not marry her, Barry's lawyer filed a paternity suit on June 3 citing Chaplin as the father of her unborn child. He was served with papers and ordered to appear in California Superior Court on June 17 to answer the charge. An agreement was worked out allowing time for blood tests, and the hearing postponed until after the birth.

Chaplin was indicted by a Federal Grand Jury on February 10, 1944 to answer charges alleging violation of Joan Barry's civil rights, and of the Mann Act, a piece of legislation dating from the twenties which made it illegal to transport a woman across a state border for "immoral purposes." The trial was set to begin on March 21, and on April 4 he was found not guilty, and discharged. Joan Barry had given birth to a daughter the previous autumn, and although independently administered blood-tests had proved that Chaplin was not the father, the federal government continued to pursue the case. Writing to Ivor, Georgia commented:

> Charlie is out of the worst of it. I wish his case were over. I don't want to see him have to give large sums of money to this girl and child. He always had the faculty of surrounding himself with enemies. And his real friends he doubted. I saw him several times before he married "Oona." He isn't happy but some foolish inferior feeling gets him into these "jams."

Georgia repeated that she still had a contract signed two years earlier with him. "I was to play the heavy [?] and Joan

[25] GH to IM, Los Angeles, 1944: KP.

Barry the lead. But as you know the season closed for her and he lost interest in the picture. I'll probably see him again soon."[25]

Georgia did see Chaplin again, but not, it seems, until they met at a funeral in April 1946. "Mr. Alfred Reeves passed on last week. Do you remember him? He was Charlie's manager and the one who brought Charlie to this country." Chaplin mentioned to her that he was "starting a new picture, a "Bluebeard" idea. Some of the scenes are going to be so funny of him killing his different wives."[26] She had opened a dancing academy during the War, thinking "it served a good purpose, teaching the boys how to dance and making them happy." It is clear that her old relationship with Chaplin had come to an end.

After the news of Eisenstein's death in February 1948, Georgia wrote to Ivor and Hell thanking them for "the souvenir of the memorial meeting. The picture of Eisenstein brought back fond memories. We had fun together." She had to confess that "I never see him [Charlie] anymore however I'm still with his studio and so I visit with the staff over there every now and then." Georgia now had two schools of dancing, "and they keep me busy. Aside from this interest, I'm also writing a short story."[27]

With the completion of *Limelight*, Chaplin set sail September 18, 1952 from New York for London aboard the *Queen Elizabeth* to attend its premiere. Once at sea, he was told that Attorney-General James McGranery had revoked his reentry permit, and that in order to be readmitted he would have to answer questions as to his moral behaviour. Chaplin's decision not to return to the United States to answer the Immigration and Naturalization Services charges, led to his removal from England to Switzerland early the following year. The INS requested the assistance of the FBI in its investigation

[26] GH to IM, Los Angeles, 20 April 1946: KP. The film she refers to is *Monsieur Verdoux*. Although preparations began in 1945, Chaplin did not start production until April 1946.

[27] GH to IM, Los Angeles, 6 October 1948: MP.

of him, and attempted to obtain from friends and colleagues evidence to support their allegations that he had been guilty of moral turpitude. Georgia was among those who were questioned.

> I was a witness for him the other day and told them the truth and of course everything was in his favor. I told them of his high morals around me and that we were just friends even though in love. They said I was thus far his best witness. I hope everything goes well for him . . . Perhaps you'll have him for "keeps", as your neighbor. He'll be happy wherever he lives.[28]

When Chaplin decided to close his studios, he gave instructions that Georgia's allowance be terminated "as of week ending March 28, 1953."[29] Feeling ill-used, she enquired about the possibility of bringing suit against him. Writing to an attorney,[30] Georgia gave four reasons for the proposed action: 1. that Chaplin and Alf Reeves had told her the "allowance was for life"; 2. that Chaplin had promised her "a royalty from the re-release of *The Gold Rush*," and that "this promise was published in *Variety*"; 3. that he had promised to put her "in a picture and that this contract [the one signed on October 1, 1941] was just for that purpose"; and 4. that Chaplin's decision not to employ her in *City Lights* had prevented her "from doing other things." The attorney's reply stated "that in my opinion you have no case against the Charles Chaplin Film Corporation by virtue of the agreement of October 1, 1941 which, in the fourth paragraph, provides that after one year your employment could be terminated upon thirty days' notice, and it appears that such a notice was given to you on January 24, 1953."[31]

[28] GH to IM, Los Angeles, December 1952: MP.

[29] The Chaplin Studios, Inc. to GH, 24 January 1953: KP.

[30] Manuscript copy of a letter from GH to Sidney Fischgrund, Los Angeles, November, 1957: KP.

[31] Sidney Fischgrund to GH, Los Angeles, 29 November 1957: KP.

How much this payment had meant to Georgia and her financial position is hard to estimate. Similarly we do not know how much money she was earning during her later years. Although they were successful, she had closed her two dancing-schools in September 1946. At the end of the year, "tired of Hollywood," Georgia decided to get out of the movie business and go "into a 'cosmetic' line." However, a screen actor's and extra's Guild card dated 1951 and 1952, and issued to Georgia LaCarr, were found among her papers; but whether she ever performed under this name is unknown. During the sixties she made use of her musical knowledge to compose and record several songs, including "Painted on Black Velvet," released under the pseudonym Georgie Hale. At the time of her death, Georgia left several properties, including a duplex she occupied on La Brea, a few blocks away from the Chaplin Studios.

After twenty years of separation, Georgia met Chaplin again when he returned to Hollywood in April 1972.

> I had the joy of spending about forty-five minutes alone with Charlie at lunch at the Beverly Hills Hotel. We talked over everything . . . He spoke of our happy days together and of how close we all were . . . He introduced me to Oona. She came up just as I was leaving . . . I wish I could turn back time.[32]

She never saw him again. When Chaplin's *My Life in Pictures* was published in 1975, the Montagu's sent a copy to Georgia.

> What a joy to find . . . that thrilling book when I finally returned from San Francisco. The book brought back dear memories of those days we spent at Charlie's house. We were all one in love . . . So now Charlie is a "Sir." From what I read he seems to want to do things again. I

[32] GH to IM, Los Angeles, 1972: MP.

> hope he is not being held back by too many well-meaning "no nos." He seemed to want to break out of his way of thinking & have fun & express himself. . . I'll treasure that book and your sweet note always.[33]

Charles Spencer Chaplin died on Christmas Day 1977. Shortly after, Georgia wrote to thank the Montagu's for their "kind words which helped me so much," and to express her own deep sense of loss.

> There is a void feeling. Just to know he was over there in Switzerland warmed my heart. But I am so happy I saw him and was alone with him for a full hour in 1972. I told him I loved him and would never marry while he lived. It made him so happy he grabbed and kissed me again and again. You know the night before he married Oona he came to my house and begged me to leave the country with him. But I knew it wasn't right not with him in his situation. So at three in the morning he left and how sad it all was . . . Charlie did recognize true values but somehow he could be flattered and it would get to him and all the while he knew he was being fooled. All that was absent at our last meeting. The real sweet Charlie was present. Of course you and Hell were the two who knew how I adored him—faults and all— As you said—he did have a full life and passed on peacefully in his sleep. I feel rich for having been so close to him.[34]

A little over two months after the funeral, in a rather macabre incident, Chaplin's body was stolen. On March 18, 1978, the day after it was recovered, Georgia wrote the last letter in which she would mention his name.

[33] GH to IM, Los Angeles, 22 February 1975: MP.

[34] GH to IM, Los Angeles, 6 January 1978: MP.

> How I loved your article! You understood Charlie in depth . . . Oona I believe really loved Charlie but her endeavour to shield him from the world was not only feeble but it seemed to me—weaken[ed] the one she smothered with her love. What could have been the motives of this vicious theft? Do you suppose it was someone who wanted it for ransom or someone who just wanted it. How little those pitiful remains had to do with the undying genius we loved. How quickly most people seem to forget him. However his pictures will make him live in our hearts forever. I'm so grateful for your beautiful tribute to him. I feel so rich to have known and loved him so deeply. You and Hell have been so dear to me and understanding. Even my sister and close friends never understood my love of Charlie nor his genius.
>
> loads of love
>
> Georgia[35]

Georgia spent her last years in Los Angeles, surrounded by friends, many of them fellow-members of the Christian Science Church there. She was still able to take pleasure in memories of a career which, although unsatisfactory in some ways, had enriched her life. Her death on June 17, 1985, at the age of 85 went virtually unnoticed. Georgia had never lost her essential strength and individuality, and while Chaplin was alive had been willing to live joyfully, sometimes painfully, on the periphery of his life. "So Hell just tags along," she once said, "that's all I've ever wanted to do with Charlie."[36]

H. Kiernan
Stow, Scotland
November 1994.

[35] GH to IM, Los Angeles, 18 March 1978: MP.
[36] GH to IM, Los Angeles, 23 March 1943: MP.

Note on the Text

Attention must be drawn to the limitations implicit in the title of this book. While it is important to remember that this narrative was not planned as an autobiography—Georgia may have been too modest to think of that—it was shaped by an understanding that what would make her interesting to succeeding generations of film-goers was her relationship with Charles Chaplin. Inevitably a portrait of Georgia emerges side by side with his. Even in this light, it is selective rather than complete.

The reader should not be surprised to find it frequently vague about details. There are many matters of potential interest about which Georgia is regrettably silent. After three decades, it has proved possible to check and correct inaccuracies, to add further detail, and clear up facts of chronology. The notes provided point to a number of these clarifications. This does not imply that where there is no comment, Georgia must be entirely reliable. Editorial silence may mean ignorance, not consent. Nevertheless, once some allowance is made, she would seem to be a credible, if not comprehensive, witness to the events of which she was a part.

As an historical document, this memoir has the obvious merit of not having had the assistance of a ghost-writer. The numerous drafts, with many manuscript additions found among Georgia Hale's papers after her death, were written by her. In consequence the originals contained many typographical errors. Modern scholarly practice might require an editor to reproduce these, with painfully frequent use of the term "sic". But this book is not a biography, and so, in the main, only her inadvertent misspellings have been reproduced, the rest being silently corrected.

The technicalities of presentation largely follow convention. Every intrusion into the text is enclosed in square brackets [ ]. Her characteristic, though idiosyncratic use of ellipsis (. . .) has been preserved. Grammar and punctuation, often eccentric, have also been largely left unaltered. Individual forms of grammar, punctuation and spelling seem to convey her personality directly, and to standardize them would have weakened this lifelike impression.

The notes attempt to identify persons referred to and explain obscure allusions without, I hope, too much interruption to the text. I have been able to present some facts hitherto not known, which help to provide a clearer and more accurate outline of Georgia Hale's life and career.

It may occur to the careful reader that the title is quite literally intended, and that it is not an accident that the text reads much like the scenario of a film, with a great deal of dialogue, directions as to movements, and instructions to the principals about what should be conveyed in their "close-up" scenes. Georgia cast herself as the heroine of a great dramatic romance involving "Charlie, the little fellow" as hero, thus giving her memoir a verve that the more restrained writer lacks. We all invent ourselves, but some of us with more conviction than others.

HK

Unpublished letters referred to in this book belong either to the Ivor Montagu Papers (now housed at The British Film Institute, London), or to a series written by Georgia Hale to the Montagu's, and now in the editor's possession. These two sources are referred to in the footnotes as MP, and KP (Kiernan Papers).

Foreword

Charlie Chaplin was not one but two. For many years I was under contract to Charlie Chaplin. Now I want you to know him as I do. These intimate close-ups of him, reveal the still calm of a sun-lit lake, the fury of an unspent sea.

Introduction

In order to understand the deep impact Charlie Chaplin made upon my life and my way of thinking, let me tell you some of the events leading up to my first glimpse of the little clown. Let me take you back a little, just a little to the days preceeding [*sic*] the great event . . . that of seeing the little comic for the first time on the silver screen. That blessed day I saw the famous comedian Charlie Chaplin.

1

As a child I was aware of the poverty of my surroundings. I felt deeply, for a little girl of five, even my own shortcomings. "Five years old and can't 'dun-down' my pants yet," my mother heard me say. This little remark became a standard joke. The family would chide and tease me with it constantly. I couldn't appreciate their fun.

Mother, a short, plump woman, was very loving and completely impartial. My father, a tall, handsome, well-educated man, was like a boarder. He'd come and go, mostly go. He held a good position as wire-chief, with the telephone company of our town, St. Joseph, Missouri. He would give mother part of his salary, a small part, the first of the month. She was a poor manager and the allowance, so inadequate, would all be spent in the first couple of weeks. The last days would find us broke and hungry. My sisters accepted this.

My sister Frances[1] was six years older than I. She was quite pretty and up to my appearance received most of the attention, which she cherished. She was very practical and loved to cook and sew. Her goal was to be efficient. She was.

My middle sister Melissa, the tallest, was a red-head, with lots of freckles. She thought of herself as very plain, but she was sweet and kind. She had no ambition other than to just get by . . . that was all.

1 See Introduction, p. x. Eugenia (Frances) was born on 16 March 1896, and Helen (Melissa), on 19 August 1898. Georgia's reason for altering the names is uncertain; possibly it was out of deference to her sisters' wishes.

Mother was a slave. She washed all of our clothes by hand, scrubbed floors the same way, and even shoveled coal. I crept down stairs to the basement and asked "Why—why doesn't papa come down here too, and help you?" She shrugged her shoulders and whispered, "I guess he figures he does enough."

I didn't agree. When her back was turned, I began to pitch in and help her. I picked some black dirty coal and started filling the pail. When she turned and saw me, she threw up her hands and exclaimed, "No, don't you dirty your little white hands with coal . . . ever! I want you to do big things and lift your mother out of this basement forever." She kissed me on the forehead and chased me upstairs. I left reluctantly. There she stood . . . with a wet stomach and black hands. I didn't like the picture.

With mother so busy, Frances had to look after me. Mrs. Hogan, our aristocratic neighbor, lived on a hill, across the street in a great big gorgeous house. We looked up to her. Everyone did, for she was rich. She called Frances one day when we were out playing and said, "Give this doll to your pretty little sister, Georgia. You know, I predict a big future for her. Mark my word, she'll be a star."

This was the last straw. Frances heard this all the time and now from Mrs. Hogan. Frances turned on me and said angrily, "Don't let all this flattery go to your head, for heaven's sake. They just feel sorry for you. They pity you, because you put on that sad face. They're only trying to cheer you up. Why in the world don't you smile once in awhile?"

I tried to explain. "So far I haven't seen anything to smile about," I said. Then I asked, "What about mother? What about . . .?" But she interjected, "Well, what about her?" Melissa stepped between us and took me away. She whispered, "Don't mind Frances. You see she used to get all the attention and now you get it . . . you're the baby . . . you see? Don't let her sharp tongue hurt you."

Finally, I was old enough to go to school with my sisters. This day we were all called into the assembly hall, to try out for the big play of the year. My sisters and I, and everyone, were given the opportunity to read lines, walk about the stage and even sing a little song. It was such fun for me to be included.

At the close of the day, we all had to re-assemble and hear who had been chosen. Mrs. O'Donnell, the dramatic teacher, made the announcement. She said solemnly, "The judges have chosen . . . Miss Georgia Hale to play the leading role. She will play the little fairy, who with the touch of her wand can change the most ugly and naughty child into a beautiful and heavenly angel." My heart thumped with joy. The kids applauded generously . . . but not Frances. She looked angry. I watched her leave the hall even before they announced the names of the rest of the cast.

On the way home, she waited for me and said, "I refused to be in that play, because you're going to make it ridiculous. Wait and see! Little you, going around touching those big kids with a wand." Then she burst out laughing as she picked up a stick and started patting me on the head, as if it were a wand. The patting grew harder. She exclaimed, "Look, this is the way you'll do it." But as she pranced around, she tripped herself, stumbled and fell.

I picked her up and started to brush her off. She yelled, "Stop it! Mercy . . . we think we're the fairy, already." This struck her as funny and she laughed louder than before saying, "You little fool. I fell on purpose. I wanted to show you what's going to happen to you on the stage . . . in front of everyone." I swallowed hard and managed to giggle . . . a little.

I had no heart now for the part . . . a fairy. I wasn't making people beautiful and heavenly, nor happy. But mother stood by me and helped me with my lines. My father thought that Frances should have gotten the part. He tried to put a stop to my doing it. He said, "Frances should have had the part. Georgia is far too serious, too heavy in spirit to be a fairy.

I'm going to call the school! Why doesn't she forget it and go out and play like the other children of her age? My goodness, I named the child George, hoping it would be a boy. Just think . . . by now we'd be playing baseball . . . too bad!" Mother simply replied, "Georgia is a happy little girl." But I wasn't.

The day came for the play. The big hall was filled. My heart was low. I peered out through the curtains and could see mother in the front row. When the play was over, to my surprise, everyone seemed to like it. I rushed out to join mother. But she was surrounded by people saying, "Your daughter made the daintiest little fairy . . . She is so talented . . . You must put her in pictures or on the stage." Mrs. Donnell shook hands with mother and said, "I hope you realize that Georgia has a real gift for the theatre. You must make use of it."

I stood aside studying my mother's face. Every line that had been running down, now turned up. Her poor little face looked young and pretty, her eyes were dancing with hope and pride. This joy, no one could take from her . . .

The next day my mother told my sisters, "Maybe, Georgia can help the family. Even if she can make a few dollars . . . it would put more food on the table." She then dolled me up and off we went to a stock company downtown.

We obtained an interview. I read some lines from the play. I shall never forget the triumph in my mother's expression when he said, "Yes, she's alright. The Marlow Group has a small part for Georgia in the production now in rehearsal." She literally bowed to the floor when he handed her five dollars for my lunch and carfare. I was to return the very next day. She grabbed me by the hand. I could barely touch the ground as she raced me home to tell the girls.

But was it worth it? When I returned to school, I was ostracized. One little chum of mine said scathingly, "Everyone thinks you're a tough, now that you're an actress. I cannot go around with you any more."

Frances came home from school and told mother, "She's disgraced the family." This did not worry me and I wouldn't let it torment mother. Far more disappointing to me was that the money I made was not enough. The need was so great and I wanted so to lift that burden from her shoulders. Life was still a struggle and bleak.

2

This poverty was not unchallenged by me, even though my sisters tried to hush me up. I felt ashamed and dismayed. The burning question was, "Why?" My little girl friends had more than I did. I would engage them in deep conversations. I'd ask, "Do you ever wonder why some people have and others have not? Why are we here at all? What is the purpose of anything? Does religion give the answers?" But they would answer with a question, "Why worry?" "I'll seek out Eva. She knows, I'm sure. She'll help me," I consoled myself.

On the way to Eva's next day at dusk, I heard a cry come from the little shack behind Mrs. Hogan's big house, where a colored family existed. I ran to the place, pressed my face against the old rusty screen and called, "Is that you, Cora?" My little friend came to the window crying and sobbed, "Georgia, I can't stand it. I'm hungry . . . real hungry and ma tells me she hasn't nothin in the house." I whispered, "Maybe I can help you, just hold on tight. I'll be back."

I hurried home and then paced the floor, waiting for dinner. Mother always divided the food. It was always a little meat and lots of vegetables. A soup bone with a tiny bit of meat, cost a quarter, and a bunch of vegetables a dime.

She filled my plate with these "goodies." I asked, "May I have a bun?" Mother's buns were the best in the whole world. She gave me one. In a few minutes I asked, "Mother, may I have a bun?" Mother answered, "I just gave you one, I didn't see you eat it."

I jumped up from the table and said, "Oh, that's alright, I was just going out on the porch to eat my dinner, it's so warm in here." Mother followed me and saw me heading towards Cora's house with the food. She called, "Here Georgia, here's the extra bun. I know what you're up to . . . but tell me honey, which is worse, you going to bed hungry or Cora?" I kept going.

Cora was taken care of . . . now to Eva's. I was more eager than ever to get to Eva's and I hoped I wasn't too late. "Surely, she has the answer to all this poverty and hunger," I told myself. You see, I always looked up to Eva, because she went to church. She wasn't pretty, so the kids said, but to me she was so out-going and had such a big healthy smile. She was a devoted Roman Catholic. Her sparkling orchid beads . . . how I loved them! Orchid was my favorite color. Then that tiny pure-white prayer book with Jesus hanging on the cross, made of gold and in relief too . . . that was so dramatic!

But, oh dear, when I reached her home, I had just missed her. She had just gone. "If I had not helped Cora then I would have been on time," I thought. But immediately I said, "I'm glad I helped her, and I'll always go to Cora's rescue, always." Then I scolded myself, "Why didn't you run faster? You only missed her by a few seconds . . . so they said." I went to bed frustrated and hungry in body and soul.

On Sunday, I decided to sit on my porch and watch for Eva. The people passed by my house coming from church. She was always preceded by Ruth, who though only ten years of age, already had chosen to be a nun. I wanted to ask her questions too, but she was so austere. I could see her coming for she was so tall. She was the direct opposite of Eva. Her hair, a mousy brown, was pinned back flat. I felt a revulsion as she floated or rather slithered by. Yet I tried to catch her eye and smile to her . . . perhaps she might speak. But she never looked left nor right. She gave the strange appearance of sitting as she went by, so flexed were her knees. She left a sinking feeling in the pit of my stomach. But Eva was so different, so approachable. I couldn't wait to see her.

Along she came finally. I ran to meet her and took her into my hall-way, where nobody would interrupt us. Eva smiled happily and asked, "What have you got to tell me?" I answered, "Nothing. I want you to tell me what you learned today." The smile left her face. I continued, plying her with questions, "At church . . . what did you hear? . . . please tell me the Bible story? Tell me about . . . Daniel in the lion's den? Isn't there something about Joseph with his coat of many colors? Just tell me about Jesus . . . and the healings he did?" Eva grinned . . . then started to choke . She put her two hands over her mouth and pressed hard. I thought I heard a giggle. Then she flung her head back and laughed out loud in my face.

Once again I had that hollow feeling in my stomach. My eyes filled with tears. When she saw my expression she said, "I'm sorry, I just feel silly to-day. Georgia, you're too serious, you make me laugh. Is this what you asked me to come in here for?" She didn't wait for an answer. She hurriedly arose, opened her hand and showed me a quarter. She whispered, mischievously, "Look, I held this back . . . I didn't put it in . . . let's go and get some candy with it. We can get two chocolate bars and six bags of jelly beans." "No," I said. "No, I can't do that . . . you go along . . . please." I could hardly hold back from sobbing. She turned from me and bounced down the stairs two at a time. She looked up and waved saying, "Cheer up old lady." Then she giggled again and said, "I wish you could see your face. You'd think your cat died." She made a sour face, grinned and disappeared.

Now I could cry. The tears rolled down my cheeks. I had expected Eva to help me to answer my questions. She didn't understand nor care. We didn't communicate. Alas, she wouldn't or couldn't relate one Bible story to me. My secret, my plans to become a nun, ended that day. It had been a secret. You see, I didn't have any religion in my home. Both of my parents had turned against it. In their youth it had deprived them of their innocent joys.

Their Sabbaths were colored blue. They were told, "It is a sin to pick berries on Sunday." They dreaded Sunday. They were not allowed on this day, to go into the woods near by and play. When the tornado hit their town and demolished their crops and belongings, their parents told them, "It is God's will. He, in his infinite mercy is punishing us for our sins." But mother and father couldn't understand this, nor did they agree. They thought their parents were good and had worked hard on the farm and deserved the best. So their parents' God, with a long white beard, sitting somewhere up on a cloud judging and punishing everyone, became a hoax, a myth, a big joke to them. God-fearing they were not, they simply didn't believe.

So they couldn't answer my persistant [*sic*] questions nor calm my perplexed thoughts. "Why are some rich and others poor? Is the colored man happy with his lot?" I'd ask. Mother would answer, "I don't know and no one else does. The black folks are happy if they have a dime in their pocket. They are a joyous people. Don't worry your pretty head or you won't stay pretty."

God became a mystery to me too. Churches were just beautiful buildings where people sat, all dressed up and looked at each other once a week and listened to words they didn't understand. But my urgent need for the answer to the tragedies I saw around me was not silenced.

3

We moved from Missouri to Chicago when I was still very young.[1] There I lived, in more of the same, only with a gangster element added. Murders, beatings and gang-wars were the theme of each day. The world was a strange place to have landed in . . . from where? . . . and whither?

We were no longer surrounded by cobblestones, so mother with her poetic soul made use of a nice backyard of rich earth. Beautiful flowers came from that soil. I called them all by name and they answered me. They sang to me, words of praise . . . to beauty! It tantalized me. I wondered, "All this loveliness amidst so much ugliness! How can it be?" There were different shaped beds of verbenas, pansies, columbines and fragrant peonies, tube-roses, lily of the valley and more . . . many more. I loved this spot.

When not busy in a play, modeling or in school, there I would spend my hours. I stayed close to the earth, my new-found world, and became acquainted with the little living things of this earth. The bees and ants seemed to be fired with more purpose than people.

Then, one day, I found "Cheepy," a tiny sparrow. She had a broken wing. I nursed her back to health but she couldn't fly. So I kept her in a sturdy cage where she was safe. She became my precious pet. One day she was missing. I ran to my parents and cried, "Who took Cheep? Where is Cheepy?" But no one answered, they didn't seem to know. I darted out

[1] Since Georgia cannot have been more than three years old when the removal to Chicago took place, we must suppose that the stories in the preceding two chapters really belonged to her Chicago years.

of the house and searched and called, "Cheepy, come to me." I went up and down the alleys and gang-ways . . . but no Cheepy.

When I returned home, mother was waiting for me at the back gate. She said in a low tone, "Papa doesn't want me to tell you. He said, "I'm going to teach Georgia a lesson. Just let her hunt until she gets good and tired. She's got to learn there's more important things than a little sparrow." I begged, "All I want to know is . . . where, where is Cheepy?"

Mother patted me on the back, and whispered, "Honey, papa found your little bird . . . dead, in the bottom of his cage this morning. Now, Georgia please, it's really not good for you to feel so deeply. He threw him over there . . . in the corner by the shed."

Tears ran down my face, as I protested, "Threw him where? Why didn't someone answer me? Why did you let Cheepy lie in that dirt and hot sun all day? Where . . . where is he?" Through the tears I saw him . . . I found him. I gathered Cheepy up in my hands and carefully placed him in a little satin lined box I had always cherished, and buried him.

Each day I'd put some of mother's flowers on the little mound. But this all left an ugly impression on me. Unkindness, cruelty and death, how I hated this triad. I vowed, "I'm not going to eat anything that has ever lived . . . never again . . . ever." Mother insisted that I eat whatever we were lucky enough to have. She warned, "Don't let your father find out about this. He'll cut down on our allowance." But I held on to my vow for a long time.

Even in my retreat, my garden of pretty flowers, I found sorrow and ugliness. The sinister gangsterism of man was reflected in my bug world. I had to rescue bugs from bugs. The questions about life became numerous. I was disenchanted. I decided, "The answer is not to be found in my backyard. It's not in nature." My heart sank to a new low.

4

My father very seldom spoke directly to me. But he often complained to mother about my attitude towards life. However, this day he called me to him and said, "You're so darn sad. What's wrong with you? I wish you'd been a boy, then you wouldn't be worried about trifles. We'd be out throwing horse-shoes right now."

Then the impossible happened. He said, "Here's some money. Take this and go to the movies. There's some comedy playing. It might, just by chance, do you some good." I stuttered, "Th . . . th . . . thank you." I simply couldn't believe it. He gave me some money! That was the first money he had ever given me. I asked myself, "What on earth or in heaven ever prompted him to reach in his pocket and pull out that change for me?" He slapped it into my hand and shoved me out the door saying, "Now get . . . go and see something funny."

"Thank you for the money . . . thank you!" I yelled as I ran, still wondering how I managed to get the change, instead of Frances, to whom he always gave. "You're so darn sad . . . wish you'd been a boy," kept ringing in my ears. I heard this for years. I found myself wishing that I had never been born . . . at all.

When I reached the "Bona-Venture" the show had started. I crept into the dark theatre. Finally, the main feature, the comedy started. Onto the screen came a funny little fellow. He was a pathetic character, like the rest of us. His clothes were castoffs and much too large for his small frame. His shoes were way out in front of his feet. He did wear a collar and a tie, but no shirt, and on his head a classy, dirty derby. His hand whirled a cane, jauntily, as if in defiance of his lot.

I could see him skating with the skill and precision of a ballet dancer, twisting, whirling majestically around and through the crowd. He was working hard at his menial job of picking up the rubbish. When he touched a big bully accidentally, he got shoved so hard he lost his balance. But he just picked himself up, brushed off his baggy pants, tipped his hat and smiled a cute little smile.

Courage and joy were the qualities he industriously used in his busy little life, for keeping body and soul together. He battled the strong, the cruel and the arrogant. The kids near me wildly laughed and applauded this tiny comic, yelling, "Charlie Chaplin . . . more . . . more." His funny gags and clothes had sent them into the aisles rolling and screaming.

But I saw something different, something invisible. I felt something beautiful. A gentle beam of light had stolen into my dark world. "What was it?" I was silent. When the picture was over,[1] I left the show quickly and ran ahead of the kids. I wanted to be alone. I wanted to hold it closely. Charlie Chaplin had said something to me . . . he had spoken to me directly.

Charlie Chaplin said to me, "Georgia, I'm using this little nobody to show you that there is a spirit in man which nothing can down. Stick out your chest, little girl, and step over your troubles." I was bubbling over with inspiration. Something had come alive inside me. I felt light and gay. I went home, donned my sisters' skates and tried strutting, twisting and kicking my feet.

When I saw my father come out on the porch to see what was going on, I tore around wildly and skated as fast as ever I could in front of him, just like the comic. Everything was fine

[1] It was probably *The Rink*, a Mutual comedy released in two reels, 4 December 1916.

until I hit a crack and sat down, abruptly. Wonders... I saw a smile spread from ear to ear on pap's face.

I couldn't wait to see that comic again and again. I'd skimp and save all my pennies. When the kids would call, "Georgia . . . want to go to the movies? Charlie Chaplin, our little comedian is there." I'd slide down the bannister and join them before they'd stop yelling.

I would walk backwards out of the show just to steal a last glance. He was daring—he'd try—he'd do any kind of work . . . scrub . . . clean . . . wall-paper, whether he knew how to or not. I'd hold his image vividly in my thoughts and then I'd go home and try anything too.

Mother had been wanting the hall painted. She'd had the paint for a long time. I gathered the paraphernalia together and pitched in, with the verve and vigor of the little tramp. I started to paint. My father heard me splashing around and joined in. When mother saw the nice clean hall she said, "Papa, how nice of you. It's better late than never." I hid. He answered, "Yes, I finally got to it. Doesn't it improve the place? Sorry I let it go so long."

Frances, who saw the whole performance said, "Whatever has gotten into you? Georgia, you surely made mother happy. Did you see her face? You know, I'm going to help her more too." The whole house gradually became neater and cleaner. It was such fun putting into practice some of the graces of my new-found friend.

The kids named Charlie Chaplin "Our funny clown." We'd all vie with each other to imitate him best. His cute antics . . . that sharp little backward kick, his twirl of the cane, his hobble, with one toe pointing east and the other west . . . we'd never tire doing them. But I clutched his message to my breast. Secretly, I named him "My flame." Little me, I was carrying a torch like the big girls on my street. He was my light, my dear one . . . He made my heart laugh, for the first time.

I wish the "Hippies" of to-day could hear what I heard and what I saw, in Charlie Chaplin's pictures. Then they wouldn't run to a pill for a few moments of forgetting, nor for a larger view. He opened my eyes, my closed eyes. He said "There is a way to face up to life." I eagerly listened and heeded his message. His sensitiveness made him rebellious and intolerant of hypocrisy and self-righteousness with its formal worship, but he protested in a meaningful, constructive way.

The little tramp was no "Hippie." His clothes were not just dirty rags. They were a brave attempt at being someone. His acts were not ruinous, nor was he stupified, expecting others to stay awake and do the job. His were energetic gestures. He tried and worked hard to overcome being trodden under foot. He was no beggar. I heard a still small voice crying out from the silent screen against the bald injustices bluffing us all. But I saw the answer in his heroic spirit and deeds. He was a nobody to the world, but proud and dignified to himself.

I knew too that this little character he had created didn't just happen. He had taken a blank sheet and written a book of life. It was loud and clear, even to those who run. He did not crawl into a dark corner and gaze into space. With every blow, his spirit rose higher. He dusted the clay off and sprang into action. He glowed.

My mother, trying to be helpful, would tell me constantly—I can hear her now—"Don't forget you are the grand-niece of an English lord."[1] But this didn't help. It didn't answer a thing, nor put shoes on my feet. Charlie's acts inspired me.

I heard of a company trying out people for "Pinafore." I wanted this chance, but as life would have it I didn't have the

[1] An odd coincidence is that Chaplin was told in boyhood that his half-brother Sydney was the son of a lord. *My Autobiography* (London: Bodley Head, 1964), p.9; cited hereafter as *MA*. Such private "myths" have been common enough. Chaplin may have had this in mind when his character Terry in *Limelight* tells Calvero that she is the daughter of the fourth son of an English lord.

carfare. "Mother," I begged, "this could be a big opportunity. Please ask dad for some change." I was desperate. Of course he said, "Tell her I won't give her a dime. She's just wasting her time." So I frantically searched through every drawer and came up with the change. One obstacle was down.

But in my hurry, I scorched my dress. My mother, who never failed on these occasions, went to pieces. She threw up her hands and cried hysterically, "Now see what you've done! What are we going to do? What can you wear?" I answered firmly, trying to hold myself together, "Why mother before every audition do you have to go into hysterics and send me out with my nerves frayed? Please mother, don't make everything a tragedy. Please?" I pinned my dress together and left the house wanting to cry . . . not sing.

When it came turn to sing, I still had a lump in my throat. I was frightened. I reached out for help . . . and almost like a voice speaking to me, came that sweet theme from the little comedian, "There is a spirit in man that cannot be downed. Let it soar." I sang out, and from a large group I was picked to play and sing the leading role.[1]

I asked myself, "Is my life changing? Have I found the key? Have I learned a little? Could thoughts of courage and hope take tangible form? Is it possible to rule out such failure and bring out beauty?" My comic, my little tramp had stirred up these awe-inspiring questions. Then one could make a masterpiece of one's life, instead of something hideous. I'd better choose the better way. "It's up to me," I told myself.

[1] Georgia's high school yearbook says that her "voice made her justly famous when she appeared as 'Ralph Rackstraw' in the opera *H.M.S. Pinafore*."

5

Just to philosophize about this man, Charlie Chaplin, was not enough. I became fired with the desire to see him, meet him and talk with him in person. But how? It was like reaching for the moon . . . impossible! Or was it?

He had changed my morbid questions into, "Is man something special? Are all things possible to him? Is he made a little lower than the angels?" No one else but this funny man had taken me out of my well of darkness.

Melancholy is ugly. I had felt this ugliness inside me all my life, even though I had heard nothing but these words, "Georgia is so beautiful." These words fell heavy on my ears. I realized from the time I was a little child, a person wasn't pretty because he deserved it, nor had earned it. He was born that way . . . and that . . . not of his own volition. "Why be haughty about it?" I'd ask myself.

However, to feel beauty and give it out to others, as Charlie did, was something else again. He was giving out hope and a way to live, with your head above the clouds but with your feet on the ground. He did it simply, so that the simple could understand and be entertained at the same time. He never seemed to preach, he wanted people to laugh and learn. He received good ideas and used them to help others. His pictures were like a breath of fresh air in the otherwise polluted and foul atmosphere.

The more I saw him on the screen, the more I wanted to hear him and converse with him. But then came the suggestion, "He's way out in Hollywood and it costs lots of money to get there." I cast out these thoughts . . . as dribble. I said to myself, "People have traveled far and wide for knowledge . . . why not I?" I was commencing to glimpse that we experience just what we think. So my child's faith burned bright.

I was back at school only a few days when the Chicago Musical College offered a scholarship to the best singer in our school. Many contestants lined up for the auditions.

Dorothy Dean, the girl in front of me, was beautifully dressed as usual. She was very popular and I thought was the best singer at school. But more importantly, she belonged to a sorority. She was in "The" clique. They never knew I existed.

I had been rushed by one sorority, but when they found out about my financial status, I was dropped resoundingly. No other one ever looked my way. This made me a nobody. You were nothing at school if you were poor. Gladys, my chum, put it this way, "It's like being an 'untouchable.' Sororities have ruined my school life. I hate them. I'll be glad when I'm out of here." This was the deep hurt and shame all those on the outside of the inner circle were made to feel. No one in a sorority ever spoke to us. How could they? They never even saw us. We could never . . . ever stand in their certain place on the landing. That was "off limits."

This horrible feeling of being inferior, and of course rebellious, tried to creep in. It talked loudly. Then I thought of how the poor little tramp triumphed over these suggestions. I felt the riches, the true riches of his great grace, and the fear subsided and all chanciness left. I heard myself talking out loud, "I'll do my best, my very best."

I sang out with abandon and joy . . . and dignity. I was awarded the scholarship. Not only that, as important as that was . . . Dorothy Dean took me by the arm and walked down the hall with me. Every one saw me arm and arm with Dorothy Dean, her sorority sisters, as well as my little friends. The wall of partition between us had been broken down by courage and effort. As we walked along, I could see out of the corner of my eye the amazement on everybody's face.

To my surprise, Dorothy put her arm around me and said, "Georgia, you deserved the award. I've always envied you that rich voice." "You did?" I asked. "I never thought you ever noticed me before," I continued. She smiled so sweetly and said, "Well now that we know each other, will you be my chum?" It was a miracle. I became her pet. I was in. From that day on, I could stand on the landing with that clique. My own little pals were right alongside of me, including Gladys.

While on the way to one of my free singing lessons at the Chicago Musical College on Michigan Boulevard,[1] out of the blue heavens I came face to face with Charlie Chaplin. It was the real flesh and blood Charlie. He was walking alone. All I could dare say, but I did dare it was, "Hello, Charlie." Then I held my breath. Finally, his face broke into that famous smile and he answered me, "Hello." He answered me. He spoke . . . to me![2]

I ran all the way to catch the streetcar for home. I wanted to broadcast the news to the kids, my family, the entire neighborhood. The streetcar dragged, as my heart flew. So I spread the word to everyone in the car.

When I reached home, I was like Paul Revere. Breathlessly I scooted about and proudly related the big event. I even was tempted to fudge a little, and add a few words to his reply, but I didn't. I just repeated his "Hello" real loudly. I was the envy of all the kids, for the little fellow did belong to them too. How could one little "Hello" mean so much to so many?

1 While the Chicago Musical College has no record of Georgia's enrollment, there were a number of musical colleges and conservatories in Chicago during the 1910s and 1920s, many of whose names began with Chicago, and several of which were located on South Michigan Avenue.

2 Chaplin traveled east with his then companion, the actress Florence Deshon, in August 1920. He stopped in Chicago a few days before joining her in New York. See Max Eastman, *Love and Revolution* (New York: Random House, 1964), p. 205.

6

A few more years of working, growing up and trying to save, passed. Money—it takes lots of money to get to California. When . . . how . . . was I to get it?

I picked up "The Herald and Examiner"[1] to scan the want ads. On the front page, in bold letters was, "The Herald and Examiner will pay $1,000 to the winner of a beauty contest." It was for "Miss Chicago." "One thousand dollars . . . that's all I needed," I thought.

My heart leapt with joy. But immediately in came that train of thoughts to discourage one. "You haven't anything pretty to try out in . . . and it calls for one test in a bathing suit . . . where can you get that?" Foolishly I listened, "Where can you turn for help? . . . nowhere . . . and to no one. It's hopeless." But I was learning to talk back to this parade of negative thoughts, thanks to the little comic. I said, "I can hope, I can expect. I won't give up . . . yet."

Late one night my front door bell rang. It was Jo, a tall, blond boy from school. He had always been sweet on me and often dropped by . . . but never so late. I said, "Hi Jo. What on earth brings you calling so late?" He answered, "I've just come from a meeting of the Englewood Business Men's Association." Mother came into the room wondering what it was all about. Jo continued, "The business men of Englewood want Georgia to be one of the entrants in the beauty contest from this part of town. How about it Mrs. Hale? . . . Georgia?" We both hesitated. Then he added knowingly, "A very wealthy woman

1 *The Englewood Herald and Examiner.*

we know will supply you with any garments you might need. Alright?" Mother and I said together, "That's fine. When and where is it?"

But father came stalking in and asked, "What chance have you in a great big city as large as Chicago? Georgia, I couldn't help from hearing this foolish conversation, and I'm not going to let you become indebted for those clothes." But Jo was all prepared for him. He knew him. He said, "You won't have to pay a cent Mr. Hale. It's all going to be paid by the merchants. They need the publicity." Father protested, "But she won't win. It's silly to expect that." Jo finished the discussion by saying, "We don't expect her to win but we think she'll make a nice entry." The three of us were all for it. What could father do but agree.

It was all so wonderful. Jo coming to the door . . . mother, who hadn't read a thing about the contest nor did she know anything of my dreams to go to Hollywood . . . yet she was so supporting. "Was that hope and expectancy of good, paying off?" I asked myself. I could only answer, "Yes, yes!"

Out on the big municipal pier we paraded . . . in street clothes . . . evening clothes and bathing suits. As the gruelling contest continued, so did that little devil sitting on my shoulder. "You're tired and look it . . . It's impossible . . . Why did you enter? . . . You'll never be chosen . . . You'll never get to Hollywood. Why did you decide to waste your time and others' money and enter a beauty contest?" But, in a still small voice I could hear . . . that first little message from the comic, "Throw out your chest and walk over your troubles . . . smile."

I got a second breath. I said to myself, "If he can battle these whispering lies, so can I, so can everyone, everywhere and now." I did. I smiled. Quickly, things started to move. They eliminated, one by one . . . until . . . I was left alone on the platform. I glanced to my left, then to my right. No one was on stage but me. Then Mr. Weiss, one of the judges, stepped up onto the stage. He extended his hand, waved to the band and marched around slowly to the front of the stage.

He stopped the music and announced dramatically, "Miss Georgia Hale is the winner! We hereby change her name to 'Miss Chicago.'" The band struck-up and the applause was deafening.

My happiness was threefold. I could now get to Hollywood. I had won the beauty contest for Englewood. Last, but most important, I had found things were changing for the better . . . because I was changing . . . within. It was thrilling!

7

Now I found myself at the station, bidding my family farewell. I hated to say goodbye to my sisters, especially Melissa. Father took me aside and said, "I think you're a silly girl squandering your contest money, and the hundreds more you received in personal appearances . . . on Hollywood. It's not too late to back out. Take your father's advice. Have I ever been wrong?"

I didn't have to answer that, for Melissa stepped forward and said, "I wish I could go with you to look after you." Frances said, "Don't worry about Georgia. She'll take care of herself." Mother assured dad, "Georgia has a way . . . I have confidence in her." But she whispered to me, "Be careful, be good, and only good will come to you."

A few moments before the train started moving, up ran Jo, my contest promoter and admirer. He waved frantically yelling, "Don't leave, don't leave!" He grabbed and pulled me to him saying, "Georgia I don't want you to go . . ." Just then the train gave a lurch and I ran and jumped on. Jo threw all caution to the winds, and as I moved away he screamed, "I love you! I love you!"

It was a happy send off. I liked the attention of Jo. But not really . . . it was only a little bubble. Deep down I was delighted to leave. I felt that I had been a prisoner of trivia, of a meaningless and irrelevant life. I was glad to flee this atmosphere of poverty, gloom and of getting no place. Now I felt I was speeding towards the blazing sunshine of Charlie's world. His shaft of light was intimately present within me. I was fired with the purpose of seeing and knowing him.

As I neared my destination, up popped the frightening suggestions of how debased Hollywood was . . . I could hear, "Georgia, you can't get into pictures without letting the big shots make love to you. The industry you know, is filled with dope fiends . . . has one wild party after another and you're awfully young to be facing this alone." These dark forebodings hung heavy and my heart beast faster.

When I took one step down from the train, a chorus of camera men shouted, "Hold it, Miss Chicago!" They took several pictures of me and wished me great success in my new adventure. It was such a surprise and such a wonderful welcome. The next day my picture was splashed on the front page.[1] "What a colossal beginning," I thought.

I couldn't wait to see Hollywood. I expected it to be wrapped in tinsel, I guess. But it wasn't. It wasn't much different from where I came. I looked on the streets and in the gutters for dope fiends . . . but there weren't any. Still there was a glamour I had not felt nor seen before. Chauffeur-driven limousines paraded Hollywood Boulevard. In the back seat was always some actress or actor wanting to be seen. Some even had two flunkies engineering their car. The street was lined with colorful eating places . . . Armstrong and Schroeder's . . . Musso-Frank's . . . The Montmartre and others.

Foolishly, I had thought when I arrived, "What a colossal beginning." I found getting inside the studios was the bitter end. It was like trying to get into a palace, guarded by gendarmes. The secretaries acted cold and mighty, like veritable sentinels. Each little job, or part, was sought after by hundreds of raving beauties. I tried every morsel of salesmanship that I knew, however tiny, but all I'd hear was, "Come back in ten days."

Finally I thought of the publicity I got upon my arrival. Calmly, and with all the dignity I could muster, I said to the

[1] *The Los Angeles Examiner*, Saturday, 19 May 1923. Georgia was greeted by Frank Wiggins, secretary of the LA Chamber of Commerce.

secretary, "Just announce to the casting director, that Miss Chicago has arrived . . . he's expecting me."

It worked! In a few moments I was sitting before Mr. James Ryan, the casting director. I was amazed at getting in to see him. But I was more surprised to find him so soft spoken, so utterly business-like and so gentlemanly. They were all supposed to be wolves. He said, "Yes Miss Chicago, I saw your picture in the paper. It's Miss Georgia Hale, isn't it?" I answered happily, "That's it. How nice that you remembered." Without further comment, he signed me to a seven-week contract.[1] When I walked out with that little contract under my arm, I was bursting with gratitude. I said to myself, "Foolish . . . how foolish I would have been to let fear stop me." I was holding fast to my new philosophy.

But immediately I was sent away from Hollywood on location, to an Island[2] off the coast of Santa Barbara, California. It was like having all my plans snatched out of my hand. At the close of each day's work, I would climb the hill, and sit alone and gaze across the Pacific towards filmland.

I knew Charles Chaplin was king there, and that he lived atop a hill, in a palatial mansion. I wondered what winding roads led there, and if I could ever find them. I was eager, restless. I wanted to leave the island and search for him.

Gradually the days lengthened into weeks. With the lull of the surf and the quiet relaxation, and a sort of giving up of my will, I found an unfamiliar peace. The clang and noise of teaming mad ambition, was shut out by stillness. It was easier to have faith in everything. The stars were so near. I was so inspired by the beauty of the heavens. This seemed more like reality. Now I wanted to stay here forever, where I would never hear a horn or the clang of the street-car again. I wished everyone I loved would come to this Island. But the last day

1 According to Paramount publicity information, the studio was Fox.

2 Georgia is probably referring to one of the Channel Islands located in Santa Barbara Channel.

came, and I felt the heavy pull . . . of gravity . . . or was it fear? . . . or are they the same?

Going back to the mainland, the sea was rolling and choppy like my thoughts. All around me the people were becoming sea-sick. I went to the front of the boat, where I could feel the cool fresh breeze. But bad thoughts came along with me. They were whirling around me and in me. Fear had opened the Pandora box for me. I felt uncertain, then a little sick. Thoughts of job-hunting again poured in . . . with hundreds competing for every part, and filled me with anxiety. I was feeling sea-sick for sure now.

I rose up and tried hard to shake off these bad thoughts and feelings. I paced up and down. I searched my mind for some helpful thought. In trotted the little comic . . . I remembered him smiling, tipping his hat, and graciously helping a little old lady to cross the street.

I looked up. Right in front of me was a tiny man wanting to go downstairs and he couldn't keep his balance. I said, "I'll be happy to help you." He answered in a husky voice, "Well, that would be mighty helpful. All I want is to get out of this wind." When I returned to my place, the words of Shakespeare were in my thoughts, "How far that little candle throws his beam! So shines a good deed in a naughty world."[1]

An unexpected big spray of cold water hit the deck and me right in the face. I was so surprised, but it felt good. I was refreshed. However I was a sight. My mascara started running and everyone burst into laughter, and so did I. The whole gloomy scene had changed into comedy. It was such a small event and yet I felt well, completely well. The rest of the trip was delightful.

I returned to Hollywood feeling inspired and rested. The moist clean air of the island and trip home refreshed my entire being. I was happy to get back to movieland. After all, I had

[1] *The Merchant of Venice,* Act.V, sc.vi.

only been in it a few days when I was sent away. It was like back home, to the destination for which I had set out.

But this feeling of getting back home didn't last very long. I packed my pictures under my arm and went from one studio to another, but I heard the same old tune, "Come back in ten days" or "There's no work, at all!"

After two weeks of getting on and off buses and pounding the side-walks, the refreshed, inspired and rested feeling was gone. I said to myself, "You can't even get a few days' work and you came out here expecting to meet Charlie Chaplin in person. Father was right . . . You're just plain foolish, and you're squandering all that contest money."

Finally I got a few days at the Fox studio, but this was cancelled. In desperation I went to a small studio[1] and there to my surprise I got a few days . . . Josef von Sternberg[2] was the assistant director. He was a dark, short fellow with a slight foreign accent. His black wavy hair was cut close to his head. He was a quiet, intense chap, who moved about slowly and thoughtfully.

The first day had been a long hot one. I had been one of a big rabble . . . in some rough, boistrous scenes. But, as on the other picture, the day had been spent in mostly just waiting. My make-up had caked. I felt dirty and ugly, not that it mattered. I went into a corner to try to fix up. When I looked into my make-up mirror, glancing over my shoulder was Mr. Sternberg. I couldn't believe it . . . but sure enough there he was smiling at me.

He said, "You noticed, no doubt, that I've been studying that face of yours all day?" I answered timidly, "No, I really didn't think anyone had seen me." He continued, "Of course, I have my reasons for looking you over. But I must say, you are

1 Grand-Asher Studios were located at 1432 Gower Street, Hollywood.

2 Josef von Sternberg (b. Jonas Sternberg, 29 May 1894, Vienna; d. 22 Dec 1969, Hollywood) was working as scenarist and assistant to Roy William Neill on his film *By Divine Right*.

a beautiful girl. There is an inner fire and courage about you . . . fine qualities."

I couldn't believe him. I thought he was teasing me and expected him to laugh. I smiled and asked, "Did you say courage? . . . or sadness?" He didn't laugh. He continued with a serious question, "Would you like to read a book I've translated?" [1] Well, I was overcome with delight. I quickly said, "I'll be so happy to read your book." He smiled at last and added, "You interest me."

The following day, I returned his book. I praised his work. I told him, "You are just brimming over with knowledge. It is a brilliant rendition." I hoped that I said the right and correct thing. He seemed pleased. He pulled up a chair and sat down next to me. This was a big compliment I thought, to sit right next to the assistant director. He continued talking and told me in such a serious manner, "I've given my life to the study of theatre and picture-making. Lighting and composition has been another love. You know, I could photograph you and make you . . . exquisite! Someday soon, maybe I shall." I was thrilled and said, "I hope so. I do hope you don't forget."

I couldn't understand his interest. He asked, "Do you read much?" I hesitated . . . He said again, "Well, do you?" I answered reluctantly, "I hate to confess this, but your book is the first book I've read in a long time." He answered, "I admire you for being so truthful. But promise me you'll start reading good books. I read four a week. Will you read a little more Georgia?" I answered enthusiastically, "I promise, and I deeply appreciate your interest. I want to improve in every way . . . truly." He smiled sweetly and patted me on the head. I was so happy. Someone really cared a little.

At the close of the next day, Mr. Sternberg approached again. He informed me, "This is the last day of work for the

[1] *Daughters of Vienna,* freely adapted from a novel of Karl Adolf by Josef von Sternberg (London, New York, Vienna: The International Editor, 1922).

crowd, so I won't see you here. I've had one more day to study you carefully . . . You see, I'm just about to start a picture. It's my first at directing and I've got to be sure. But I'm convinced that you have what I've been searching for to play the lead in my story. Are you interested?"

My mouth dropped open. I couldn't believe he really said the "lead." I answered breathlessly, "I'd be glad to play any part. Of course I'd love it. How nice of you . . . for the opportunity . . . I mean, it's so good of you to have faith in me . . . I'll try my best . . . I'll . . . He broke in, and it was well that he did, for I had lost my head with joy. He said calmly, "Very well, we'll start next week. I'll call . . ."

I finished the day's work walking around with my head in the clouds. At last a chance to be seen in a picture. "Who knows what it might lead to?" I asked myself. "Did he say that he saw inner courage in me? Could it be possible my sadness was going?" If I could only learn more, from Chaplin.

I felt upright with hope, less a victim of circumstance. I remembered Edwin Markham's poem "Man with the Hoe," [1] where he questioned whether this bent slave of the earth was the man to whom God gave dominion. I felt a little more like the latter. The day had certainly sent me dreaming. I was happy.

[1] Edwin Charles Markham (1852-1940), an Oregon poet, won widespread popularity with the publication of *The Man with the Hoe and Other Poems* (San Francisco: Book Club of California, 1916).

8

The air gradually went out of my bubble of hope. My toy and joy wilted and so did I. For days, weeks, months passed and I did not hear a thing from Josef von Sternberg. So I was forced back to working a day here and a day there.

A contest was being held at Metro-Goldwyn-Mayer Studios. It was a beauty-talent project. I was in no mood to enter it. But the publicity man called me aside and said, "Georgia, enter it. It won't hurt you, and it might get you a few days' work . . . even if you come out last."

So I went with a mob of gorgeous girls out on location. They took yards and yards of footage, in different scenes and outfits. Our final shots were at the beach in bikinis. We worked like dogs. We all knew we weren't going to get a cent for the gruelling hot day, but every girl gave as if she were being paid a thousand dollars. The prize was a nice long contract.

I needed the money and the contract, but I realized more clearly with every passing moment that this was a different ball game. Winning a contest in Hollywood was entirely different from . . . Chicago. Every girl I looked at was more magnificent than the last . . . the competition was fierce. I knew it too well. I was convinced that I didn't have a chance.

I wasn't surprised when the days passed and I received no word. Long after the day was through, and there was never a chance of an important call, my phone rang. It was the publicity man who had coaxed me to enter that contest. He said, "This is Jerry." Before he could apologize, I immediately assured him, "Oh, don't worry about that gruelling deal. It was a good experience and I was aware that I didn't have a chance."

While I took a breath he whispered, "Please stop talking a minute. I stepped out of a meeting to call you. I just learned that it's dwindled down to two girls[1] . . . you and another gal. Be at the studio at 10 o'clock and you'll find out the verdict. I do hope you're the winner. Don't mention this call . . . I've got to get back . . . good luck."

I hung up the phone and stared into space and this is practically what I did all night. Who would be chosen? Who was the other girl? I thought I could guess? It was Miss Knight I was sure. But I was grateful to be in her class, and to be second.

At 10 o'clock on the dot, I was there at the studio. I gave my name to some girl in the cage and asked, "Do you know who won the contest?" She answered in a vague, disinterested manner, "The what? . . . Well whatever, I don't. Just take a seat." I waited and waited. I fidgeted. I made myself up and renewed my make-up a dozen times. Almost two hours later I was famished and exhausted. Just as I was about to slip out for something to eat, a girl from inside the office asked, "Is Georgia Hale in the waiting room?" I jumped up and said, "I'm here." She said, "Follow me."

Down a long hall she led me. While my heart was pounding loudly, she was completely silent. Suddenly, she turned to me and said soberly, "The casting director is waiting for you in there." I entered, and over he came to meet me with hand extended saying, "Congratulations Miss Georgia Hale, for winning our beauty contest . . . I reached for a chair. He continued, "Yes, sit down and I'll get your contract papers . . . they're all ready for you to sign. It starts to-morrow . . . nice?" I stammered, "Thank you, thank you very much."

1 Miss Charlotte Stevens and Miss Waunda Wiley were the two runners-up in the brunettes category.

He got the papers and said, "Don't thank me . . . but I'm sure if I'd been one of the judges, I would have chosen you too." I was so nervous that when I took the papers they rattled from my trembling. I hoped he'd turn away and not watch me trying to sign my name, but instead he saw the whole thing. He said so cutely, "Now Georgia, be calm! After all this is a small contract. But mark my word, I predict you'll be signing a big one before very long." I laughed at myself, and said, "It's mighty big to me. I didn't sleep all night wondering who would get it. Thank you for your encouraging words." I managed to scribble my name. He shook my hand and I left his office feeling that I really was someone.

I pranced out through the waiting room. Now it seemed bathed in sunshine. I carried my contract high in my hand as I beamed a smile at everybody. They took no notice of me. But Jerry the publicity man came barging in the door just as I was dashing out. He snatched my papers from my hand and asked, "Did they decide on you? Are these the contracts?" I threw my arms around him and said, "I just signed them. And I really owe it all to you. You're a dear." He looked at his watch and ran off saying, "Bully for you, I can see your name in spot-lights."

That evening I was so inspired. I said, "Now I have something definite to work for." I put on my leotards and started practicing and dancing. I went through every routine I ever knew. I whirled and turned, but just as I did a quick leap, I felt a strange movement in my leg. In a few minutes my ankle and leg were so inflamed and swollen, I couldn't even bear to put my weight on my foot. With all my will and might I tried to throw this off, but in vain. In one tiny moment, I was rendered helpless.

My contract, my beautiful contract . . . was all blown up in smoke, and so was my ecstasy. I had to phone the studio and tell them of my accident. Of course, it was of little moment to M-G-M, but to me it was like losing the world. I found out that "Walls do not a prison make"[1] as has been written. I was as trapped as if someone had snapped hand-cuffs on me and thrown me into a bottomless pit. "Search for the blessing," my new philosophy tried to whisper, but I wouldn't listen. I was fiercely rebellious and furiously tense. This didn't speed my recovery at all. It all added up to my staying on crutches for six months and the end of my career . . .[2]

[1] Richard Lovelace (1618-1658), "To Lucasta, Going Beyond the Seas": Stone walls do not a prison make, Nor iron bars a cage.

[2] This version, a rather bold compression of the facts to lend them a more dramatic shape, passed into circulation. It can be found repeated in the programme notes to *The Gold Rush*.

9

My life was completely changed. I became resigned to my fate. I was docile and humbled by the turn of events. This was the time when I needed my mother, and this was the happening that caused my entire family to tear up their roots and move to California. This was the blessing that came from my adversity . . . that blessing I refused to search for . . . I was guilty like those of long ago, who having eyes could not see. For my family spent many years in sunny California and thrived on its beauty.

When they arrived I was still on crutches. A woman and her daughter had watched over me for months. In return I paid them a nice amount. They needed this money badly, so we were twice blessed. On the day of my families' arrival, all I had left in the world was eight dollars. But I was grateful I didn't owe a penny. My heart was filled with gratitude at having my family near me. They were overjoyed to see me and at long last to get to California. But I could feel their dismay at seeing me still on crutches. I heard them questioning each other, "Is she going to be a cripple for life?"

We moved a few doors away, in a place I had found. I wanted to keep my old phone number, although it had ceased to ring. My mother, father and sisters acted as if they had arrived in paradise. They thought the little cottage I had found was a dream house. Actually it was an old wooden house, but it was covered with roses and surrounded by lush green foliage. It was on the back of a large green lawn, almost hidden in this beautiful bouquet. But it was dainty, and a romantic place. They settled in as if they were home at last, truly home . . .

I had forgotten my first impressions of California with its palm trees, orange groves, mountains and long stretches of beaches. It had become a place of war for me, with victories and heart-breaking defeats.

My father cornered me one day and started scolding, "Remember at the train what I said? I told you it was foolish to squander your money out here. Now look at you! I knew and I warned you that you'd never make a dent in this place. You see, it's different . . . a lot of of competition. It was mighty easy to win things in Chicago . . . no one to compete with . . . I told you, Georgia." I couldn't answer. I was too ashamed of myself.

Mother joined us. I could talk to her. I could explain, or rather I could communicate with mother. I said sadly, "Honey, I'm so sorry I let you all down. I know you put so much hope and faith in me. Now here I am, as papa has just told me, a failure and broke." But mother came over to me and smoothed my hair. She knew father had said something to squelch me. I couldn't hide my emotions from her. She said bravely, "I still have faith in you. You are a lovely young girl and you're going to be alright."

My family were courageous, but they were worried. I heard mother ask my sisters, "When is she going to be able to walk again?" Frances, who was always a "doubting Thomas" said, "I'm commencing to wonder if she ever will? I have my doubts about it." But Melissa spoke with love and authority, "Of course she will."

Soon after, I went with Melissa to the drug store. I went hobbling in on my crutches. One leg was now much smaller than the other and much weaker. My pharmacist called to me, "See here young lady . . . what are you trying to do to yourself? Why are you still using those crutches? Do you know, that if you continue, you're going to be a cripple?"

I knew he didn't understand so I protested, "But when I walk on my foot, it swells and turns red and pains." He demanded in a fatherly manner, "Here, give me those things!

Now I want you to walk home . . . without these props. Just let it swell, turn red or whatever." He handed Melissa my crutches and added with a big smile, "You'll be alright in a few days, just stop all this babying stuff." Bless my dear druggist, he was like an oracle! It turned out exactly as he had predicted. I had been a creature pacing up and down in a cage that wasn't there.

10

I came face to face with the fact that I was now able to work. I was timid and frightened. My family were all pretty well located. Father was in real estate, and my sisters were both employed. I was eager to help, for I knew they had spent everything getting relocated in California. Mother was my biggest concern, as she had been all my life.

I searched for work but I wasn't trained for a job of any kind, and I was turned down. I figured, "All I know is show business. It's too late for pictures. I spoiled all my chances in them. I'll have to go back to New York."

One lonely rainy day, mother and I were alone at home. I told her of my plans. I said, "Honey, I'll just have to go back to New York to get work. I have to go." Mother was silent. I felt she had lost her faith in me. This hurt. She rose, shrugged her shoulders and started to leave me. I ran to her and we threw our arms around each other and almost sobbed out loud.

The phone rang. I could hardly say "Hello." It was for me. He said, "You have forgotten me . . . but I've not forgotten you . . . this is Josef von Sternberg." I answered breathlessly, "But of course I remember you. I suppose by now that picture you were speaking of to me is finished." He said, "Then you do remember. It's been a long time. What have you been doing?" I answered quickly, "Oh, I've been busy." I didn't go into details. He said happily, "May I see you to-night? I have something to discuss with you."

My cheeks were flushed when I hung up. Mother asked excitedly, "Who was that? You were so elated." I said trying hard to be calm, "That was that director. The one I told you about showing an interest in me. The one whose book I read and everything . . . remember?" She remembered. Her face came to life as if some magic words had been spoken. That one little phone call had chased away our blues. What a joy to see her happy. Since her arrival I had not seen her so filled with joy and hope.

It had been a long time since I tried to doll up and look glamorous, but I tried my best. I was afraid to face Jo von Sternberg. After all I had been through, I felt faded. When the front door bell rang, my heart stopped. I opened the door and when he saw me he exclaimed, "You look radiant! Have you been resting? Tell me the secret. Whatever it is, keep it up." I felt so relieved, even if he didn't mean it. It was good to hear those sweet compliments. And was I glad all the pain and frustration wasn't showing. I said, "Thank you for those kind words and thank you for remembering me and calling."

When we sat on the couch he silently studied me for a few moments and said, "I've been all these months raising money to make my picture. Now I have it and I still want you to play the leading role. Are you interested at this late date?" These words were like a needle thrust into me filled with hope and joy. I wanted to shout and kiss him, but instead I answered softly, "I'd love it. I'd dearly love it. I thought I was through. I mean . . ." He broke in and said, "I'm glad you feel this way . . . you'll be perfect, just perfect in the part." He left abruptly and said, "I'll pick you up to-morrow and we'll go together to the location. Be ready at seven."

I ran to the kitchen and almost knocked mother down. There she had been with her ears pressed against the door. Her joy made mine seem small. At last a chance. I wasn't through. My prison doors had sprung wide open. Whatever the lesson was I had to learn in this school room of ours, I evidently had passed the grade. I was glad to shove it all in the past and forget it . . . I was living in the "now." "That time was mine from here on in," I vowed.

However I never wanted to forget . . . Charlie. Just before I dozed off this exciting night, his face came so clearly before me. I had not thought of him for months. Now he was back. Of course he had been my reason for coming to Hollywood or getting into pictures. But the hope of ever seeing him or talking to him I now realized had been a foolish childish dream. Nevertheless, if it hadn't been for him, I would not be going with Josef von Sternberg on location to-morrow. "What a happy thought," I told myself.

11

My career in Hollywood really started this day. Sure enough at seven sharp, Josef von Sternberg appeared and off we went to the location. There I started playing the lead opposite George K. Arthur [1] in a picture titled *The Salvation Hunters*. What an appropriate name for my first picture.

This picture was a desperate attempt by Jo Sternberg to gain recognition. He told me, "I have been assistant director long enough to men without one tenth of my background and knowledge. I'm going to change the whole picture of me. From now on don't call me Jo Sternberg. I want to be addressed, 'Josef von Sternberg.' " [2] I replied, "O.K. I believe in you. I look up to you as a man of great talent and just you wait, Hollywood is going to hear about you. Someone is going to discover you!" He liked to hear this, even though I was a young girl who knew very little. Like all men he was encouraged by the woman at his side. It's a strange phenomenon, how some little female can make a great man feel whole.

George K. Arthur, who had gained fame in London for playing "Kipps" by H.G. Wells, needed a come-back. George

[1] George Brest (b. 27 April 1899, Aberdeen, Scotland) came to Hollywood in 1922 under the name of George K. Arthur. After *The Salvation Hunters* was released he was signed to a seven-year contract with Metro, and was reunited with Sternberg in *The Exquisite Sinner* (1925). Arthur retired from the screen in 1935.

[2] According to Sternberg himself, it was Elliot Dexter, the star and co-producer of the film *By Divine Right*, who added the "von" without his knowledge or consent. *Fun in a Chinese Laundry* (New York: Macmillan, 1965), p.154. This work is referred to below as *FCL*.

was a young Englishman filled with ambition and know-how. It was he who promoted this whole effort. He talked Jo into writing and directing this picture and he promoted the money. He was a [curly] sort of character. You never knew which way his thought would take, but you were sure he would produce, come hell or high water.

The third day into the picture we ran out of money. We were on location on the docks at Wilmington, California, using a big dredge . . . and we were asked to leave.[1] But George, who was used to hard knocks and whose vocabulary did not include "quit" or "no," blithely said to the owner, "I'll be back with the money in a jiffy," and to Jo, "continue shooting." Jo was very proud and sensitive, but he bravely followed George's advice.

George was more of a business man than an actor. He must have begged and borrowed, for back he came with his pockets stuffed with bills. His cheeks were like two red apples. He didn't look a day over sweet sixteen. There was something impish about George. Jo was the straight man of this team. His pride and dignity would never have permitted him to do the things George could do, and did. They were a perfect act.

Jo was very conscious of his appearance too. I remember that day he saw his profile in a glass as he hurried by. He went back and studied his reflection. Then and there he decided not to cut his hair short in the back . . . so it would balance his nose. It did improve him. So he was the first suggestion of a "hippie." What a change was coming over Jo. He was even sporting black shirts on the set, which hadn't been seen before in movieland.

Jo tantalized George. It seemed to me that he enjoyed teasing and tormenting him. Jo would grind and grind the camera and use so much footage on every shot. George would squirm, for it was he who had to dig up more cash. This was a fault that continued with Jo through the years. He could not, or would not conserve on film. Poor George!

1 The film was shot on location at San Pedro, in Chinatown, the San Fernando Valley, and at Grand-Asher Studios.

Downtown in L. A. was our last location. Trouble? Sure . . . there was no more film. Jo always appeared completely calm at these crises. He just let George do all the conniving.

The final shots were filmed on "poverty row" [1] in Hollywood. We all held our breaths the last hours . . . but we inched through to the finish. It cost about $5,000 and was made in three weeks.[2] At last it was finished . . . but . . .

[1] Originally the name given to an area of Hollywood around Sunset Blvd. and Gower Street where films were made inexpensively by lesser known producers. The term later came to refer to a type of production made by minor companies such as Mascot, Tiffany, or Grand National.

[2] While many of the financial details of production are both unclear and questionable, it seems likely that the final cost of the film was just under five thousand dollars.

12

They had no release for *The Salvation Hunters*. Here they were film in hand. Their precious dream completed, but no place would accept it. George K. Arthur had the dirty job again. He scurried from one place to another but they continued to slam doors in his face. They'd ask, "Who made the picture? Who is in it? . . ." Poor George would tell them. They'd answer bluntly, "Never heard of them." Out he'd go.

George, secretly in a frantic effort as a last ditch chance, fought his way in to see Kono,[1] Charlie Chaplin's faithful valet. He cornered him and literally begged Kono to show the film to Chaplin. But Kono quickly told George, "Mester Chaplin too busy with own picture . . . sorry . . . sorry." George would not be waved away. He would not, could not take "no," for an answer. This was his last stop. He pleaded, "Please just take it and in case he wants a few moments' relaxation . . . show him this. It's a little gem, he'll thank you Kono. It's entirely different—new director, new faces and new treatment. Kono believe me, he'll be grateful to you. Please?"

Kono thought it over and answered, "Well I not sure, won't promise . . . but . . . maybe. You come to the kitchen door and slip it in to me . . . maybe I put it on without him knowing . . . I try. But don't think so . . ." George bowed to the floor with gratitude for these crumbs.

[1] Toraichi Kono (b. 1888, Hiroshima, Japan) was major-domo and factotum to Chaplin from 1916 to 1934. He appeared in *The Adventurer* and *The Circus*.

He rushed . . . returned in an hour and gave his precious treasure to Kono. He drove slowly down the hill. He was drained of all feeling. "You're a fool, a dreamer. The impossible can't happen. Chaplin will never see it," kept clanging in his ears.

Days passed or rather crawled by, and George knew, was convinced, he'd been a clown. He decided to pick up the film but the thought of what to do with it deterred him. He had no other place to go. Jo von Sternberg had grown silent with despair.

It was good that George had not picked it up, for that very night, Charlie Chaplin came home from his studio weary, and at his wit's end. His own picture was at a standstill. After dinner he rang for Kono and asked wearily, "Do you have some little short I can see before turning in?" Kono wondered what to show him. Then he remembered the picture of his little intruder of a few days past. Without telling Mr. Chaplin that it was by an unknown, with an unknown cast, he fearfully put on the film. He really had no choice. He had nothing else in the house. He hurriedly told Mr. Chaplin, "If . . . don't like . . . I take off."

Mr. Chaplin slouched down into a big comfortable chair in his gorgeous showroom with its high ceiling and soft lights, and dreamily watched. The room darkened and the film began. Kono described the whole thing the next day. He said, "My heart stopped. I thought . . . I'd taken too big a chance . . . too big. But soon after picture start. . . I noticed Mr. Chaplin sit up and I heard him say, 'Every frame is like a painting! . . . Where did this film come from? It's like seeing a lovely poem. The characters are so real . . . the mood so intense . . .' "

Kono related, "When I hear Mester Chaplin, I so delighted, for he has not been in happy spirit for days." When the showing was over, Chaplin could not contain his enthusiasm. He wanted to know all about it. Who made it? Who was the leading lady? But of course Kono could not answer any of these questions. He was delighted anyway that he had made Mr. Chaplin so happy. Charlie said to Kono, "I want to see this picture again. Can you arrange it? And Kono, I want to thank you for bringing this artistic little film to my attention. Yes, the director is a poet . . . very good. The leading lady . . . she has a sultry quality that is very interesting. She moved with such grace." Kono knew for sure he had pleased Mr. Chaplin, but he admitted later he didn't exactly know why.

All of this was unknown to George K. Arthur the day he decided that there was no use to leave it up at Mr. Chaplin's any longer. He drove up Benedict Canyon, then Summit Drive, on to Charlie's hill top and stopped. It was the end of the road, in more ways than one for George. He didn't want to go in or even move out of the car. But he forced himself and dragged his feet along the path to the back door . . . the servants' entrance.

Gingerly he rang the bell. Kono appeared with a broad smile and extended his hand. George was puzzled. Kono said, "Thank you, thank you very much. I so glad. I so grateful for that film, *The . . . Salvation . . . Hunters*. It make Mester Chaplin very happy." George swallowed hard and asked, " You mean he saw it? You mean he liked it? " Kono reassured George, "Yes sir, and he wants to see it again, very soon. Can you arrange another showing if I return it?"

George was bouncing with joy and said, "Keep it, or I'll bring it back . . . or whatever you wish . . . just say the word . . . you name it." So overcome with emotion was George as Kono handed him the film, he dropped it. It rolled like a wheel. George scrambled after the magazine and retrieved it as he stammered, "Any time, any place Kono . . . I'll be there." He slid down the banister holding the film high in his hand, then raced for the car.

Josef von Sternberg deeply admired Charles Chaplin. In fact he was his idol. Jo often said, "Chaplin is the only genius in Hollywood. He's without a peer in acting and directing." George K. Arthur knew this. Hence his daring episode of attempting the impossible, that of trying to get the film before the great Charlie, Jo's model. He had kept it a secret from Jo.

Now it could be told. Now he could tell him the glorious news.

George arrived at Jo's place filled with excitement. In contrast, Jo's face was tense and drawn when he answered the door. George concealed his emotion and asked dryly, "How about trying to get the film to Charles Chaplin?" Jo replied waving his arm, "Please spare me . . . it's like asking, 'Let's scale Mount Olympus?' It would be just as absurd and calamitous." George continued, "Jo, what would you say if I told you that Charlie Chaplin has seen . . . *The Salvation Hunters*?" Jo gasped and then laughed answering, "Even the question makes me gasp . . . don't tease, please don't kid with me . . . George, you are a dreamer."

George pulled his chair over to Jo standing by the fire place and whispered, "He did. He saw it." Jo reached for a chair and sat. With pale face he asked, "He didn't really? You're joking." George shouted, "Chaplin saw it and what do you suppose was his reaction?" Weakly Jo asked, "Negative? He didn't like it? Did he really see it?" George started waving his hands in the air saying, "Chaplin not only saw it . . . he loved it. He's calling you a poet, and the picture a gem."

Jo who usually hid his emotions, jumped to his feet and embraced George. Almost weeping he cried, "Charles Chaplin saw my picture! He liked it! Charlie Chaplin . . . I can hardly believe it. Please tell me how it happened?"[1] But Jo's mind started ticking. He exclaimed, "One word from the great Chaplin and we've got it made . . . a release is in our pockets! How? . . . when? . . . where? . . . did it all happen?" Bubbling over with happiness, he had to share it. Once again he didn't give George a chance to answer, he said, "Georgia, let's get

[1] Although there are some discrepancies, similar accounts of how Chaplin came to see the film are given by Sternberg (*FCL*, p. 204-206), and by George K. Arthur. *Evening News* (London), November 13, 1924. Lita Grey recalled that before her marriage to Chaplin, they attended a dinner party given by Sam Goldwyn, after which a screening of *The Salvation Hunters* was shown *My Life with Chaplin*; An Intimate Memoir (New York: Grove, 1966), p.76-77.

Georgia. I've got to tell her the good news." This was typical of Jo von Sternberg to remember others.

While this was going on, I was home waiting . . . just waiting as most people are. The picture had been over for days. There had been no salaries paid,[1] for George and Jo had run out of that kind of money. It had been four weeks without a salary or even a call from a studio. Things looked black and the room was closing in on me, so were my thoughts. "A long walk would do it," I told myself. So I walked and walked while my phone rang and rang.

As I dragged my feet homeward and neared the house, I could see Jo standing at my door. I wasn't sure but his eyes seemed to be laughing. There was a smile on his lips. My face was immobile, frozen . . . Jo grabbed me and shook me saying, "Cheer up, I've got good news for you. The picture has been seen and we're sure to get a release. This means you'll be paid your salary and a nice bonus too."

I could feel the numbness leaving and my face relaxing. I replied quietly, "Please, say it again. It sounds so good. I can hardly believe it. I've been walking for hours wondering who . . . who . . . could help us. Who could or would help the picture? Who could get some money for the cast?" Jo just listened and smiled a broad smile. Wide eyed with curiosity I begged, "Tell me who . . . who is our benefactor?"

Jo took me inside the dark house and turned on the lights. He really turned on the lights for me. He took me by the shoulders and looked straight into my eyes and said, "Charles Chaplin is our angel, none other than the great Chaplin." Jo was studying my eyes to see the big reaction. But I dropped my eyes, I couldn't bare [*sic*]to have him see my emotions. I laughed a bit hysterically and turned my face away saying, "Wonderful, it's a miracle." I was startled by the thought that

1 Sternberg claims that he paid her the rate given to a "dress extra"—$7.50 a day—for every day throughout the duration of filming (*FCL*, p. 155).

once again he . . . my miracle man . . . had turned my sadness into gladness . . . It was a miracle!

Jo knew nothing of my secret. He continued, "Yes, just by luck it was Chaplin . . . Georgia, you don't realize how terrific this man works. His word is law in Hollywood, and by the way, he thinks you gave a very good performance." Then Jo took me in his arms and said lovingly, "We're on our way Georgia Hale, and if you stick with me I'm going to make a big star out of you. Your name will be on everyone's tongue." He gave me a big hug and added, "Tomorrow night the picture is being shown to Mr. Chaplin and guests at F.B.O. Studios.[1] We all have to be there at eight sharp." He dashed off.

My heart stopped. How could I go? I had nothing to wear, nothing . . . and no money. But Jo had bounded out the door and left me bewildered, gazing into space. What to wear? No money . . . and this my first meeting with . . . Charlie Chaplin!

[1] Film Booking Offices of America was formed in 1922. The company was acquired in 1926 by Joseph Kennedy who eventually merged it with the Keith-Albee-Orpheum circuit of vaudeville houses. In October 1928 these two merged with RCA Photophone to create the holding company RKO.

13

At eight o'clock I arrived at the F.B.O. Studios looking my worst. I realize now that my taste for street clothes was bad. I never had enough money for stage and street clothes, so I never gave the latter a thought. I wore a bright blue hat to match my eyes. I thought that was a brilliant idea. My orange hat? . . . well, my face was brilliant, all red and blotchy from all the excitement . . . that matched my skin.

I had put on and pulled off dozens of old stockings, trying to find a pair without a run . . . no luck. Time was running out and so was my sanity. What could I do? I wasn't about to spend my last two dollars on a new pair of hose . . . A familiar feeling of desperation and poverty gripped me, but another marvelous idea came to me. I tucked my two dollars securely into my purse, grabbed a bottle of leg make-up and smeared it all over my legs, and that was it.

By the time I managed to get myself pulled together and to the studio, the picture was about to begin. Thank goodness the room was dark when Jo von Sternberg and I entered. We stumbled our way over some people and sat down.

The film began to roll, of course I wasn't seeing a thing. The stillness was frightening. The silence was broken by a whisper behind me. A man said softly, with a beautiful English accent, "Isn't it colorful, the lighting, the mood and the treatment?" Jo leaned close and said, "That was Chaplin speaking to Nazimova."[1]

[1] Alla Nazimova (b. 4 June 1879, Yalta, Russia; d. 13 July 1945, Los Angeles) made her U.S. film debut in 1916. In 1922 she produced Ibsen's *A Doll's House* for release by United Artists.

Frantically, I started to rehearse silently what I was going to say to Mr. Chaplin. I had memorized it all, "How fortunate for us Mr. Chaplin, it was you who saw *The Salvation Hunters*. No one else would have seen its worth . . ." Huh-huh, I was all ready! When the lights came on I felt that I had the speech at my command.

George K. Arthur rushed over with Mr Chaplin. I was so thrilled and delighted. I was going to start my speech . . . but they went right past me to Jo von Sternberg. I pressed my lips together and my throat went dry. I was crowded back to the rear. All I could hear was Mr. Chaplin praising Jo and George.

On my tiptoes I could peek through and see their faces lighting up from the words of magic being spoken by Chaplin. I felt so alone. Then I heard him inquire, "Is the girl here tonight?" That meant me. I froze. My speech, I couldn't remember how it started. I hid behind some people.

George K. Arthur, the promoter, wanted to please Charlie. He found me, snatched me from the fringes and brought me over to him. Graciously George said, "Mr. Chaplin, this is the girl, Georgia Hale. Georgia, of course you know Mr. Chaplin." I just stared and nodded my head, nothing came from my lips. He took my hand in both of his and drew me close and asked, "So this is the girl Georgia? You know young lady, you gave a very fine performance." This pleased George and he discreetly slipped away.

So far I hadn't said one word. My big, big moment had arrived for which I had memorized a speech and I couldn't think. I put my hand on my forehead . . . and wished I could remember the first word. Thank the stars, just at this moment of embarrassment, George returned. I never knew why, but he said rather loudly, "Georgia can you find a way home? Jo and I have to go with a group." He disappeared without waiting for an answer.

My face turned red . . . why did he have to say that in front of Mr. Chaplin? But he smiled tenderly, as if sensing my feeling and came to my rescue, as he had done so many times before. He asked graciously, " May I have the pleasure of taking you home?" My first words were a timid whisper, "How nice you are." He gently took me by the arm and escorted me through the crowd to his limousine. All dreams come true, no matter how wild. Heaven was within me, not here nor there . . . but within me.

On our way home Charlie did most of the talking. He praised Jo von Sternberg generously. When we reached my house and we started to part, he quickly asked, "Would you care to go some place for tea?" I still couldn't believe what was happening—that I was with Charlie Chaplin. I couldn't come down to earth. I could hardly breathe or speak . . . but I didn't want the evening to end. I hurriedly said, "Yes, yes very much."

We went to a cozy little restaurant and sat for a long time—a moment to me. He excitedly and persuasively convinced me that *The Salvation Hunters*, Jo von Sternberg and George K. Arthur would have a great future. Then he turned to me. For a moment he just studied me. His dark blue eyes roamed slowly over my face and he asked enthusiastically, "Now . . . what about you? Tell me . . . do you work steadily? . . . enough to get along?" Somehow this question put me a little more at ease. It was so down to earth and kind.

Now he seemed so approachable, so human. I told him, "I've been assured of work by Mr. Huginin, a casting director. He told me that I can work every day at his studio, but that I'm free to accept any good part that might come my way. So, I'm sure of seven-fifty a day." I courageously added, "I really feel quite secure." He liked this remark and said, "You have the right attitude. Go right on working and I'm sure something very good will turn up. It can't help it. You're a very photogenic and talented person."

It was closing time. The waitress came with the check. Mr. Chaplin reached into his pocket, pressed his vest pockets, then started patting himself all over and muttering, "Oh dear, I've come away with . . . no money." I smiled, almost out loud. I thought, "Just as I had dreamed he would be." My two dollars . . . where was the two dollars I had carefully stuffed in my purse? Hurriedly I dug into my pocket book and pulled out my bills and joyously handed them to Charlie. Like a mischievous child he took the money saying, "I'm really so absent-minded. Will you ever forgive me?" I was so tickled . . . so happy. Imagine Charlie Chaplin being indebted to me and asking for forgiveness. Wow! What a feeling.

The last thing I thought of before I fell asleep that night was how truly rich he was, not in money, but in spirit. He was an artist and yet so child-like. Someone had said in jest, "Money isn't everything, love is two per cent." Charlie would have reversed that statement. I just knew it.

I continued to work every day at the studios, but with a heart that was light and expectant of good. I knew if I heeded his advice and was courageous and industrious, another opportunity would surely come. It would follow "as the night the day." He said so.

I had no thought of ever seeing him again, for the trade papers pictured him as very busy finishing his picture. But there was this stirring . . . I heard from everyone on the sets, "Charlie Chaplin is raving about that picture of yours *The Salvation Hunters*." Then they would ask, "Have you heard the very latest . . . he's going to marry his leading lady?"[1] So I knew I was out of his world forever.

[1] Lita Grey (b. Lilita McMurray, 15 April 1908, Los Angeles) had appeared in *The Kid* and *The Idle Class* before signing a contract with Chaplin for *The Gold Rush* in March 1924.

14

I worked and worked . . . and waited and waited. Then it came, that important opportunity he said would surely come. Douglas Fairbanks' studio called and asked, "Georgia Hale? Please be at the studios at 10 o'clock, for a test to play the part of a princess opposite to Mr. Fairbanks."[1]

I was so excited. I piled my arms high with stills, as I always did when going for a job. Of course I thought these photographs would help sell me to Fairbanks. But George K. Arthur happened to see me. He took my pictures from me saying, "For heavens sake, are you trying to spoil things? You're no longer an extra, and don't act like one. Charlie Chaplin has already sold you to Douglas, because of your work in our picture. Now go in there with your head up in the air. You've proven you're a great actress in *The Salvation Hunters.*"

Obediently I heeded his advice and went in empty handed. The time was at hand for me to live up to all the words of praise Charlie had been so generously bestowing on me. I felt so uneasy, not in acting ability, but I was afraid I wouldn't photograph. You see my face was so blotchy, as happens so often at that tender age. I was filled with passion and unsettled emotions. But I had the best camera man in the business for my test. It turned out that my face was spotless.

[1] Douglas Fairbanks (b. Douglas Elton Ulman, 23 May 1883, Denver, Colorado; d. 1939), the silent screen's best loved hero, made his film debut in *The Lamb* (1915), in which he exhibited the talent for acrobatic stunts which was to account for a large part of his appeal. One of the four original members of United Artists, his last production for them was *Mr. Robinson Crusoe* (1933). Fairbanks' career ended with *The Private Life of Don Juan*, made in England for Alexander Korda in 1934.

As for the acting, Mr. Fairbanks was so delighted, he signed me to a year's contract with options.

In the meantime, plastered all over the front pages was the news that Charlie Chaplin was about to marry his leading lady of *The Gold Rush.* This ended any hope for me of ever seeing or hearing from him again. I consoled myself, "You can see this picture and learn more. Then you can try hard to put into practice some of the lovely lessons you'll surely see in it." But my whole goal of talking with him and learning directly from him had been dashed to bits.

Mr. Fairbanks was so enthusiastic about the test. Now it was Mr. Fairbanks raving about me to Mr. Chaplin. Fairbanks immediately took my test over to show him and to tell him the good news. "I've signed her to a year's contract. Wait till you see her as a princess," Doug said.

They ran the scenes, but Charlie was clearly disappointed. Doug asked, "What's wrong? You don't like it?" Charlie answered, "Yes, it's lovely. She's very versatile. She's entirely different from the girl in *The Salvation Hunters.*" Mr. Fairbanks was relieved and said, "I'm very fortunate in getting her." Charlie continued, "You know Doug, I'm seriously considering reshooting my picture." "*The Gold Rush*?" enquired Doug. Charlie went right on, "I was thinking of making a test of Georgia Hale myself." Mr. Fairbanks was surprised and half teasing said, "I'll allow you to take a few shots of her. Why not?"

The thing I thought could never happen . . . did. The Chaplin Studios called me. The girl asked, "Can Georgia Hale be at the Chaplin Studios at 10 to-morrow morning? Mr. Chaplin would like to make a test." Was I thrilled? I was going to see and listen to this man once again. I knew it could not be for a part right now, for he had just finished his picture. But I really didn't care. I just wanted to be with him. I had a nice contract with Mr. Fairbanks, so I felt secure and happy about work.

My contract with Doug—did it permit me to go to other studios and take tests? Perhaps I'd better see Mr. Fairbanks and ask his permission. I might lose out all around, I told myself. I hadn't received any money yet and I'd better be careful, I reasoned.

Early in the morning I went to see Mr. Fairbanks. I managed to get an interview before he began his morning work-out in his gym. I haltingly asked, "Is it alright if I go at 10 o'clock to the Charles Chaplin Studios and have a screen test?" I thought I saw a smile touch his lips, or was he always pleasant? I never knew whether he had tongue in cheek or not. He said, "Is that where you're going this morning? I've been thinking of what a lovely princess[1] you're going to make for me." I continued fearfully, "I'm sure it won't interfere with our work. It's not for *The Gold Rush*. That's finished, so I'm positive it's for some future story."

Mr. Fairbanks lowered his head and said, "Let me think." I waited for his O.K. I so desperately wanted to see Charlie again, and now I knew the answer was going to be "No." My eyes filled with tears. He looked up and said, "Mercy, you certainly are an emotional little thing. Please save your make-up. Run along or you'll be late." He seemed to be laughing. Had he been teasing me?

I rushed over to Charlie's. I was still emotional over the whole thing. I was out of breath from hurrying and by this time a fire was burning inside me. My make-up was melting and caking . . . All my rushing was for naught, as it usually is. When I arrived at the studios I was met by a bevy of pretty girls. I could have appeared two hours later and no one would have known the difference. I waited and waited.

Every girl had been called and there I sat alone. I knew I had to be the next one . . . now. A screen test is an awesome thing anyway and by the time my turn came . . . the last.

1 When *Don Q. Son of Zorro* (Elton Film Corp.) was released on 20 September 1925, Mary Astor played the young heroine, Dolores de Muro.

Although many others had come in after me . . . the tension had mounted and mounted inside me. I wanted to leave but I firmly took hold of myself and the chair and held on.

Finally, Mr. Chaplin in person appeared and said, "Thank you for waiting so long. But you are something special and I wanted to take time with you and put you through some extra scenes." I was tense, sullen and moody. When it was over I was completely frustrated and almost hysterical. He left the set without saying a word and I burst out of the place as fast as I could. It had been terrifying, that's all. Just the opposite from what I dreamed it would be. I knew he would tell Doug . . . now I would lose everything. I didn't sleep that night.

The dawn came, then the morning. I said to mother, "I simply can't face this day." She couldn't calm me. But he . . . he could, he always could. The phone rang and I heard, "Mr. Chaplin would like you to be at the studio at 10 o'clock when they run the film." My mother smiled. She alone knew what this man meant to me. This meant one more time to be with him. I felt it would be the last, because when he'd see the test that would be it . . . the end.

I was ushered into the projection room. Mr. Chaplin called softly, "Come and sit next to me Miss Hale." I wanted to sit near the door, where I could make a quick exit. How I dreaded seeing myself. As I watched . . . each girl seemed more gorgeous and talented than the one preceding.

Finally I came on the screen. In contrast to the others who were so vivacious and active, I stood still. When I did move, it was slowly and anxiously. My close-ups were like stills. I grew so small in my own estimation of myself, that I felt I could crawl out under the door . . . like a worm. I wished I could . . . and that I was one! The lights came on. With my mouth down at the corners, I stood waiting for the verdict.

Mr. Chaplin was very thoughtful. He glanced at me and smiled. I thought it was a forced grin. He said in a business-like manner, "It was very nice . . . interesting. Thank you, Miss Hale." Without another word, he turned and went off with the crew. I stood there bewildered, wondering why I'd been called to see the test. It was terrible. The few words he said confirmed that. On the way home I asked myself, "Why did I do it at all? Why did I ask Mr. Fairbanks for his permission?" I had spoiled everything. But the worst part of it was that I had made a fool out of myself in front of Charlie.

In the following days, the more I thought of it, the more the tears flowed. If I had only thought of something clever to do . . . as the other girls had in their scenes. I wore myself out pacing the floor, crying and regretting. I hadn't eaten anything all day, so I went out to a little restaurant. At the same time my waitress served my dinner for which I was famished, the little newsboy came along selling his papers. He held up the head-lines, "Mr. Chaplin elopes with his leading lady, Lita Grey."[1] My face must have turned white, for they both asked, "Are you alright?" . . . I paid my bill and left immediately.

It was the end of my appetite and everything else. Now it didn't matter how that test was . . . Of course I realized that from now on his wife would be his leading lady in life and in his films. I could stop worrying about the test. I'd never work for Charlie, nor hear from him again, I knew. I couldn't get any lower, so I had to start up. I forced this whole episode out of my mind. I tried hard to recall only the good which I knew to be true, as Charlie had taught me. He met defeat with victory, a bully with bravery, a slave-driving employer with more efficiency and effort, arrogancy with a smile. I can do the same. "It's not going to be the end for me," I told myself.

[1] Chaplin married Lita Grey on 26 November 1924 at Empalme, Mexico.

15

In the meantime, the entire cast of *The Salvation Hunters* became beneficiaries of that fateful day Chaplin saw the picture. Jo von Sternberg had received an interest in the picture and a nice sum of cash. The moment he got it, the actors were paid. This was like Jo. He continued to be the man he was when he landed in this country from Vienna.[1] He gave the purser his last ten dollar gold piece and proudly walked to his new home in America. Now his new-found fame did not change him . . . not Jo the generous and proud.

One day while talking with Mary Pickford[2] at the studio, her jeweler came to show her some gorgeous new pieces. Jo saw a sparkling diamond ring and bought it. I was figuring out some way to get along until some money came in. Jo was coming over to bring me up to date on all the news. When he arrived he had a twinkle in his eyes. He handed me a tiny box and said, "This is a bonus for you. It is part payment for what you did in making the picture a success."

[1] The Sternberg family emigrated to New York City from Vienna in 1901, returning there in 1904 "probably because of my father's inability to endure constant frustration" in trying "to provide for us" (*FCL*, pp. 11-12). They made a fresh start in the U.S. in 1908.

[2] Mary Pickford (b. Gladys Smith, 8 April 1893, Toronto, Canada; d. 30 May 1979), known as "America's Sweetheart," began her film career with Griffith at the Biograph Company in 1909. Together with Adolph Zukor, she was the first star to become a producer, forming the Mary Pickford Corp. in June 1916. She entered into partnership with Chaplin, Fairbanks, and Griffith to form United Artists in 1919, marrying Fairbanks the following year. Pickford announced her retirement from the screen on 13 February 1935, a month after divorcing Douglas Fairbanks.

I was excited about the little box and eager to see what was in it. But I really needed money, my bills had piled high. When I opened the gift and saw the ring, a two carat diamond surrounded by loads of smaller ones, thirty-two to be exact, for I immediately counted them, I threw my arms around Jo and kissed him, again and again. It was my first diamond ring. I admitted to Jo, "Nothing could have made me any happier. I'll treasure it all my life." I didn't care if my stomach was flat and I needed cold cash. I loved that ring.

Jo was getting along famously. He had been signed to write a scenario[1] for Mary Pickford, which he was to direct. He had been given three weeks for this task. He assured me that was all the time he needed to come up with something artistic and different. But he didn't do a thing for days. We went for rides in his new Packard and out to dinners but without one word about his story. I asked, "Jo, haven't you an assignment? Why are you not confining yourself in a room and writing?" He answered, "Let me worry about that." I said, "No, I'm not going to play around anymore. You don't seem to care and I am worried."

I had never been around a writer before. I had no idea how an artist works. When the dead-line drew near, Jo nonchalantly said, "I'm going to take a little trip to San Francisco. I need a few days' vacation." I couldn't understand, for we had been having fun and seeing the sights for days.

When he returned in a few days, I dreaded to ask, "What about . . . the story?" He calmly replied, "It's finished. The most wonderful thing unfolded while I was quietly looking out the window of the train." Then he related the most heart-touching story of a blind girl. Jo never made this picture. But

[1] The story outline he wrote was called *Backwash*, and revolved round "a blind girl and a deaf-mute, the subject to be visualized through the eyes of a girl who had never been able to see." Mary Pickford, concerned about her image, rejected it as too squalid and depressing. The contract Sternberg had signed with her was cancelled by mutual consent. Chaplin had agreed to appear in one scene (*FCL*, p.207).

because of Chaplin's continuing praise of him, he was securely in with the big league and on his way. He deserved this break. What a store of knowledge and talent he had to give Hollywood.

His constant companion since a boy was a camera. He studied lighting, composition and painting.[1] His photography was the best. He could make the plainest woman beautiful. He taught me how to light myself and he told me he gave this valuable knowledge to Marlene Dietrich[2] also. Jo gave.

But his treatment and faithfulness to his mother endeared him more than anything else to me. When he was an assistant director making a small salary of one hundred a week, he always . . . the first thing . . . right off the top, would send the major portion to his ma.

The other side of the coin is so different. Why can't they both be beautiful? This evening Jo took me to a swanky restaurant where I had the joy of showing off my new ring. I hoped this evening might be an exception. But no, as usual the delicious meal and lovely music was spoiled by Jo's caustic tongue. Sarcasm was humor to him. He delighted in embarrassing waiters with what he thought was stimulating satire. But he would always end up tipping them handsomely.

We lived in different worlds even though we were so close. When we were about to say good night, he took my hand and said, "I'm so glad we're engaged now." I asked, "Are you teasing? I don't understand your humor I guess, anymore than the poor

1 Sternberg singled out the French director Emile Chautaud, whom he had assisted in *The Mystery of the Yellow Room* (1919), as having "carefully instructed me in the rudiments of his craft," including "the value of light and shadow" (*FCL*, p. 42). Sternberg was the only director of his day to earn membership of the American Society of Cinematographers.

2 Marlene Dietrich (b. Maria Magdalena von Losch, 27 December 1901, Berlin; d. 6 May 1992, Paris) appeared in nearly a dozen films before starring in Sternberg's *Der blaue Engel* (1930), produced simultaneously for Paramount-UFA in Berlin. They collaborated on six other films for Paramount.

waiters." He continued, "I'm sure, that's what we both want. I'm so sure." Do all men take for granted that their feelings are always returned? I realized then, he had thought all along I was in love with him. I haltingly asked, "Was . . . this an engagement ring? I thought you said . . . that it was a bonus."

He didn't hear me. He had visions of his own. He said, "Yes, I want to make a great star of you. I want to teach and mold you into something truly big. That's what I've been counting on since the day I first saw you. You have everything I need or want. I said softly, "I know with your talent you could make me famous. I know everything you say is true. But I'm sorry I just can't say 'Yes.' My heart won't let me. I don't want to hurt you. I really am so fond of you, and you've done so much for me already." I offered him the ring and said, "Please take this and forgive me?" Jo folded the ring in my hand and said, "It's yours Georgia. You made the picture . . . you were so lovely in it. You earned the ring . . . keep it." I hated to see him leave.

"Life is a disappointment . . . to Jo . . . to me . . . to everyone," I thought. This episode with Jo was saddening.[1] But I thought of Charlie and remembered that here was one happy marriage. I knew he deserved it but I was a little envious . . . I felt so alone now with Jo gone. And the phone was so still. The Fairbanks studio had not called. I asked myself, "I wonder what Mr. Chaplin is going to do with my test?" I thought, "I'll call the Chaplin Studios and ask . . .?" As I picked the phone up . . . it rang in my hand.

[1] Sternberg devotes a great deal of space to Georgia in his autobiography, but there may be a taste of sour grapes in his sometimes uncomplimentary allusions to her (*FCL*, pp. 153-157).

16

The phone suddenly became alive after being dead for days. It made me wonder if there is anything to mental telepathy or was it that there is just one mind? I heard these blessed words, "Miss Hale . . . Mr. Chaplin would like to see you at 3 o'clock."

A 3 o'clock on the dot, I was ushered into his office. There I sat waiting! I had plenty of time to sum up the past . . . how I had come to Hollywood just to meet this man, because I knew he had saved me. I knew what I had been planning! Now he was going to appear and tell me how sad my test was. I wished my tragic and smoldering thinking had not etched their ugly lines on my young face. I wished I could have been more animated and joyous in the scenes. I wished . . .

He entered the room. As he seated himself, he said politely, "Nice to see you again Miss Hale." Then he glanced at some letters. My heart was jumping. He looked directly at me and said soberly, "I've just been speaking to Mr. Fairbanks about those scenes you made for me." I said softly, "Oh . . . I wish . . ." But I pressed my lips together and braced myself for what was coming.

He arose and sat on the desk close to me. He clasped his hands together firmly and said emphatically, "I told Mr. Fairbanks that I was greatly impressed with your test." I grabbed the arms of my chair and held tight. He continued, "You showed such depth of feeling. Your sullen mood and slow graceful movements were very dramatic." I quickly put my hand over my mouth to hide my emotions. He said joyously, "I can see you in the part. You have just the qualities it calls for." I wondered, "What part?" but I anxiously waited for him to say. He said, "You have just what I've been wanting in her for a long time. Do you think you'd like being my leading lady?"

I jumped to my feet and stammered, "I've always wanted this . . . I mean . . . that's why . . . of course . . . but of course." He was delighted and said, "Please sit down, I'm not quite through with you. You know I'll have to lift your contract with Douglas Fairbanks, which by the way he has consented to. Is this to your liking young lady?" I exclaimed, "I'm so happy, I can hardly speak. It's all like a dream come true." He asked, "Excuse me a moment. I'll be right back. I have a little thing for you to sign."

I sat there thinking of the lovely girls who had tried for that part, among them I heard was Carole Lombard,[1] or Jean Peters as we knew her then. When Charlie returned, I asked timidly, "Why did you ever choose me? There were so many pretty girls?" This question hit a responsive chord. With his uncanny sense he asked, "Why are you doubting yourself?" I quickly said, "Oh no, it isn't exactly that . . . but . . . the others." He interrupted me and said with deep sympathy and understanding, "You know Georgia, in a beautiful garden of flowers, one is not jealous of another. Each flower lifts its face to every passer-by and impartially sends forth its sweet fragrance and loveliness to all. Each one plays its important part. You were just one of the beautiful girls, but I chose you because you suited my decor . . . my need. Always remember there is no need for fear or jealousy. Each one has his right destiny and will be chosen by the right one at the perfect moment."

I was enthralled. This was the reason I had wanted to meet him and talk with him. Here was my teacher giving me a lesson, a loving lesson. My world was aglow. How can words express our feelings, but I said, "Thank you once again for . . . making me the happiest girl."

1 Carole Lombard (b. Jane Alice Peters, 6 October 1908, Fort Wayne, Indiana; d. 1942 in plane crash).

That night Jo von Sternberg called me and asked me to dinner. It was so good to hear from him again. It had been a long time since he telephoned me, but he was his old sweet self. At dinner I broke the news, "I signed a contract with . . . Charlie Chaplin today." He asked very surprised, "But how could you do that, you're already signed up?" I joyously told him, "Charlie lifted my contract from Douglas Fairbanks. Isn't it great?" Jo had mixed feelings and said, "There's one thing about it, you'll give another fine performance with the master directing you. But Georgia be careful. Don't let anyone change you."

I could see Jo was eager to tell me something. He liked to tell jokes on himself. He said, "I drove into my garage, in the blackness of the night last evening, and started to get out. Suddenly I became apprehensive and filled with terror. My car started to roll out of the garage, and of course I immediately knew someone was pulling it." He put his hand to his head and continued, "I screamed like a maniac and jumped out and ran from the thief. When I glanced back there was no one in the car. I ran back after the moving car. It safely crossed the street and hit a curb and stopped. All it had needed was for me to calmly set the breaks. I sheepishly crawled into the car and drove it across to the house. My little landlady had answered my shrieks and asked bravely, "Is there anything I can do for you Mr. von Sternberg?" I gave a silly grin and said, "No, I'm alright . . . but I wondered?" I laughed so much at Jo, that he thought it deserved another . . .

Since I had last seen Jo, he had driven to New York to see his mother in a spanking new, long and powerful Packard. He said, "I wanted to show off to mother, my friends and everyone else in town. While driving along Fifth Avenue, everyone started looking my way. I wore a black beret and the car was flaming red. I thought I was making some splash. When the people along the street started pointing at me . . . Was I thrilled! At the height of my glory I glanced into one of the big plate glass show windows where I could get a better look at my long slinky car and . . . there was no back wheel! My God, I had been cruising around on three wheels. I immediately removed my foot from the excellerator [*sic*] and carefully brought it to a safe stop along the curb. Had my balloon burst in my face. Everyone surrounded me shouting, 'God, man, how did you ever bring the crate to a stop without tipping over?' " Funny Jo, and how nice!

17

My dream had come true. My reason for coming to California had been fulfilled. It was even more than I had asked for . . . I was now Charlie Chaplin's leading lady. Was it a dream? Was it really all mine? I was afraid I'd wake and find it gone . . . only in my mind.

My fears almost came true. The first day at work was a down to earth affair. Mr. Chaplin arrived. He was wearing a business suit. I had anticipated working with the little tramp. Nothing ever happens the way one anticipates. He greeted me in a very stern manner. He said formally, "Turn around and let me see your dress . . . uh huh . . . I like your hair-do too. Keep it that way." A strange feeling crept over me. It wasn't like a dream come true, it was like working in any show. I chided myself for expecting something different. I felt a cold chill. It wasn't like a fairy tale nor an answered prayer, it was going to be just work.

Count D'Arrast,[1] or Harry as they called Mr. Chaplin's assistant, must have noticed my bewilderment, for he came over to me and said, "We're all so glad to have you aboard. Now, maybe we'll get something done. Thank goodness he's very business-like to-day for a change. He's really inspired." These few words put me a little at ease. Maybe I was welcome. I thanked Harry. "You've helped me so much, you're very kind."

[1] Henri d'Abbadie d'Arrast (b. 1897, Argentina; d. 16 March 1968, France) arrived in Hollywood in 1922; he was a researcher and technical adviser to Chaplin on *A Woman of Paris*, then his assistant on *The Gold Rush*. His first picture, made in 1927 for Hearst's company Cosmopolitan Pictures, was *Service for Ladies*. Between 1927 and 1934 d'Arrast directed eight comedies, but despite their critical acclaim, his career in Hollywood was over by the mid-thirties.

In a few moments Harry returned and said, "You're wanted on the set. Mr. Chaplin is ready." It was a snow scene. My first shots were to be scenes outside his cabin. The snow was fake, made by a company down the street. I felt as false and cold as the snow . . . so-called. I walked stiffly onto the set. He glared at me. But when he started directing me everything changed. I soon found out that all the cold, false feeling must go. He wanted perfection and he carefully explained and showed me every detail.

Just as I was settling down inside and really feeling the part, some high and mighty friends of his arrived on the set. It was such a terrible interruption to me, but not to him. He gayly introduced me to Thelma Morgan[1] and some others, and then disappeared with them for the day. This procedure and these social encounters were repeated all the time. He had more friends! Mr. Chaplin's life seemed so full of famous people and he acted so elated with it all. While I was deflated by it. He didn't seem to be interested in the picture. My exuberance for the part and working with this genius turned into a strange down-to-earth feeling.

For days there was no call for work.[2] No one cared and no one was in a hurry. I went back completely adjusted when the call finally came. I had thought it all out. I was working, not for the little tramp, but for Mr. Charles Chaplin the business-man and above all the socialite of Hollywood. I dismissed my feelings of the past as childish!

1 Thelma Morgan Converse (b. 23 August 1904, Lucerne, Switzerland; d. 1965) was the twin sister of Gloria Vanderbilt. Chaplin had made use of his friendship with her as a smokescreen while courting Lita Grey. "'I'm a planful man,'" Chaplin told Lita, "'and Thelma Morgan happens to be part of my plan'" (*MLC*, p. 72). In 1929 she became mistress of the Prince of Wales, later introducing him to Mrs. Wallis Simpson. It is possible that Chaplin had her in mind when he used her name for one of the murdered wives (Thelma Couvais) of *Monsieur Verdoux*.

2 During the making of *The Gold Rush* the number of days idle was 235, compared with 170 shooting days.

I walked onto the set and looked for the dapper and charming Mr. Chaplin. He wasn't there. Huddled in his director's chair, sat a little figure. It was "The Little Tramp," big feet, derby hat and all. A warm feeling came over me. He glanced over to me and with a child-like smile, bowed his head to me.

It was the little fellow who spoke out of the screen to me years ago and made my heart laugh for the first time. It was a different set, a different studio, a different world. Now it was my dream come true. A wonderful feeling enveloped my whole being. I felt at home. I foolishly hoped Mr. Chaplin would never return. Mr. Charles Chaplin was exceedingly charming, but now I was to be with my childhood miracle man. The scene was where the girls visit him in his cabin, where Georgia his secret love repents for not showing at his Christmas-eve[1] party given in her honor. I felt every moment of the story. He was so warm and easy to work with.

When the day was over, the funny little clown took me aside and said softly, "Georgia, you are ideal for this part, and I find it delightful to work with you. I feel like a child . . . I'm really so happy with you as my leading lady." It was like music. Imagine . . . me inspiring my teacher. Could it be possible that I was returning in a small, small measure, the abundance of good he had poured into my life? It is a rich feeling to give. What a recipe for happiness!

"Perfection is what an artist strives for . . . but I'm satisfied if I can achieve fifty per cent," Charlie would say. He used various methods to attain his goals when directing. Sometimes he'd be almost feminine, sad and wistful. Then again he'd act like a baby, press his lips together, straighten out his arms between his knees and rock back and forth, uttering little baby sounds of coaxing and teasing. However he could also be cold and crisp. Even in his own work and scenes, he'd stand apart and drive himself—like a slave. "Genius is perspiration, not just inspiration," he'd often remind himself.

1 An error for New Year's Eve.

Henry Bergman,[1] the heavy-set man who played in so many of Charlie's pictures, was like a father to him. When Charlie was fired with ideas and seemed to be working too hard, Henry would say lovingly, "Don't you think that's enough for today?" Charlie would motion him away. But he loved Henry for this concern and tender solicitude. Later Charlie fulfilled plump Henry's desire. He surrounded him with food, by setting him up in a nice restaurant on Hollywood Boulevard.

At the close of a hard day's work, Harry D'Arrast gave the call for the following Wednesday . . . but he qualified it. Harry said, "We'll be shooting only if the sun is out . . . shining. The call then folks is 9 o'clock, weather permitting." This gave me a few days at home. It was a joy to see mother free of worry. Her back had actually straightened. Money had now started to roll in for me. When I'd find her sitting at the table frowning over some bills I'd ask, "What are you scowling about?" She'd answer as she had for years, "Oh, I'm just trying to figure out how and when to pay the bills." It was such fun, now I could say, "Give them all to me and I'll pay them honey." This was true medicine for she grew younger and healthier. Poverty is sickness!

Whenever I had a few days off, Jo von Sternberg would come over and ply me with questions. He wondered how I was getting along with Charlie Chaplin. He knew Charlie's reputation and he was sure I would change. He seemed to see what he was sure he would see, for he said, "My, you're like a different girl. What on earth has transpired?" I inquired, "In what way have I changed? It's only been a few weeks." He said, "I do hope all this doesn't go to your head. But you do seem happier, of course this is no sin, but I do hope no one spoils you. I hope you keep your head, Georgia." I replied,

[1] Henry Bergman (b. 1868, Sweden; d. 1946, Los Angeles) made his first appearance in American films in 1914 after abandoning opera. He started his long association with Chaplin in 1916, figuring prominently in most of Chaplin's films of The Mutual, First National, and United Artists period, and he assisted him in *City Lights* and *Modern Times*.

"Charlie is not only a great director and actor, but he inspires me. I love his philosophy. He helps me to think and act correctly." Jo questioned this, "Chaplin teaches you how to think and act correctly?—Chaplin? I think of him as a genius, but this religious angle . . . I don't get it. I don't understand you Georgia." I said, "Jo, you are not interested in this side of life. You're not even interested in politics." Then I teased him saying, "However, I do notice a change in you too. You're wearing your hair long and black shirts. Also your wardrobe has become pretty elegant." I laughed but he didn't.

Jo never questioned life, he accepted it. He knew the dark shades and brilliant colors, the shadow and the sunshine, the hideous forms as well as the beautiful. He liked what he saw in the great modern paintings. And he spent his money lavishly on them. It was said that he collected one of the largest collections west of the Mississippi. Patiently, he would try to open my eyes to see as he did. The beauty of most of these modern paintings was hidden to me. But I did try, and thanks to Jo, I appreciated them more and more. But Charlie opened my eyes to living beauty within us, which was also hidden to me. This was what I longed to see, more than the inanimate beauty in Jo's paintings.

The day arrived to go back to work. The call had been "weather permitting" and it was almost raining, so heavy was the mist. When I looked out and saw the pavements wet, I knew the call was off . . . no sun was visible. So I didn't make-up . . . in fact I climbed back into bed and dozed off. The phone blasted the silence with its loud ring. I sleepily reached for it. I softly managed a "Hello." But I could hear Harry loudly asking, "Why aren't you here? Mr. Chaplin is on the set waiting to begin." He hung up . . . in my ear!

My heart sank. What an awakening! Of all persons on earth I didn't want to hurt Charlie. I raced with time. I threw on some make-up and flew to the studio. Harry rushed up to me and said, "Don't go near Chaplin. He's furious! Let him speak first . . ." Finally, it seemed like forever to me, Charlie spoke to me, almost in a whisper. "You wouldn't have been late at another studio. You're so sure of my feeling for you, so sure I'm pleased with your work . . . it wasn't very nice of you to take advantage . . . not nice at all Georgia."

I could hardly compose myself enough to think of a good excuse. I don't think he heard my reply, I spoke so low. "I'm sorry, I didn't understand the call. But it wasn't Harry's fault . . . it was mine. I should have been here." He knew I was truly repentant. He always sensed a real emotion. He said so sweetly, "You'd better go to your dressing room and put on good make-up."

I rushed away trying to hold back the tears and a strange fear. I could hear the warnings of Jo and the words of Henry Bergman who had said, "Never fall in love with Chaplin, Georgia. He's a heart-breaker." I tried to forget this advice. I reasoned, "Having an ideal, one who inspires . . . doesn't mean you are falling in love." I talked silently to myself and tried to be convincing, "It means you are learning to love . . . all, all mankind." I felt reassured.

I returned to the set. But as fate would have it, the scenes were where I realize the little tramp is in love with me. I find my picture under his pillow. I had been cruel to him. I had not showed up for a New Year's Eve party and he had scrimped and labored to give it in my honor.

This scene called for remorse and a true feeling of affection towards the little clown. It was so easy for me to feel this affection . . . too easy. Charlie was not fooled. He knew it was real, not just acting. After the days' work, he kindly came over, as if to wipe away all trace of hard feelings because I had been late. He said, "Thank you. I really liked your work today. You were excellent in the scenes, Georgia. May I tell you how inately [*sic*] kind I think you are. In fact I've been thinking too much of you lately, even away from the studio . . . do you ever think of me?" I had to be truthful. I had to answer, "I thought of no one else . . . but you this past weekend." He was pleased and said, "That's all I wanted to hear."

18

Mr. Chaplin the Hollywood socialite would take over and cause "The Little Tramp" to suspend his work for days and weeks. The publicity, the reputation, the actions of Mr. Chaplin revealed a man the very opposite of the tiny fellow with the big shoes and the derby hat. Chaplin made enemies of friends and courted those who only flattered him to get something.

His greatest weakness was his sympathy for the young and beautiful. One day I told him of a quarrel I had at home with my sister. She had said, "I simply cannot come home from my hard job and clean this house. Your work at the studio is so easy, just sitting around and looking pretty. Why don't you keep this place clean . . . or better yet . . . why don't you get out." This hurt, and one remark led to another until it was heated. When I complained to Mr. Chaplin he said, "Move out immediately. I'll put you in a lovely apartment and it won't cost you a cent." I looked quizzically at him. He said quickly, "And there will be no strings attached." I smiled and said, "It was only a foolish quarrel. You are too sympathetic. This can get you into trouble."

At another time I just made a small remark, "Show business keeps a girl on her mettle. So many men try to take advantage of every little job offered." He asked then and there, "Tell me Georgia, what amount of money can I give you to give you a feeling of complete independence from these wolves? Let me put in your name $250,000 . . .?" I never accepted this, nor did I feel it was right. But it did show a man of many facets . . . this sympathy got him into lots of trouble.

It took a long time to make *The Gold Rush* because Mr. Chaplin had to take care of his private life. It really wasn't very private for he was good head-line material. His life was juicy and a delight to the reporters. He tried to avoid them saying, "My private life is my own." But he never convinced the media. I guess Mr. Chaplin would get bored and allow Charlie to assert himself.

After weeks of delay we were called to work. Charlie with his baggy pants, derby hat and all came tripping onto the set accompanied by his brother, Sidney.[1] It was so pleasant to see the whirling cane and the cute little face of Charlie again. The whole crew was eager to get on with the picture.

But he leisurely introduced me to his brother, who had brought some pictures of their mother[2] to show Charlie. They acted like two children, so eager were they to see these new shots of their mama. Proudly Charlie asked, "Would you like to see my mother? You would love her . . . and I'm sure she would like you Georgia." I joined them and said, "I consider that one of the nicest compliments I've ever received from you Charlie. I hope someday I can meet her."

Sydney treated Charlie like a little brother. He said to me, "Pick out the funniest little chap and that will be my kid brother Charlie." He handed me a picture of a large group of boys of about nine or ten. I searched for the cutest and pointed to a tiny boy. Sure enough I was right. Even at that tender age

1 Sydney Chaplin (b. 17 March 1885, Capetown, South Africa; d. 16 April 1965, Nice, France) was Chaplin's half-brother. After a brief stint with Keystone, he gave up acting in 1916 to take charge of Chaplin's business affairs, and was instrumental in securing lucrative contracts for him with Mutual and First National. He played occasional roles in Chaplin's films—*A Dog's Life, Shoulder Arms, The Bond, Pay Day, The Pilgrim.* After some trouble with the Internal Revenue, he returned to England in the late 1920s.

2 Hannah Harriett Chaplin (b. 1865; d. 28 August 1928) appeared briefly in British music halls as Lily Harley. After spending much of her adult life in an asylum, she was brought to California by Chaplin in the spring of 1921.

he stood out from the rest of the boys as a personality. I remarked to Sidney, "You treat Charlie even to-day just like a kid brother, don't you?" He answered, "I still think of him as my little brother, no matter how big he gets to others. I can't forget our early days. You know those were difficult times for us. I was the big star of our act and Charlie was the little guy. I carried the responsibility then. Now I run to him for help and he never lets me down. He's still my helper, I guess. You see, our childhood poverty and hard knocks in show business wove a very close bond between us." Charlie joked and chided Sidney saying, "After his picture *Charley's Aunt*[1] is finished, he's going to be the big cheese." This rang a bell . . . Sidney was late, so he hurried off.

We all thought this was our cue to jump to attention. I started to leave Charlie, while all the crew took their places. But he asked, "What do you think of my mother?" I sat down again beside him. I could see his heart was with his mother and not on work. I looked at her picture again and said, "She's very pretty and has such a warm motherly expression." He was pleased and said, "She is pretty, isn't she? Yes, she was a true mother. She loves her boys and we love her. You know I was her love child."

I could easily believe he was born of great love. He was just radiating it. "Now" he said, "I have the great joy of making her life rich and free from worries. She lives in a lovely place in Pasadena, with constant care and companionship." There is no joy comparable to this. I know. Then he added, and I think with a little pride, "Every time I see her she admonishes me, 'Remember you can gain the whole world and lose your soul. So be good and put God first.' She loved the Bible and would quote it profusely."[2] Charlie would always agree with her and say, "I promise, dear." This would make her so happy

[1] *Charley's Aunt*—Christie Film Company, 2 February 1925.

[2] Chaplin's own account of his mother reading the Bible to him can be found in *MA*, pp. 14-15.

and she'd answer, "Now you have given me more than money can buy." He loved her sweet faith.

A lot of her sweetness rubbed off on Charlie. One day he came into the studio, hands deep in his pockets, head down and shoulders hunched. He was unable to work. Finally I asked, "Is there something bothering you? Is everything alright?" He quickly came over close to me, as if glad someone sensed his feelings and answered, "Just as I arrived at the gate this morning, a little old man stopped me and asked for my autograph. I was preoccupied . . . thinking of the day's work . . . and I shrugged him off. Now I feel all upset. I know I should have given the chap a few moments. It wouldn't have hurt me. I went back to find him but he was gone."

Then he stopped talking and listened, as if asking for some words of consolation. I said, "Charlie, you're very sensitive and it is sweet. But just stop for a minute and remember all the hours of wholesome joy, plus the beautiful messages of hope you have given to so many. Very few have given so much to so many. You must forgive yourself this moment of being remiss. Don't forget we're all still learning in this schoolroom." I patted his hand like a mother and added, "Someday maybe I'll tell you what you have done for one lost soul."

All anguish left. He looked humbly into my eyes and inquired, "Really? Is it about you? Will you tell me soon?" Then a soft smile stole over his face and he pressed my arm and said, "Thank you Georgia." A joyful little fellow again, he rose from his chair, rubbed his hands together and happily said to the crew, "Well, let's get on with some work."

Charlie the genius, had no sense of limitation when at work. He would work, sweat and keep everyone waiting or whatever until he was satisfied. He was inspired and filled with true riches. I didn't know why then . . . but his studio became more like home to him. He seemed not to want to leave it. The making of *The Gold Rush* had taken on new lustre. "Mr. Chaplin," his private life, nor his social whirl did not interfere, not when Charlie the artist was inspired.

In the back of his studio grounds, Charlie had an old shack. There he would go and work, write and rewrite. One day he invited me into it, to talk over a scene. I had pictured it furnished beautifully inside. No indeed . . . it was bare, with only a few old chairs, a table and empty walls. He laughed at my amazement and explained, "I keep it this way so I can think. I'm not tempted to relax."

I stood at the door. He said, "Come on in and join me. Please sit down with me." I started to sit in one of the hard chairs but he sat down on the rug. I sat right down with him. It was such fun and so informal, we could really communicate. This was what he wanted. This was the first time we had been alone. For a moment or two there was silence as he put his hand to his chin and just looked at me. He said thoughtfully, "Georgia, in you I find all the good qualities of all the women I have ever known. Why is this?"

I pondered this question and answered slowly, "I wonder if it could be like . . . Narcissus seeing himself. You see . . . from my early childhood . . . you . . . started to mold my character. I tried to emulate you . . . all the confidence, courage and hope . . . you depicted. So, perhaps, you're seeing yourself . . . your own reflection." Charlie didn't laugh at me, he said, "Narcissus fell in love with what he saw."

Charlie moved close to me and took my hand for a moment. He said, "I've known you for quite awhile and yet I don't know you very well. Please tell me more." It was like a confession. I confessed to him, "When I was a little girl, you reached out from the screen and took me by the hand and led me out of total darkness. I didn't like what I saw. I didn't like life. I wanted out . . . I had planned . . . You were a beam of living light into my dead world of unanswered questions."

He replied so gently, "You're so very comforting to me. I like you to be around . . . sometimes I feel so lonely. You know there is a great gulf between an artist and the world. He lives apart. Thank you for your . . . confession. I feel rewarded. He lifted me to my feet and said, "Now we have a secret." For a brief moment he held me, then gently put me away from him.

He laughed happily and said, "Mr. D'Arrast and I are going to John Barrymore's[1] home to-night for a chat. Would you care to join us?" But this was not for me. Charlie was married and although it was a threesome, my feeling was not right about it. I had to renege [*sic*]. I said, "It is very kind of you to include me, but not tonight . . . not as things are." He understood and smiled saying, "You have more character in your little finger than most of the girls of Hollywood."

I had refused this first invitation. I knew I had no choice, yet temptation whispered, "Don't be foolish, go ahead . . . you have heard of troubles in his marriage . . . he likes you and you could break it up . . ." But principle spoke, even the ideals, the very ideals he had put in my head, "Be honest, be decent and fair with your fellow man." I was glad I listened. I remembered how as a child I wanted Edna Purviance's place. How I envied her his attention and love. I even prayed for it. No wonder our prayers aren't answered.

But now I was on firmer ground. My steps were still faltering and so was my refusal of that first invitation to go out with Charlie. But I did manage to take that big step for principle . . . and my reward was at hand . . . he complimented me for it. I got a good mark from my teacher. Bully!

Charlie had many colors.[2] When he was inspired he'd forget his own needs and those of others. He'd work himself like a slave and also the rest of the cast. One day an elderly woman came to me and said, "He hasn't given us a moment

1 Chaplin first met John Barrymore (b. John Blythe, 15 February 1882, Philadelphia; d. 1942) "at the height of his success sitting broodingly in an office in the United Artists building" (*MA*, p. 280).

2 "Colors" must refer to moods. In his autobiography, Adolphe Menjou said that Chaplin's moods could be gauged by the colour of the suit he was wearing: green meant melancholy, blue—jovial, grey—in-between. *It Took Nine Tailors* (New York: McGraw-Hill, 1948), p. 107.

off. Dear, I don't think I can wait any longer. But I'm afraid if I slip out I might lose my job. What am I going to do?"

I said, "When you see me talking with Charlie, leave . . . I'll keep him busy until you return." I asked Charlie, "Don't you think the day's work had gone real well?" He answered enthusiastically, "Real fine, things are clicking." These words led to other words and I managed to hold his interest. Soon the woman returned. But as luck would have it, he glanced up and saw her. He immediately asked, "I wonder what is going on? I didn't dismiss anyone. I want to take . . ." I interrupted him and said, "This little woman has wanted to excuse herself—an hour ago, but she was afraid she'd lose her job. I'm quite sure there are others here who feel the same. Do you realize how long we've been working? Do you know what time it is?" He looked at his watch and said, "Mercy . . . I'm so sorry . . . I had no idea . . . how thoughtless of me." Then he dismissed everyone for lunch.

Then he turned to me and said humbly, "I don't want these people to be afraid of me. I shouldn't be so selfish. I should consider other people's needs more. Georgia, whenever I get too big for these baggy pants . . . tell me." I laughed and said, "I shall." He smiled and confessed, "It's funny, I want you to correct me . . . as you did to-day. I don't know why but I can tell you things I can't tell anyone else. It's a good feeling I have for you . . ."

19

Edna Purviance[1] was Charlie's leading lady in his early pictures. She was very dear to him and he always spoke tenderly of her. She was very motherly to him—she must have loved Charlie. He loved to recall their days together and Harry D'Arrast and I enjoyed listening.

He said, "You know, Edna and I had many happy as well as trying times. She was a good girl and very kind. One day she and I dropped in at a swanky restaurant, The Riverside Inn. I was dressed in an old sweat shirt, Edna in a cotton house dress. We'd been driving in the heat of the California sun and we looked like hoboes.

As we entered the spacious dining room, the head waiter took one glance at us and raced ahead of us, to the back of the restaurant. He seated us behind a large pillar. While we were scanning the menu, some of the customers recognized us. The word spread like wild fire. Back rushed the waiter bowing and waving us to a nice table by the window, where we'd be visible to all his guests. But Edna remained seated and motioned to me to be seated. The waiter came close to her bubbling with apologies. He said, 'I'm so sorry, I thought you were just common people.' Edna looked up at him and said sweetly,

[1] Edna Olga Purviance (b. 1894, Lovelock, Nevada; d. 11 January 1958, Hollywood) joined the Essanay Company at Chaplin's invitation in 1915, making her film debut in *A Night Out*. During the following seven years, she played romantic parts in nearly thirty of his pictures. Although her career ended in 1926 with Henri Daimant-Berger's unsuccessful *L'Education du prince*, Purviance continued to be on Chaplin's payroll until her death.

'We want to thank you for treating us like humble people. You have just paid us the highest compliment. That will be all. Please send us the waiter.' Nothing more to the point could have been spoken. The head waiter lowered his eyes and discreetly backed away and never returned for the rest of the stay." Then with a twinkle in his eyes, Charlie smiled and said, "Georgia, remember the lesson you gave me the other day in humility?"

Charlie continued his tales about Edna. He said, "She had the most easy-going disposition. No matter how many pies she'd get in the face or how often I'd repeat the take, she'd remain calm and patient. Knowing this, I'd take everything out on dear Edna. I'd become exacting and severe, and not watch my tongue . . . but she'd never complain. This smoothness went on for years without a ruffle."

He seemed to enjoy telling Harry and I about Edna. He went on eagerly, "One day . . . one time I was in a terrible hurry and in a horrible mood. I was on a tight schedule and was behind, so fear and rush had taken over. As usual, I took it out on her. While directing her, I started a tirade saying, 'Don't look so dead . . . show some emotion.' Pies were flying into her face and I kept up my yelling. Finally I screamed, 'For heaven's sake, act spirited.' That was the climax. That's exactly what she did. She came out of the set and with arms flying and fire in her eyes, she came after me . . . me. I took one look at her face, and I sprang to my feet, turned on my heels and started running. She chased me off the set, out of the building, down the lawn and I just managed to make it into my dressing room and slam the door."

Harry and I were laughing out loud, as we watched Charlie re-enact this episode. With big eyes and hand on his heart he gasped, "I ran for my life. When I felt I could dare, I peeked out from behind the curtain, then I poked my head out the door. The coast was clear. I gingerly tip-toed over to her dressing room and called, 'Edna, Edna dear, are you alright? Will you ever forgive me? Please? I'll never act like that again.

I promise. Please forgive me dear?' Edna slowly opened her door and stared at me. There I stood dripping with repentance. She smiled softly and said, 'I can see you are sorry.' Once again she was her sweet self. So I was taken into her arms and given a motherly hug and was forgiven. But I was wiser, much wiser."

Charlie starred Edna Purviance in *A Woman of Paris.*[1] This picture made Adolphe Menjou[2] famous. Mr. Chaplin tried to put Edna in a picture written and directed by Josef von Sternberg at a later date.[3] But she had let herself get too heavy and in other ways ruled herself out of a further career. Charlie was a loyal friend, and helped her until she passed on.

Now I knew Edna as a lovely person. It made me sorry that I had ever coveted her place in Charlie's pictures or affection. What makes us do what we would not, and not do what we would? But I was learning and slowly getting much wiser too.

1 A founder member of United Artists (1919), Chaplin did not fulfill his contract with First National until *The Pilgrim* was completed in July 1922. *A Woman of Paris* was his first film for UA.

2 Adolphe Menjou (b. 18 February 1890, Pittsburgh; d. 1963) played supporting roles in several major Hollywood productions before gaining prominence in *A Woman of Paris.* He later became a member of the militantly anti-Communist Motion Picture Alliance for the Preservation of American Ideals, and appeared as a "friendly" witness, before the House on Un-American Activities.

3 In 1926 Chaplin invited Sternberg to direct *The Sea Gulls.* The film, re-titled *A Woman of the Sea*, was intended to provide an opportunity of a come-back for Edna Purviance. Chaplin, for reasons not known, never released it. The "original and only negative" was formally burned on 24 June 1933, probably to satisfy the demands of the Internal Revenue.

20

While shooting *The Gold Rush*—I heard many tales of Mr. Chaplin's unsavory reputation. But it all seemed to be about someone remote . . . someone I didn't care to think of or know. It was like being tempted to give value to a counterfeit.

I was vitally interested in trying to understand more of what made the little comic think and act so ideally. Mr. Chaplin and the news about his loves and worse [his] marriages, was a dark cloud that always hovered around. It couldn't extinguish the light I basked in from Charlie, who was just the opposite . . . but the only real and substantial one to me. My adoration continued. I cherished the spiritual message he gave to my listening ears and hungry heart. The larger village of the world too, continued to adore him. He treated me like a gentleman. He responded to me, as I saw him . . . I guess people do this.

As we worked together, this little bum looked so devoid of worldly possessions. Half teasing, one day I asked, "How does it feel to be a millionaire and own a huge estate?" Rather wistfully he answered, "You know, we never really own anything. We more or less hold them in trust. But I love it here and I do want to live in my home all my days." Then he added sadly, "But who knows?" Charlie had the ability to see things in detail . . . but to see the whole . . . in picture-making and in life. He was gifted.

Charlie was so articulate and was eager to talk. He pulled his chair close and asked, "Do you want to hear of my first days in Hollywood? Georgia, I want you to know all about me . . . and I'd like to know all about you. Are you interested?" Of course he didn't know that he had absorbed my thoughts for years. I answered, "Tell me how you became the man you are today? I'd love to hear."

He settled back in his easy chair and said, "I was working as a comic at Mack Sennett's,[1] in the early days. Seeing I was perfectly willing to take pies in the face and do any dirty gag that was handed to me, Mack Sennett took note . . . and started figuring out something for me."

As usual Charlie filled in . . . with gestures, cute expressions and pantomime. He was delightful to watch. As if it had all happened yesterday, he continued, "Big Mack Sennett came down on the set one day just as I had been pushed in the mud and received a pie in the face and yelled, 'Hey you, come into my office.' I cleaned the pie from my eyes and asked, 'Who me?' He waved his hand and marched off ahead of me into his plush office and sat down. I was so slimy I couldn't sit, so I just stood."

Charlie made it so realistic, I could see his face dripping and feel the mud clinging. He went on, "I was so out of breath trying to keep up with this large man and also I was scared stiff . . . wondering what I had done wrong. Mr. Sennett began, 'I've been watching you young man, and I've decided to give you an opportunity . . . a small one . . . a very slim one. If you can make a picture a day for three weeks and if I can sell them . . . I'll give you a little more money and another assignment . . . O.K.?' "[2]

Charlie threw back his narrow shoulders courageously, as if he were living it all over again. He said, "I answered Sennett just as business-like as I knew how . . . just as to the point and

1 Mack Sennett (b. Michael Sinnott, 17 January 1880, Quebec, Canada; d. 1960), considered by many the "King of Comedy," was an experienced director when he left Biograph in 1912 to enter into an association with Charles O. Bauman and Adam Kessell and create a new production company, Keystone.

2 Chaplin appeared in thirty-five films for Keystone. The first, *Making a Living*, was released on 2 February 1914; the last, *His Prehistoric Past*, 7 December 1914. He directed or co-directed twenty of the last twenty-three films.

short . . . as he had put it. Anyway I was afraid to say too much for fear he'd change his mind. I said quickly, 'Very good, very good, I'll be ready any time . . . tomorrow? Is that alright? I mean, anytime or . . . thing you say.' Sennett said stiffly, 'Tomorrow.' Then dismissed me with a wave of his hand."

Charlie was living it all again. He said, "The next morning I was there, bright and early, giving all that was in me. I frantically thought up stories, found locations, cast the parts, played the lead and directed a comedy . . . every day for three weeks. Each night I'd be completely exhausted. But in the morning, as if a shot had gone off, I'd jump up, race to the studio and like fire and lightning, I'd go at it again."

He sighed, as he vividly remembered and told me, "Finally, the assignment was over. But I couldn't turn off the steam. I felt sure . . . I knew that nothing would come of this work. Sennett hadn't said one word and so I was convinced that I was through. Not a sound . . . the phone didn't ring . . . everything had gone dead. But I was keyed up. I couldn't turn it off now. I had been going full speed ahead for three weeks."

He slapped his hands together and exclaimed, "Then and there I made a big decision. I was through with acting forever. I said to myself, 'Immediately and without delay . . . I am going to turn my endeavors to raising chickens . . . that's it, I am going to raise chickens.' " With his jaw bone set and dead serious he continued, "I set off to the library, obtained all the books I could get on the subject and burned the midnight oil pouring over these books. 'How to be a success . . . raising chickens,' became my Bible. I studied and pondered its pages. It took a little money. But I figured my last check would do it . . . I had it all figured out to the last penny. I rushed over to the studio to pick up my closing check. This was all I needed now to launch me into my new career."

Charlie put his hand to his head and said, "My heart sank. My check was not at the cashier's window. I was told to go to Mack Sennett's office. I had planned on that money, and on my way to his office, I went over what I was going to tell him . . . and in no uncertain terms. Hysterically, I hurried. My firm resolve was turning awry. My knees were about to cave in when I saw Mack Sennett standing big, tall and foreboding in the door way. My pace slackened. Then I saw his face break into a broad smile. I looked behind me. I knew the smile wasn't for me, but I couldn't see anyone. I stopped completely, then I advanced gingerly.

Sennett became exasperated and beckoned saying, 'Hurry along, I've got something exciting to show you Charlie.' When I heard my name I raced to him. When I reached him he pointed inside to the room. It was piled high to the ceiling with mail. I was bewildered and asked, 'What does that mean? Who is it for?' He threw his arms around me roughly and said, 'It's all for you, it's your mail. The children across the nation have opened their hearts to you. The distributers are wiring, begging for more of your films. Now Charlie . . . what is your pleasure? . . . you can write your own ticket.' "

Charlie continued, "Of course I was flabbergasted, but I took hold of myself and tried to gather my wits. Timidly but courageously I mustered up the nerve and said, 'I think I should get a little money . . . and a contract?' Mack Sennett was delighted and wrote out a check for three times the amount I'd been getting, and handed it to me saying, 'This is just a starter.' I waltzed out of that office thinking I was king of the world. My head was in the clouds without a trace of chickens in it."[1]

Then he came back to me from his journey into the past and said, "You've just heard a short story of poverty to riches. That day was the beginning of my trek up to that hillside home." The more I knew this little fellow, the more I realized that "The Tramp" was the expression of his great sympathetic character and thought. It had to take the form the children could love, understand and enjoy. "There is where the hope of the world is," he'd often say. He himself retained this child-likeness.

[1] Compare with Chaplin's account in *MA*, Chapter 10, and Mack Sennett's in *King of Comedy* (New York: Doubleday, 1954), Chapter 14.

21

Douglas Fairbanks was Charlie's closest and most precious friend.[1] Charlie said, "Many times through the years I would feel the need of some certain person to inspire me. While making a picture I'd say, 'This is for Doug.' Then I would try to do what I thought would delight him." But Charlie also inspired Doug. One day he invited Charlie to go for a short run around the hills. Douglas lived just above Charlie in a place he named "Pickfair." Doug formed this name from Mary Pickford and Douglas Fairbanks.

Of course Douglas was considered the great athlete by his friends, his fans and himself. He worked out everyday at his large gymnasium which he had built at his studio. Charlie was out of condition and fragile . . . he thought. But Charlie accepted the invitation and they started off.

After they had jogged quite a distance, Douglas sprinted ahead. Looking back at Charlie he lovingly warned, "Don't try to keep up. You mustn't over do it. Drop out anytime and I'll meet you later." Charlie ignored the advice and kept running along. Doug started to slow down. Charlie went sailing by. Doug yelled out, "Charlie, I told you not to overdo it." But on Charlie ran.

Just as he turned the hill, he glanced back and saw Doug at a stand-still. Half an hour later, Charlie had circled the hill and came jogging up to Doug, who was now sitting by the

[1] Mary Pickford recalled that when she telephoned Chaplin with the news of Fairbanks' death in December 1939, she realized "perhaps as I had never before, how very deep the friendship of Charlie and Douglas had been." *Sunshine and Shadow* (New York: Doubleday, 1955), p. 226.

road-side. Douglas said good naturedly, "I always noticed your legs . . . were developed . . . now let me have it." Charlie had never told Doug before that running was his forte as a youngster and that he had quite a reputation for long distance running in England. Douglas threw his arms around Charlie and said, "I'm proud of you . . . I never knew or dreamed you had it in you." Douglas Fairbanks was not only a good sport, but I found him to be one of the friendliest of the stars of Hollywood.

Charlie and Doug played many youthful pranks and jokes in their early days in California. He told me, "We'd call up some big broker, order a large block of stocks . . . hundreds of shares of this and that blue chip. The salesman would hurriedly take down the impressive order. Then when it came time to give our names, we'd start coughing, sputtering and garble this information." With a twinkle in his eyes he'd ask, "Weren't we impish? But Hollywood in those days was our playground."

Maybe he was kidding but he said, "We hijacked a street-car one day and drove it a bit . . . until we got scared stiff. Then we jumped off and beat it." He was probably pulling my leg, but I enjoyed hearing these "weirdos." He told me Mary Pickford and he tried to play a joke on Douglas. "We decided to flirt and make Douglas jealous. So we danced around the parlor in front of him, gazing adoringly into each other's eyes. But he turned the prank on us, he wasn't fooled at all. He started singing loudly, grabbed us both and danced a three-some awkwardly around the room, until we all ended sitting on the floor and laughing wildly."

Charlie loved Douglas like a brother. It worried him that he worked out so hard at his gym. And just as Douglas had warned Charlie not to run too much . . . so Charlie admonished Doug, "Don't over-exercise . . . take it easy."

22

Charlie's many moods and endless stories revealed the deep sensitive feeling he had for his fellow man. Every day was a school day for me. I was learning what a monumental masterpiece is man's true self and how much it can do for so many. Of course I realized each one must do his own thing. But he taught me . . . each one can. He said, "There is genius in everyone. Study people, study yourself and you'll find it. This genius can make visible, beautiful things that before were invisible." I complimented him. I told him, "I have seen the loveliness of pathos and courage in your genius." With all the praise he received he never seemed to tire of hearing of the good he had done. Life was commencing to be a real adventure with purpose and fun.

That bubbling spirit of Charlie's was undaunted. In a clowning mood one day on the set, he started humming and then singing softly. It must have sounded good to him for presently he threw all caution to the wind and began vocalizing. With one hand on his chest and waving the other frantically, he bellowed loudly . . . the clown song from Pagliacci. Imagine!

He looked around for approval. Everyone's mouth had dropped open. Some could hardly contain a giggle. Then he burst into laughter at himself, which allowed all around to let go and do the same. But this laughter did not deter him. He would clear his throat and try again . . . stopping only to ask, "Don't you think I have a voice?" This was typical of Charlie. He would fearlessly attempt the impossible. He had many times said to me, "Don't be afraid of making a fool out of yourself. Just try . . . anything. Even if you can't do it, you might find that you can." In a few words, he had stated his life's action.

But the rich experience of working with Charlie was not going to be forever. *The Gold Rush* was rushing to the finish line. He was inspired and grew eager to get to the last shot. It made my heart sink. "Perhaps I'll never be close again to my great teacher and guide or even see him any more," I thought to myself.

The last shots did come. They were taken in San Diego, on a boat.[1] There the story picks up Charlie, the little tramp, returning home to the States. His rush for gold had not been in vain . . . for he located a mine and is now a millionaire. I, his love, am in the steerage just by chance. I was leaving the dance-hall life forever.

For a reporter's human interest story, Charlie takes off his expensive fur coat and puts on his tramp's outfit. In the meantime, I hear an officer speak of a search for a stowaway. Posing for the camera, Charlie steps back for focus and falls down a staircase, into a coil of ropes near me . . . Georgia. I recognize him and I realize I love him. Believing him to be the stowaway, I push him back into the ropes and shield him with my blanket. I plead with the officer who finds him, to let him go. To my consternation, the captain identifies him as one of the millionaires aboard. I feel like running away, but he stops me. At last he has his love . . . Georgia. His heart is warmed because I tried to save him . . . the poor little tramp.

A reporter asks, "Who is the lady?" Charlie answers, "It's Georgia, my love . . . my wife to be." We walked up to the upper deck and there we were asked to pose for pictures. Charlie had these shots taken over and over. He whispered to me, "I love you Georgia, truly love you." It was all a part of the story, so I dared to say, "I've loved you since I was a little . . . I love

[1] The boat named "The Lark" travelled between San Diego and San Francisco. This scene, the last with Georgia, was filmed on board in April 1925; the final shots were not filmed until 14-15 May.

you too." Then we kissed our first kiss.[1] How many times he retook this I lost count. Then the fade . . . the end.

I had a feeling of ecstasy and tragedy. Harry D'Arrast and Charlie were driving back to Los Angeles, some one hundred and twenty-five miles together. I was going back with a girl on the train. A knock came at my cabin door. Harry called, "Georgia, Charlie wants to know if you'd care to join us?" I was so thrilled with the thought of being with Charlie a few more hours. I replied, "Yes, thank you."

Immediately came the realization that I had nothing glamourous to wear. I cried out, "Harry no, I cannot . . . no." But he didn't hear me, he had gone. However, Consuelo, my dear friend and room-mate, grabbed me back into the room and said, "Don't refuse . . . I won't let you. Wear my new dress." I knew instantly the dress she meant. It was a princess of soft blue, with velvet roses applicade [*sic*] on georgette. She had paid one hundred and fifty dollars for it and this was a huge sum to us. I put it on and it fit like a glove.

When I came walking up to Charlie and Harry, they both stood silent. They had only seen me in the dance-hall costume day after day for months. Charlie exclaimed jokingly, "Harry who is this beautiful young lady?" Harry answered, I've never seen her before. Dare we approach her?" They each offered an arm and escorted me. Charlie said, "We'll just have to go to some nice place and dance a little. I want everyone to see you to-night, Georgia." Still jesting, they both bowed to the ground as I stepped into the limousine.

I may have seemed changed to them, but Mr. Chaplin looking so dapper, was like a strange person to me. I had been working with the little comic for months. I had just kissed the little tramp good-bye. Now I was confronted with the charisma of Chaplin. I had read constantly about

[1] It has been suggested that Chaplin, expecting some critics to object to the kiss as out of character for the Tramp, forestalled them by having the reporter shout "Oh! you've spoilt the picture." When Chaplin reissued *The Gold Rush* in 1942 he omitted this ending.

Hollywood's socialite during the filming of the picture, but I had not been close to him.

The more he spoke in his charming manner and showered me with compliments, the more awed I became. The feeling of teacher and pupil slipped into a memory. He made me feel . . . like a Circe, whose past was illusive . . . or with no past at all . . . and possibly no future. I was no longer . . . simple little Georgia. That dance-hall girl I had been playing for one year . . . I felt like her. This whole encounter seemed like a dream.

Yet Mr. Chaplin was so real, so close . . . too much a man and I a woman. I wanted to be free of this feeling. I started reasoning and reminding myself, "He is a married man, and no doubt happily so. I'm sure any woman could be happy with him." I told myself firmly, "It is ugly for a single girl to flirt with another's man . . . it's like stealing and selfish." But I said, "It might be easy." Again I argued, "There are plenty of single men." Opposite thoughts raced threw [*sic*] my head, "He is so attractive and he likes you . . . it might be very easy to flirt with him . . . he might be easy . . . With all my strength I forced these suggestions out as being no part of my nature and ideals. I maintained an impersonal attitude and hoped he knew nothing of my battle. I tried hard to be affable and composed.

However, I continued to study this man. I felt he was the exact opposite of little Charlie. Mr. Chaplin was outgoing, worldly and gay. The little one was sad, lonely and to himself. I reproached myself, "Why do you feel such a strong attraction for this one?" . . . I wished the back seat of the car were bigger . . . that he wasn't so close.

It was dinner time. Mr. Chaplin asked, "How would you and Harry like to dine at the Grant Hotel? I know you must be hungry." I was famished, but not for food. When we entered the room, the orchestra struck up the band with "Charlie My Boy, Oh, Charlie My Boy." The head-waiter greeted us with a bow and proudly escorted us to the best table—right in front of the band. Everyone in the place applauded him. Mr. Chaplin was not only the toast of Hollywood, he was without a peer every place.

The band leader leaned down and said softly, "Please dance—everyone is waiting for you. Will you honor us?" Mr. Chaplin turned to me and said, "May I have the pleasure?" How different was this dance from the crazy one I had with him in *The Gold Rush*. There, Jack Cameron,[1] my insolent admirer comes up to claim me. To show my contempt I dance off with enraptured Charlie, the little tramp.

Bad luck however, follows him in this dance. His trousers start slipping. Seeing a rope on a table, he uses it as a belt. Unfortunately, the other end of the rope is attached to a large dog, who complicates the dance steps and brings our brief time together to a close as the sight of a cat takes him off his feet and the dog pulls him around the floor. He is so embarrassed and the crowd is so amused.

"Now I'm in his arms again dancing. This charming self-possessed man cannot be the same one . . . there must be two," I told myself. He did such fascinating routines, his professional dancing was so apparent. His favourite dance was the tango. He requested the band to play . . . "La Cumparsita." Not even Valentino could have out-danced Mr. Chaplin this evening. He was inspired and danced like a native Argentine performer. His contra-shoulder movements made his Gaucho steps dramatic. He bent his knees and straightened them, making the exhibition sensuous and cleverly punctuated. It was thrilling and yet he was so easy to follow, so subtle and firm was his "lead."

When we finished, everyone applauded loudly. He was so delighted. His eyes beamed with the joy of a child. Harry was the only one who didn't seem to appreciate our fun. He and I had gone out dancing several times to the famous

[1] The role of Jack Cameron was played by Malcolm Waite (b.1893, Menominee, Michigan) who studied engineering before entering films in 1924. A friend of Mary Pickford's brother Jack, he appeared with her in *Dorothy Vernon of Haddon Hall* (1924).

Cocoanut [*sic*] Grove. We liked each other very much. This threesome was an unhappy evening for Harry. When Charlie and I returned to the table he asked, "Isn't she graceful?" Harry just nodded politely. All the way home while Mr. Chaplin and I were breathlessly talking and getting acquainted . . . Harry was silent. Mr. Chaplin noticed this and said, "I wish Harry had his girl with him." He didn't know we had been out dancing and romancing together.

When Mr. Chaplin took me to my door in Los Angeles he said, "I enjoyed every mile of our trip. It was too short. I've never known you before. You are so different from the other girls in motion pictures. I'm going to miss working with you and being around you young lady. I feel a little sad that the picture is finished."

My emotions were so mixed as I said good night . . . I could hardly define my feelings . . . they were not the same as for the little tramp. I said, "Your wife must be happy it is over. You were apart so much . . ." Then I added, "She must love her husband very much . . . I wish you every joy and great success for *The Gold Rush*." It was an exciting evening, but I wasn't happy with it . . . I wished it could have ended on the boat with "Charlie, the little comic."

23

The Gold Rush was acclaimed as Charlie's greatest. He said many times, "This is the picture I want to be remembered by." Immediately I was signed by Paramount Pictures. There I made *The Great Gatsby*, *The Rainmaker* and others. I had the opportunity of playing many roles for the other studios also. During my career I played the gamut of parts, some heavy and some light parts. I was always confident of my acting ability and probably should have loved it.

But I was never free from being dismayed at life. My heart and head were filled with this awful yearning for a fuller answer. I longed to be associated with Charlie again. I seemed to be walking on quicksand once more. I felt I was losing the sure footing I had found with him. I reached out for help. I searched and found where his most recent picture was playing, *The Circus*. It inspired me. Again I found that something that always gave me hope and courage. It was like fresh air breathed into an atmosphere of mediocrity. "Why are there so few of these precious pictures? . . . those with a beautiful message," I'd ask.

A reporter called me from one of the papers and asked for an interview. I agreed and wondered what angle this one would take. Promptly at the appointed time he was at my house. He eagerly started his questions, "Tell me what you think of the break-up between Mr. Chaplin and Lita Grey?" He quickly saw my dismay and asked, "You haven't heard? Of course it won't be in the head-lines until this evening. But I thought perhaps you knew."

I was so shocked by this news and my emotions so uncontrolled . . . without knowing why, my eyes filled with tears. I rushed from the room saying incoherently, "Please excuse me for a moment?" When I returned I explained, "I needed this handkerchief, there was something in my eye." He seemed to believe me and said, "Oh, I'm so sorry." He continued, "You are a good friend of his and were his leading lady . . . we're interested in your feelings?" I answered, "It's hard to believe. I'm sorry . . . so sorry . . . this marriage . . . is breaking up." But quickly the thought followed . . . now he will be free . . . a single man.

He asked inquiringly, "Are you really sorry?" "But of course," I hurriedly answered. "My last words to Mr. Chaplin I recall . . . were wishing him great happiness." But I remembered my last words were, "Your wife must love her husband." Why should I tell this reporter what I really said? Why am I defending myself at all? I asked myself. I felt confused and wished he would leave.

His questions became more penetrating. He asked, "How come you are the only girl that has been close to Chaplin, where there has been no scandal?" I answered with a question, "If you thought a marriage was beautiful, would you try to step in and break it up? Even if you felt you could?" I thought silently, "How glad I am I never tried to break up the marriage between those two. How happy I can be I never did that."

The reporter didn't answer my question. He said, "All Chaplin's leading ladies have been in love with him." Then he added rather bluntly, just as he was leaving, "Were those tears of yours . . . of sorrow or joy?" I laughed nervously and answered defensively, "It's disappointing to hear of something you had dreamed of as wonderful . . . failing." I felt like a double-minded man, like a wave that had been tossed roughly about by the winds. "The mortal is so frail, so unlike our ideals," I thought. Secretly I was commencing to thrill at the thought of perhaps seeing him. This time free.

As my interviewer departed he said, "You make a reporter read between the lines. I find you very interesting . . . not from what you said, but from what you didn't say. You're hard to know. Did Mr. Chaplin find you this way? This explains a few things."

The papers became filled with this scandal. These news stories portrayed Mr. Chaplin, not Charlie the little tramp, as one who thought a woman was born just to have children and more children in his image, which wasn't too pretty. But even two children in a very short time couldn't hold this marriage together. Mrs. Chaplin's attorneys prepared an amazing forty-two page "Complaint for Divorce"[1] . . . usually complaints run about four pages. Mr. Chaplin denied all the complaints. That was all there was . . . there wasn't anymore . . . it was through.

Mr. Chaplin, unlike the artist Charlie, didn't heed his finer intuitions. He put it this way after this miserable experience was over, "I felt inside of me that this relationship would never be right, but I couldn't stop myself. I wish I could follow this true feeling." As of old he suffered from "The old man and his deeds that should have been put off." After much adverse publicity and money . . . he was free.

[1] Reprinted in *Chaplin vs Chaplin*, edited by Ed Sullivan (Marvin Miller Enterprises, Inc., Los Angeles, 1965). It includes in full the "Answer of Defendant, Charles Chaplin."

24

I was in-between pictures. For days I had been sitting listlessly at home. Many friends had called but I wasn't seeking entertainment. I was really uninspired, without motivation. I didn't want a date.

Then a girl friend of mine called and asked, "Would you like to go some nice place for brunch?" I gave her the same answer I had been giving to my boy friends, "No thank you dear, I just feel like staying home." But she continued, I could hear tears in her voice, "Oh, alright Georgia, but I did so want to talk with you. I'm having such a problem. I felt if I could talk it out with you, you could help me."

That was all I needed to lift me out of my lethargy. I wanted to help . . . I wanted to help her. I hurriedly said, "I'm truly so tired of this house. I'm so happy you called. I'd really love to chat with you." So, I dolled myself up and tried to think of some extra nice place to go. Some place that would bring joy to my friend Mary. We went to the Montmartre Cafe[1] on Hollywood Boulevard, a very popular restaurant, with delicious food and afternoon dancing. The music was exhilarating and the place was filled with Hollywood celebrities.

Mary, a petite blonde with large sad eyes, sat opposite me and pored [*sic*] out her heart. She really had something to complain about. Her husband, after ten years of being the most self-effacing, docile companion, had suddenly taken up the hobby of gathering snakes and keeping them in their basement. The climax came . . . when one was missing. Now

[1] The Montmartre Cafe was located on the second floor of 6757 Hollywood Blvd. During the 1920s it was a favourite spot for long, elaborate lunches.

she was living in dread that it would crawl upstairs into her quarters.

I could hardly keep from laughing. But she looked so worn-out, almost ill. I said, "It's so tragic, it's almost funny." She smiled a bit and then she joined me in a little laughter. I let her do the talking, she was so filled with emotion. She said lovingly, "I think he's been so subdued all his life, he's trying to express manliness . . ." I agreed whole heartedly saying, "Yes you're right, his father was such a big shot. Wasn't he?" She thought quietly and asked, "Could I stay with you a few days? I'm going to encourage him to get all the snakes he wants. But I'm going to tell him I'll return when he removes them from our home . . . for good too." "That's the solution," I replied happily, "and you've solved your own problem." This proved to be true. It was fun being that friend who just listens, as another works out their own problem. I was filled with joy when we were leaving the Montmartre because I had helped Mary in small way. Her little face was round again with all the lines running up. But my reward followed so quickly. It was just around the corner.

I came face to face with Mr. Chaplin. We hadn't seen each other for over a year. A thousand thoughts came rushing in as he spoke. It seemed I'd made the wrong turn a year ago and had been walking down a dark, empty street. Now, somehow I'd made the right turn. The entire view was different. It was flooded with light.

I heard, "Georgia . . . fancy meeting you. It's been so long since I've seen you . . . too long." How enchanting the place became . . . the music, the people. How empty the crowded place seemed a moment before. I hadn't looked at anyone but Mary. I said softly, "It's good to see you. But . . . but I'm just leaving."

Immediately, he took my hand and asked, "Where are you going . . . can't you stay? What are you doing tonight? May I call you at eight? . . . may I see you at eight?" I just kept gazing at him and whispered, "Yes." Mary was overjoyed, she grabbed me by the arm and led me down the steps.

25

This was my first date with Charlie Chaplin. As I waited for him to drive up, I remembered that I had never been with him when he was a single man. All during the shooting of *The Gold Rush* he was married. It made a difference in my feeling. It now seemed right to think as I pleased. Heretofore I had to be studiously impersonal in my every act or word.

When he came to the front door, he too seemed freer. He said, "This is so nice. I wonder if you ever knew how much I wanted to come and call on you? . . . to see where and how you live? . . . take you dancing and to parties?" I answered, "No, I never dared to think of that. Now, it is right." Then he said graciously, "You are still so beautiful, I think even more than before . . . I'm going to show you off to my friends to-night."

We went to the most unusual party. It had been arranged by Kono, his Japanese valet. He had prepared a most sumptuous feast and show . . . all Japanese . . . in the Japanese part of town. Many notables of movieland were invited. Most of the guests were unaware of this area and few had ever seen such enchanting acts, nor tasted such odd oriental dishes. The table was a masterpiece of beauty. The daring combination of colors in their floral displays were only matched by their different colored roses, arranged as different species of fish.

Among the guests were Marion Davies[1] and Count D'Arrast. I was seated to the right of Mr. Chaplin and Marion

[1] Marion Davies (b. Marion Cecilia Douras, 3 January 1897, Brooklyn, New York; d. 23 September 1961, Los Angeles) made her film debut in 1917, and was starring in films of the Hearst-owned Cosmopolitan Pictures by the following year. Introduced to Chaplin during the making of *The Gold Rush*, they were rumoured to have been romantically involved. She retired from the screen in 1937.

to his left. Harry sat to my left. Miss Davies at the beginning of the party was overly nice to me. She said very sweetly, "You're a very beautiful girl . . . with such classical features, Georgia. I have the face of a 'Mickey.' " I noticed she called me Georgia, though we had just met. I thought, "How nice and friendly she is." Then she turned to Mr. Chaplin and said, "She's like a cameo." Somehow . . . I didn't know why . . . I questioned this. But I said, "You're very generous and nice to say that. I think you are beautiful . . . I've always enjoyed your pictures so much."

Then I noticed her lean close to Mr. Chaplin and in front of all the guests at the table, whisper in his ear. It seemed strange to me but I thought it must be alright, otherwise Marion Davies would never do it. But he laughed uneasily and shook his head negatively. She saw me glancing their way and said loudly, "Don't mind me, I'm just his wet-nurse." This . . . I couldn't answer. I hurriedly turned to Harry and engaged him in a conversation, and he seemed eager to hold my attention. All the while I could hear whispering going on between Marion and Mr. Chaplin.

She suddenly burst out in a raucous laugh, which demanded my attention. She looked at me and continued to laugh loudly. I became ill at ease . . . shaken. Harry reached under the table for my hand and gently squeezed it. I looked appealingly at Harry and he gave me a reassuring smile. I picked up my fork and tried to eat, but I could feel her eyes on me. I glanced up and sure enough she was now scowling at me.

"What is wrong? Did I say something that hurt her?" I asked Harry. I couldn't refrain from asking her, "Is everything alright?" I shouldn't have said anything . . . for she just glared at me and wouldn't answer. From then on she snubbed me . . . she completely ignored me.

I was chilled. There was a big lump in my throat. "My first date . . . and I have done something wrong," I thought. I called on all the courage I had been trying so hard to develop. I continued to be gracious to Mr. Chaplin. I praised everything, "It's such a lovely party. The lacy and meaningful way the

Japanese women dance is so enchanting. I should love to learn it." I could see the more I raved about the dinner the more pleased he was.

Then came time to leave. This was what it was all about. Marion came dashing up to Mr. Chaplin expecting him to go with her. I thought she came up to say something . . . but Mr. Chaplin didn't say a word to her. He turned to me hastily and escorted me out the door. Harry joined Marion. They just stood watching us depart. I simply couldn't understand. I turned and waved "good-bye." Harry waved a friendly farewell but Marion tossed her head high in the air.

Now I was sure I had said the wrong thing. I was positive I had spoiled our first date. I knew he'd never invite me any place again. As we drove home, Mr. Chaplin seemed to be trying hard to be polite. He kept talking, "The evening was a huge success. Their acting and dancing is so different . . . so interesting. I liked the way the guests enjoyed it. It was really something, wasn't it?" I said, "Yes, indeed." But silently I was telling myself, "You simply don't belong. You don't know how to act nor speak. He's being kind and pleasant. He'll drop you off as soon as he can and never see you again."

I kept my face turned away . . . I kept looking out the opposite window so he couldn't see the despair that had gripped me. When we stopped in front of my house I wanted to jump out and run into my house before I started to cry. He leaned close to me and said softly "Would you like to see my place and the way I live? Or are you in a hurry?" I looked into his face . . . and saw the opposite of what I had expected. He was filled with joy and inspiration. I answered quickly, "Oh, I'm in no hurry at all, not at all."

I had always dreamed of Charlie Chaplin's mansion. We drove through the beauties of Beverly Hills and then started winding up the tree-lined slopes. His home was completely invisible. The chauffeur made a sharp turn and circled around the lush greenery and there appeared a large, majestic structure. It was hidden . . . and now it was so big, so imposing. Tucked away on the top of a hill, surrounded by over seven acres of flowers and foliage, it was just like the dream-house I had envisioned.

The first thing he showed me was a small living creature, "Pet" his colorful parrot of bright green and red, which he kept on a large enclosed porch. He greeted him with a warm "Hello Charlie" every evening on his return home. Charlie said, "I've had 'Pet' for many years. He's now part of the family, and I just love him. He has cheered my heart many times with his happy 'Hello.' " This warmed my feelings towards Charlie. It's so easy to like those who are kind to animals.

Then he took me for a tour of his house. It was like being in a castle . . . for me. It had beautiful tapestries, Oriental rugs, priceless antiques and paintings. I felt awed by this grandeur. I wondered why he was bothering to show me all this splendor, especially after my faux-pas at the party, or whatever it was I had done to hurt Marion Davies. I had this feeling of guilt, and I waited for some rebuke . . . but he made no mention of anything discordant. On the contrary, he seemed overjoyed.

He said, "You've only seen half. You haven't seen the grounds." We stepped out into the night. From his hill-top it seemed the whole world was his . . . at his feet. He showed me the little lattice house in which he conceived the story of *The Gold Rush*. Here, as he spoke of our picture, I felt closer to him. For a few moments he was the little tramp to me. The heavens were so close, the stars seemed to be asking to be touched with the warmth of love. Even the lights of the city below were beckoning . . .

He reached out and took my hand and held it tightly as we climbed up and down the slopes. His hand was warm. I felt more assured. I felt even more . . . But I didn't know what he was thinking. We came to a little bench and he said, "Let's sit . . . for a moment. I want to speak to you . . . about the evening."

My heart sunk. I thought, "Now he is going to tell me . . . now he is going to scold me." Quickly I said, "I'm so sorry if I made anyone unhappy this evening. I don't know what I did . . . or said wrong. Please forgive me?" He said, "Georgia dear, you're making me feel like a cad. I'm sorry if I made you unhappy. I hope I acted alright?" I said, "But I thought I had . . ." He protested and said, "I felt as if I was with a goddess to-night. You made me so happy. I was inspired with you, young lady."

I was surprised and even more puzzled, but I was delighted that I had not hurt anyone. Then he said, "Let's not . . . let any one ever come between us Georgia. I promise I won't. Will you . . . promise?" Not quite understanding his words, I went along with him and said, "I promise." He was relieved and said happily, "Good, then everything is alright."

On the way home I said, "You don't know how happy I am that I acted alright to-night. You're sure I didn't say anything to make . . . Marion Davies angry with me?" He answered tenderly, but a little reluctantly, "I'm truly sorry that she caused you to worry . . . I'm disappointed in the way she acted to you. I want to . . . and I intend to make it up to you." Finally he told me, "It was she that was wrong, not you Georgia. I'm sad that our first engagement had to be marred . . . by her."

"Well," I said, "I feel so relieved, but she wouldn't say good-bye." He confessed, "I know you didn't know what was going on. She . . . was trying all evening . . . to get me to take her home . . . and have you go home with . . . Harry." My joy left me. I realized I wasn't with the little genius, but with Mr. Chaplin the counterfeit. I knew there was two not one. Beside me was the Casanova of Hollywood, with women fighting for him. He had been hiding something from me all evening.

I said, "I don't want this . . . perhaps I shouldn't have gone to-night. I'm sorry . . . but I'm a bit confused. I never want to spoil things for you . . . or make any enemies . . ." We had reached my home. I could see Mr. Chaplin was worried.

Our first engagement . . . and into its sunshine and fun had come this cloud. He leaned over to kiss me goodnight but I could not. I was convinced I could never fit into his life. I didn't like it. I was relieved when I shut my door, and that the evening was over. I'm sure he knew this.

26

Evidently Mr. Chaplin was determined to make up for the mistreatment I had received at the hands of Marion Davies. He planned a gala dinner party, with me as his guest of honor. All the notables of the movie colony were invited . . . King Vidor[1] and his wife, Mary Pickford and Douglas Fairbanks, Lillian Gish[2] and scores more.

I was pleased to hear from him, even though our first evening had been such a "bust" as they so descriptively put it. I felt sure nothing could be so disconcerting as our last encounter. But he said in a most charming manner, "I'm planning a formal dinner for you, as my guest of honor. Are you free Friday evening?" I knew he was trying to please me and bestow a nice compliment on me. I also knew that he was trying to make amends for the last meeting. So what could I say but, "Yes, I'm free and looking forward to seeing you. Thank you very much for thinking of me." An elegant dinner . . . and

[1] King Vidor (b. 8 February 1894, Galveston, Texas; d. 1 November 1982) made his debut as a feature director with *The Turn in the Road* (1919). A favourite in Hearst's entourage, he directed Marion Davies in *Show People* (1928), in which Chaplin made a guest appearance. His wife at the time referred to by Georgia (1926-32) was the silent-film actress Eleanor Boardman (b. 19 August 1898, Philadelphia; d. 1991). Known as the Kodak Girl, she is best remembered for her leading role in Vidor's *The Crowd.* In 1940 she married Harry d'Arrast.

[2] Lillian Diana Gish (b. 14 October 1893, Springfield, Ohio; d. 27 February 1993), widely recognised as "the first lady of the silent screen," made her film debut, along with her sister Dorothy, in D.W. Griffith's *An Unseen Enemy* (1912). After an absence of six years Gish returned to Hollywood, signing a contract with M-G-M in 1925. She chose King Vidor to direct her in *La Boheme* (1926).

in my honor . . . this was the last thing I wanted. I had never been to a formal dinner . . . and in the mansion of a millionaire. It was frightening!

I figured, "I'll wear a black lace dress. That will be safe, for that's appropriate for any occasion and will make me less noticeable. That much is O.K. But how . . . do I conduct myself. At this kind of function there's all kinds of knives and forks . . . it's entirely different from a restaurant. This calls for knowing etiquette backwards and forwards . . . what fork do I use? . . . what knife? . . . and what about all the other paraphernalia? . . . greetings? . . . introductions? . . ."

My head was swimming with questions and no answers. Good heavens, I didn't want to go. I didn't belong. I had convinced myself long ago that etiquette and all those niceties were just being high and mighty, and I held them in contempt. That's the position I took and now I was stuck with it. Like a blast of cold air I was now confronted with my ignorance. I said aloud, "Manners do count after all. But I can't go and get books and study now, it's too late!" Panic set in.

When the time arrived I was completely disheveled . . . not on the outside . . . inside. Of course all the big shots of Hollywood were at the party. The girls gazed at me with envy. They little realized that they were looking at pure pain.

Mr. Chaplin, with his poor background would understand my plight . . . which made matters worse. He lovingly offered me a cocktail saying, "It will make you feel good . . . and confident." Well, I didn't like that at all. I didn't relish it one bit that he had noticed my fears. I answered haughtily, "No thank you. I don't need that. I feel fine." Charlie smiled. Too much I thought. He said timidly again, "Of course, I know you feel alright, but I thought you might like a sip?" I firmly stood my ground and repeated, "Thank you . . . no, no thank you."

Soon after, he offered his arm and led me into the gorgeous dining room. The guests all took their seats and started staring at me. Of course they were waiting for the guest of honor to begin . . . but to me, they were just staring!

What was I to do . . . there were "umpteen" knives and forks, and I didn't know which ones to pick up. I got hot all over! The perspiration stood out on my forehead. But my blessed one, the little comic, had thoughtfully placed Harry Crocker[1] next to me. This was all pre-arranged. Harry Crocker, a handsome chap, was a kind person. He was a dear friend of Charlie's, and also worked for him at the studio. Harry was to the manor born. He was from the big banking family of San Francisco.

This evening Charlie had carefully selected him to help me. Unbeknown to me, Charlie said, "Harry, whatever Georgia has to do . . . you do it first . . . exaggerate it . . . so that even he who runs could see it. I understand her. I know her past and I know full well she hasn't had the opportunity to know the social graces. I couldn't help her before the party, there wasn't time. Anyway I shouldn't have dared. Georgia has a lot of pride." Harry said unselfishly, "You don't have to worry. Leave the whole thing to me. I'm delighted to help her. I like her very much."

But I didn't know about all this tender solicitude. So I sat there for the longest moment there ever has been . . . and stared at the gobs of silverware . . . in fear and trembling. I was blind with terror and embarrassment, but my loving friend Charlie had watched over me once again. Harry did as instructed. He hurriedly picked up the silver and started eating. I could see him out of the corner of my eye. Immediately I did the same. Simple, eh? Not really . . . but my night was saved.

1 Harry Crocker (1895-1958), a member of a prominent San Francisco banking family, came to Hollywood in 1924, and appeared with Marion Davies in *The Big Parade* and *Tillie the Toiler.* A part of Hearst's San Simeon circle, Crocker was introduced to Chaplin, becoming his assistant writer-actor in *The Circus.* A disagreement during the making of *City Lights* led to Crocker's departure. He became a columnist for the Hearst newspapers, before returning to work for Chaplin as his business manager during the making of *Limelight.*

How Charlie and Harry must have laughed at my performance. But . . . I never knew. After the party, Charlie said kindly, "I was so proud of you to-night Georgia." It was such a welcome white lie. He wisely told me that he wanted me just as I was . . . and then he slowly and quietly bought me a library on etiquette. Gradually, cleverly and lovingly he taught me how to conduct myself as a lady. I put aside all pride and eagerly sought this knowledge. He made me practice how to enter a room, greet others with universals, to introduce and how graciously to receive introductions.

He even made me like all the social graces, which heretofore I had scoffed at. He told me, "Robert Burns had spoken of manners as . . . just doing the loving thing . . . being kind and unselfish to others." Then he summed it all up one day, I guess it was my graduation time. He said sweetly, "Now Georgia, forget yourself and make others happy. That's all there is to etiquette."

But after the first big dinner in my honor, as the days went by and I didn't hear a word from Mr. Chaplin, I decided he'd had quite enough of me, after my awkward behavior. I complained tearfully to my mother, "He'll never want to see me again. If only I had known what to do." Mother answered, "You did the best you could. I'm sure you'll hear from him." I knew she was all wrong.

All my worries were childish and dear mother was right. Mr. Chaplin wanted me as his constant companion. He thought of such pleasant things to do and places to go. He took me to an amusement park[1] at the beach one evening. We danced and went on all the rides. He was such a good marksman. When he finished he had a handful of prize tickets. He asked, "What would you like for all our tickets?"

It was such fun. There was a huge display of prizes . . . wild colored bunnies, dolls, stuffed animals of every description

[1] Possibly Fraser's Million-Dollar Pier at Ocean Park. It had many gaudy amusements to attract visitors from Hollywood, where such entertainments were more strictly regulated.

and cans of food. Innocently and seriously I looked them all over and chose . . . cans of beans, carrots and peas. He watched me with keen amusement. He said, "My, you're a thrifty little person." But he added quickly, "But I like you for it. I understand you." He had known poverty and so I guess he felt close to me in spirit. Of course he had been a millionaire for a long time now and I realized why he was smiling. I apologized, "I'm sorry I made a poor choice." But the cat was out of the box . . . I could have kicked myself for not taking a big fuzzy bear or doll . . . then he wouldn't have been so amused at me . . . and my cans of beans.

27

Mr. Chaplin was a man of action. This day we met early in the morning. He had planned to go to Catalina Island, a four-hour trip off the shores of California, in a speed-boat of all things. When he arrived at my house, he handed me a couple of large boxes. He really didn't like my taste in clothes, nor my meager wardrobe. He said a little apologetically, "Please put these warm clothes on?" I had been rushing around all morning getting ready, and thought I was. I said, "But I'm all right . . . I won't be cold . . . I don't want a gift of clothes from you . . . thank you for thinking of me." I was truly taken back, I had worked so hard to look good. But he insisted, "I want you to be comfortable and not catch cold. If you don't accept these few little things from me, I'll just toss them into the ocean."

Then he said nonchalantly, "You know we're not going on the big boat 'The Catalina,' we're taking a speed boat. It's open and it might be cold. Now hurry!" I rushed back into my room, tore open the packages, and there before my eyes was the most beautiful outfit I had ever had. Without time to think further, I put on a lovely white woolen suit and a short coat of bright red . . . also a large brimmed white felt hat. When I came into the room Charlie exclaimed, "How lovely! You're pretty as a picture in that outfit. It was made for you." Then he added thoughtfully, "You looked sweet in your own outfit too." I admitted, "But now I feel like a queen. Thank you for doing all this shopping for me."

But the most unusual garment was in the second box. It was a top-coat of llama cloth, soft as down with long white hairs. This coat proved later to be a sensation at parties. It was like draping yourself in a cloud of fleecy velvet. One night at a party at Mr. Chaplin's, Lillian Gish admired it so much she asked me to try it on. It felt so comfortable, so soft, she snuggled into it and wore it most of the evening. Well this day I threw it over my arms and hurried out with Mr. Chaplin.

We finally launched out on our trip. The sea was smooth as glass. Kono, the skipper, Mr. Chaplin, two others and myself was about all this small boat could hold. The sea started to roll a little. Mr. Chaplin was at the helm, instead of the skipper. We were all smiling and trying hard to be as sold on this little boat, as Mr. Chaplin appeared to be.

Then the rolls turned into swells. We would ride up one side and as we descended, the wave would slap the bottom of the boat and ours too, with a resounding bang! Mr. Chaplin whose idea this whole thing was . . . wouldn't show one sign of concern. In fact he held the wheel with one hand, as he nonchalantly lit a cigarette. He puffed away . . . filling the fresh clean air with cigarette smoke for the rest of us to inhale. But I noticed the skipper didn't like this . . . one hand on the wheel . . . not one bit.

Mr. Chaplin, looking very diminutive, with the great Pacific surrounding him, threw out his little chest and acted like its triumphant master, until an extra large wave drenched him from top to bottom and we almost capsized. Whereupon, the skipper grabbed the wheel from Mr. Chaplin . . . which he more than gladly released. After a shudder, he quickly recooped [*sic*] his composure and said, "How refreshing."

But one large wave followed another until we were all wet through and through. In fact the brim of my beautiful hat withstood all it could and was now dangling around my neck. Then our discomfort turned into fear. We started wondering if anyone else had ever tried such a stunt. The boat got smaller and smaller and the sea bigger and bigger.

Mr. Chaplin was as one frozen in dripping icy water. I couldn't tell whether he was exhilarated or just plain frightened . . . and that's what he wanted. He acted it out to the finish. For when we finally arrived he exclaimed, "How exhilarating! What an experience in seamanship . . . I wouldn't have missed it for anything." However, on our return I asked, "Are we going back on the speed-boat?" He quickly answered, "No, no . . . just for a change we're going back on the big steamer."

This . . . Mr. Chaplin baffled me. His iron will and pride, his defiance and daring . . . all added up to . . . the opposite of Charlie, the little tramp, whom I had found so approachable and warm, so tender and easy to be entreated. Of course, he said, "You confound me. I don't know when I have found one so hard to understand." There we stood, miles apart.

28

A week passed and not a word. Then a call came. It was a soft sweet voice . . . thoughtful and warm. It was Charlie, not Mr. Chaplin. The moment we met that evening for dinner, once again there was that old feeling. I didn't know why I felt so wonderful . . . but I did know the Hollywood celebrity was not along.

We dined at the Double Eagle,[1] a darkly lit and colorful restaurant. It was owned by a Russian count. Notables were seated everywhere. Roving players went from table to table. It was so romantic. Charlie ordered "Bilini," his favorite dish of pancakes, sour cream and caviar.

As he spoke I knew why the evening was good and why I felt I was with the artist, Charlie. He said, "I'm not happy with the way things are going in my picture *City Lights*." The moment the creative spirit stirred . . . it was Charlie, the genius that was present. He continued, "I'm not able to get my leading lady Virginia Cherrill[2] to do the big dramatic scene." Then he turned to me and asked pleadingly, "How would you like to come over to the studio to-morrow and do some scenes for me? I'm desperate." His words were sweeter than violins. He made my heart sing. I whispered, "You know I'd dearly love to."

1 A mistake for The Russian Eagle. It was originally located on Sunset Boulevard, and removed to Vine Street after a fire in 1930.

2 Virginia Cherrill Martini (b. 12 April 1908, Carthage, Ill.) was put under contract by Chaplin on 1 November 1928 to play the role of the blind girl in *City Lights*. She made several Hollywood films before departing in 1935 for England. There she appeared in two "quota quickies," then retired from the screen in 1936.

The rest of the evening was spent listening to the meaningful story he had conceived. I could feel the deep love the blind girl in his story must have felt for her benefactor, "The Little Tramp." It was so easy for me to put myself in her place. I had been blind to any meaning of life, until Charlie had opened my eyes. It was as if it had been written about me. He seemed eager to get started. He said, "Please be at the studio early . . . at eight. I do want to get started."

The following day I donned the clothes of the blind girl. Charlie and I shot many scenes together. It was reminiscent of *The Gold Rush* . . . reshooting a picture that was almost finished. I understood exactly and felt deeply . . . the gratitude the blind girl had for the little tramp's kindness. He brought her groceries and constantly watched over her in every way. Her love for him . . . and hunger for his affection filled my heart. Charlie loved the shots. Then came the big scene . . . the impossible one for Virginia Cherrill. The blind girl now could see, because the little bum had saved and scrimped, so that she might have an operation. It had proved to be successful.

This dramatic scene began. I was now this blind girl. I wasn't acting, I was living it. When "The Little Tramp" came to my flower shop . . . he touched my hand as he paid for the bouquet. I remembered . . . this touch! "Could it be my love?" I closed my eyes and quickly reached for his hand again. Now I knew! My benefactor stood before me . . . my love whom I had never seen. When I opened my eyes they filled with tears of joy. I clutched his hands as if . . . I'd never let him go . . .

When it was over Charlie almost cried saying, "This is what I've been trying to get for weeks." He grabbed me and embraced me. He said, "The part is yours. I'll re-shoot the entire picture with you as the blind girl." I exclaimed, "Thank you a thousand times. I know I can do the part. No one else could possibly feel that part as I do." The whole staff rejoiced.

I didn't see Charlie nor did I hear from the studio for two weeks. During this time I was studying and living the part of the blind girl. Finally Mr. Chaplin called me and we had dinner at our usual place. I was not sitting with the warm and truthful Charlie I had last been with. Not at all . . . the atmosphere was strained. I was dining with the totally cold but aggressive Hollywood heart-breaker. He . . . constantly reappeared like an iceberg between us. Breathlessly I waited for some word about the part of the blind girl, for I had been working night and day on it.

His opening remark in the restaurant was, "I don't care for you in orchid, please don't wear it again . . . that is, with me. You're not pretty tonight." It wasn't what he said that hurt, it was what I heard when he was silent. He made me feel ugly, hated. It was like being stabbed with a piercing knife. I said, "Of course I won't wear orchid again, not if you don't like it . . . I do hope everything is alright?" He didn't answer. He wouldn't talk. No one knew better how to be totally absent, yet aggressive . . . I could feel his intent was to bewilder and hurt me. Mr. Chaplin was an artist at this game. During the entire evening, there was not one word about the picture nor the part of the blind girl. With no explanation for his coldness, he dismissed me with a cold, "Good-night."

With this same icy manner, he continued to call and invite me to parties. All the while I wondered, "Why?" He continually criticized me. After a nice party at De Milles' he said, "You don't act very friendly to my friends . . . You certainly haven't the art of dressing down . . . Why don't you go to some school and learn . . .?" I could take no more and said, "I am definitely not making you happy. Please Mr. Chaplin . . . I really think you'd be better off inviting some other girl to your parties and affairs. I'm sorry."

No calls for days and days! Then he called and in the same frigid tone asked to see me. He took me for a gloomy silent walk in his garden. All of a sudden he stopped, turned on me and in a harsh voice said, "You're not going to play the part of the blind girl." At first I couldn't believe my ears, but when I looked into his eyes, I knew he meant it and much more. He was enraged.

I turned away from him and ran back to the house. I threw myself on the bed and cried as if my heart would break. After a long time he came into the room. I could hardly speak but I managed to ask, "Please take me home? I won't be very good company." He took me home without giving a word of enlightenment nor a touch of kindness. I didn't hear from him for weeks.

At last Kono, Mr. Chaplin's devoted servant called. Kono always favored me. Whenever Mr. Chaplin was to call someone to escort to a gathering . . . Kono would always say, "Shall I call Mess Hale?" One time Mr. Chaplin answered Kono with a question, "Why do you prefer Miss Hale, Kono?" A little embarrassed he giggled and said, "Because I think Mess Hale is good company for you. She is vely honest and she truly loves you, Mester Chaplin." Mr. Chaplin appreciated this and said, "Thank you Kono, you're very kind and a discerning person too. I was going to ask you to call her anyway, because I feel the same about Miss Hale."

Mr. Chaplin called for me and we went to see a preview of an Edward Small[1] production. Mr. Chaplin, instead of watching the picture was studying me. I could feel his eyes on me. He was waiting anxiously for me to say something. He was expecting a rebuke for his rudeness and cruelty. But I said nothing. He had left me with very little to say. I tried to enjoy the showing. We were both talkative after the preview to Mr. Small . . . but not to each other. The silence between us was deadening.

We had almost reached home when he broke the silence. He said pleadingly, "Georgia, I want to talk to you. Will you come home with me for a bite to eat? Please." I was learning through bitter experience what a heart breaker this man could

[1] Edward Small (b. 1 February 1891, Brooklyn, N.Y.; d. January 1977, Los Angeles), after being promised financing by Joseph Schenck and Art Cinema, formed in 1932 with Harry Goetz, the production company Reliance Pictures, Inc. Edward Small Productions were not founded until 1938.

be. I had no idea what was next . . . what other dramatic climax was coming. I knew he was capable of many, each topping the last.

For weeks I had been remembering his face filled with rage and hate when he told me crisply, "You're not going to play the blind girl. You're not going to be in my picture." Having spent the last three hours with him in cold silence was quite enough. I answered, "I'm almost home. Let's make it another evening. I'm really a little wilted." He said to the chauffeur, "Go to my house!" Then he turned to me and said, "You'll feel alright . . . better when you've had something to eat. Georgia . . . I must talk with you! Forgive me for being so forceful?"

When we were inside his house, he took me in his arms and kissed me again and again tenderly, as only Mr. Chaplin could do . . . when he felt like it. He said, "I've missed you terribly these past days. I've been miserable. I realized how dear you are to me. Never leave me and try to forgive me?" I could only ask, "You mean for your outburst of passion and hate? I admit I just don't understand you." He said hurriedly, "Yes, I know, I know . . . Let's dine before the fireplace in the living room?"

He looked positively handsome in the glow of the embers. His expression was soft and loving, and he knew so well how to turn on the charm. He said, "I studied your profile tonight as you watched the show. You're truly a beauty." For weeks he had been criticizing me but that was turned off now. I thought, "He doesn't think I'm beautiful enough to play the blind girl though, nor capable of acting the part." I tried hard to cast this kind of thinking out. I cast my eyes down to hide my feelings . . . but he read my thoughts.

He said, "I know . . . I've hurt you terribly, but please hear me out . . . please listen to my side?" I answered, "But, of course. I'm completely confused. What do you mean . . . listen to your side?" He said hesitatingly, "It's hard for me to confess this to you . . . I have been filled with suspicion and distrust of you. Now I realize that the very person who poisoned me against you is my enemy, not you."

I was dismayed . . . bewildered and silent. I just stared into his eyes inquiringly. Finally I whispered fearfully, "What have I done against you? Tell me, I must know. I've never knowingly done anything to hurt you. Why should I? You are the one who has helped me . . . all my life . . . lifted me up out of dispair [*sic*]. Now what have I done?" I could hardly control myself . . . He said sadly, "No Georgia, you haven't done anything wrong. A so-called friend of mine[1] warned me of you. He said, "Even though you find it impractical to reshoot *City Lights* with Georgia as the blind girl, she's not going to let you out of your verbal contract . . . she's going to sue you . . . and for plenty."

So this was the reason for his cruelty, his sudden hate. His great friendship for me had turned to disdain without even an opportunity given me to do or say a word. I couldn't eat a bite. I rose from the table and walked away. I couldn't look at him. I didn't want to . . . I said, "Now I do believe others . . . that you give up friends at the drop of a hat . . . in small or big things that you have no heart. I couldn't understand when you coldly but quickly gave up your little pet parrot . . . who had called you by name and greeted you for years every time you came up the steps. You did this without a trace of feeling, just because a silly friend told you a parrot's disease was going around. You didn't try to help the bird. Of course, after you got rid of the bird, the chap said, 'I was just kidding. I didn't expect you to part with your life-long friend.' But you weren't sorry nor did you miss your little 'Pet.' Are you the same to people?"

[1] Carlyle Robinson was Chaplin's press representative from 1917 until 1932, also appearing in *The Idle Class* and *The Pilgrim*. For reasons unknown, he had taken a dislike to Georgia from the time she was cast as the dance-hall girl in *The Gold Rush*. He was dismissed by Chaplin when he attempted to interfere in the May Reeves affair. See Robinson's article published in *Liberty Magazine,* July 1933, "The Private Life of Charlie Chaplin." See also Introduction, p. xvi.

Charlie sat with his dead down and said, "Go ahead, scold me. I have it coming to me. I don't know how or why I could so misjudge you and be so poisoned against you . . . I just don't know." He came over to me and asked humbly, "Please, Georgia, give me another chance. I've been through so many disappointing love-affairs. I admit I'm disillusioned and suspicious." Then and there, I realized clearer than ever before, that Mr. Chaplin, this attractive man of Hollywood was a frightened shadow of the little comic and that he would always be hovering around to darken our relationship. Instead of hating him, a feeling of compassion came over me.

Mr. Chaplin, this hangover of a poverty-stricken past was as much in need of help as I had needed it from the little tramp years before. I had to say, "Let's not talk about this anymore . . . Please never mention or tell me the name of the person who caused all this nightmare. Let's try to wipe it out, like a bad dream . . . something that never really happened?" An ugly burden dropped from his shoulders and mine. A warm glow came over his features. I could almost see the little tramp "face." His touch, his arms thrilled me once again.

29

Dr. Albert Einstein[1] and his wife[2] arrived in Hollywood just a few days before the opening of Mr. Chaplin's picture. He asked me, "I wonder why the Einsteins are in town? There is a man I feel very close to . . . I deeply admire him. He's not only one of our great benefactors, but he is truly a great and noble person. I wish I could see him." He had hardly finished his wish . . . when Kono appeared with the news . . . "Mester Einstein is on the phone. Would you like to speak to him?" Before Kono had finished his question, Mr. Chaplin was speaking to Dr. Einstein. Then Charlie realized one big reason they had come to Hollywood. It was to see him. He was honored and delighted.

The premiere of *City Lights* was at hand. The gala opening was to take place at the gorgeous new Los Angeles Theatre. Dr. Einstein, his wife, and Charlie and I had dinner at his home before the opening. In a way it was a study in contrasts.

[1] Chaplin mistakenly remembered being first introduced to Einstein in 1926 (*MA*, p.346). Before leaving Germany permanently to take up residence in the United States, Einstein had made three visits to the U.S. During the second one, from December 1930 to March 1931, he came to Hollywood to accompany Chaplin to the premiere on 30 January, of *City Lights*. Einstein was in California at the invitation of the California Institute of Technology, and had an opportunity of working at the newly built telescope on Mt. Wilson which promised physical confirmation of his own theoretical work.

[2] Else Einstein Lowenthal (1874-1936) was a cousin of Einstein, whom he married in June 1919 after divorcing his first wife in February the same year.

Mr. Chaplin sat there filled with fear and uncertainty about the reception of his picture. Dr. Einstein was the embodiment of calmness and child-like humility. He appeared so far above all mortal strife, so great, so dignified and yet so approachable. Every pore of his being exuded spirituality. It was like being in the presence of one . . . who could heal. His wife was far more animated and did most of the talking, since his English at this time was limited.

Not only did Mr. Chaplin feel the warmth of these gracious ones, I felt it too. They included me in their remarks and made me feel completely at home with them. There was a kindred spirit between Dr. Einstein and Mr. Chaplin. The conversation even turned to religion—a topic rarely ever brought up. He asked Dr. Einstein, "Do you believe there is a God?" Dr. Einstein waited a moment and then answered thoughtfully, "Yes, I think there is a "Supreme Intelligence."

His broad high forehead and soft keen eyes seemed to reflect the infinite universe, which were such a part of his being. He spoke with conviction, as if he had experienced and proven this a thousand times. Mr. Chaplin gave this deep thought and then nodded approvingly. "Yes, yes that's what I think also," he said soberly.

I sat there drinking in the profound meaning of what this great man had said, "God is a Supreme Intelligence." For a moment he had taken me to a high mountain top. I saw through his vision. It was as if he had said humbly, "Don't praise man for his achievements . . . praise his source."

I had to ask myself, "Have you erred all these years? Have you made an idol of Charlie and not just loved his ideas and ideals?" His observation was a rebuke to me and started me thinking in new lines. It lifted my head high above the things of the moment. I could have been down on a low level. I suppose I could have been feeling sorry for myself and "hurt feelings" could have taken over, for not having played the part of the blind girl in *City Lights*—the lead that Mr. Chaplin had given me and then snatched away so cruelly. But instead I was uplifted. I found myself mothering him and quieting his fears.

On the way down to the theatre, the closer it came to the time of the showing, the more apprehensive Mr. Chaplin became. He whispered something he'd never admit only under duress . . . "I'm worried. I have an awful feeling the film isn't going to be received well. I know I've stated time and again that I don't care about being . . . popular, wanting acclaim, in the spotlight . . . but I do. I do care . . . I must have it . . . the applause of people. I love it . . . I live on it. But I'm afraid to-night." But Dr. Einstein's words, "God to me, is a Supreme Intelligence" was ringing in my ears. I could only think of the loftiness of this man's nature, so far above self-glory.

I could comfort Mr. Chaplin. I said softly, "I wish you could feel as assured as I. It's the inspired message of your beautiful story that will be acclaimed by each one present to-night. They will all love it and they'll be grateful to you for giving and sharing your precious ideals with them." He was humble and receptive. He held my hand close to him and said, "Thank you, I feel happy again." Unbeknown to me, Mrs. Einstein had been watching my solicitude for Mr. Chaplin.

When the picture was only a quarter over, I could see he was relaxed and composed. His fears were done. He was basking in success. The audience was once again in the palm of his hand and he knew it. They were enthralled and enthusiastic about *City Lights*. He had made another great one. I was so happy and whispered in his ear, "The people love you. Don't they?"

Mrs. Einstein heard this and reached over to Mr. Chaplin and said, "This girl truly loves you." And then she turned to me and whispered, "Never give him up . . . for any reason. He needs you, your honesty and love." Mr. Chaplin didn't question her observation. He knew nobody could hide their true feelings and motives from her or Dr. Einstein. Later during the intermission she said, "Dr. Einstein and I would love to have you make our home yours, if you are ever near our place."[1] Charlie smiled approvingly. He thought this was a high compliment and so did I.

Dr. Einstein and his wife were so apart from Hollywood. They did not know nor had they even heard of the other well-known celebrities. They had come to Hollywood only to call on Mr. Chaplin, whose genius they admired very, very much.

Mrs. Einstein was devoted to her husband. She told us, "Dr. Einstein stays alone in his room for days at a time. There he works, plays his violin and just waits for ideas. I take good care of him but I do not disturb him." Then she explained, "I quietly place hot food and delicacies I think he might like, outside his door. Then I silently steal away."

Although Mr. Chaplin and Dr. Einstein spoke and thought in different languages, they readily understood each other with but the tiniest assistance from his wife. They both knew the pain and pleasure of greatness. Dr. Einstein was unstinting in his praise of Charlie's genius, his comedy and pathos.

On the ride home from the premiere, I was with a different companion . . . than I had driven down with. The fear-filled actor of movieland was not present. Charlie, the humble little tramp of the picture we had just seen was beside me. As the blind girl—I loved the performance Charlie had obtained from Virginia Cherrill. The idealistic story of his self-sacrificing love for his girl, filled me with admiration for Charlie once again.

During the drive home, Dr. Einstein and Charlie discussed many subjects. Dr. Einstein said, "United States is great because of its composite of people from all over the world. They come here all seeking freedom— a new way of life." This brought up the subject of nationality. He added, "Because of

[1] Chaplin dined with the Einsteins during his visit to Berlin in March 1931.

the persecution of the Jews I always say I am Jewish. I gladly admit it. But I really think of myself as a citizen of the world."

One could readily feel with his vision so wide and high, he could only belong to the universe. When I asked Charlie, "And what is your nationality?" he answered, "British, of course. But I'm a gypsy . . . that's what I am, a gypsy." This was true too, for his art belonged to all people and he roamed the earth in his thoughts and interests. He was just interested in everyone and studied and appreciated their talents.

When Charlie dropped me off at my home I exclaimed, "What a rich evening. Thank you, so very much." He held me at arms length and looked me up and down and said, "You stood tall tonight. I was so proud of you, Georgia my dear." I asked, "Proud of me? It was I who was the proud one . . . of you Charlie and your greatness." He continued, "You know the Einstein's liked you very much. They even invited you to their home, didn't they? Georgia they never would have done that . . . if you weren't a real nice person. How they recognized your fine qualities."

He took me in his arms and whispered softly in my ear, "I've never told you before . . . remember the last shot in *The Gold Rush,* when we were to be married? I said, our children will be beautiful, if they look like their mother. I wasn't acting. Did you realize 'The Little Tramp' really meant it?" I answered with a question, "Do you remember what I said? . . . I'd like our children to be like their father?" He answered, "Yes, I do . . . that is why those scenes were so true, so convincing."

He held me close, just as he did in the last shot on the boat. This real Charlie, so unlike Mr. Chaplin, had an expression that was truly handsome. His face seemed to shine. What a contrast with the pinched, unattractive face of Mr. Chaplin in the early evening. I said, "I can't help but wondering . . . how lovely we all might be if we'd express only beautiful thoughts. If entertaining a few happy thoughts could change you so . . . what outline form and color has pure peace, joy and all the other graces?" He laughed happily and said,

"I'm going to try to do better, if it makes me good in your eyes. It was a lovely evening. I'll never forget it."

When I closed my door and was alone, I could still feel the presence of those lovely people. "What would the earth be like filled with such . . .?" Artists have painted their conceptions of Jesus . . . I couldn't help but wondering what did Jesus look like actually? I dozed of with this adventurous and happy question.

30

Mr. Chaplin called for me early this day. He was giving a large party at his home. It was not the Charlie I had last seen. I never knew which it would be. This was definitely Mr. Chaplin who liked nothing better than to attend or give a big Hollywood party.

He wanted to look his best and he liked to primp for these occasions. It was fun to watch him. His dressing table was covered with sparkling bottles of perfume. All gifts from friends, for he wanted it understood he would never purchase any. But he liked perfume, even though he swore that only fighters use it.

However, he'd fondle the bottles, take a few sniffs of each fragrance, then slyly he'd pick up Guerlain's Mitzuko. Rapidly he'd pour some on his hands, rub them together briskly (to convince himself that it was all gone) then he'd nonchalantly smooth down his tie. It was all accomplished as if he hadn't used a drop. This was always his finishing touch.

The guests started to arrive. There was an extreme coldness about these gatherings to me. They were well attended but they seemed to have no substance. They grinned but I couldn't see a smile. Their faces were always hidden with a . . . mask of artificiality.

The guests had all arrived for this one . . . Some played cards avariciously . . . others engaged in play acting, hoping to be discovered by some big-gun and get some coveted part. One aspiring actress noticed a well-known comedian and a big producer. She started her antics on him. He was really one of the nicer persons of filmland. I had spoken quietly with him for a few moments and I could see he wanted to escape this girl's attention. He was out of place in this crowd. But this ambitious girl had only one thought. She proceeded to monopolize his evening.

She cuddled up to him and asked, "When are you starting your next picture?" He shrugged his shoulders and smiled nervously. She grabbed two cocktails and offered him one saying, "You're nervous . . . here have a drink." When he refused she drank them both. She continued, "Are there going to be any parts for blondes?" He was such a gentleman he couldn't walk away. She proceeded to drink and ask more questions. Then of course, the drinking took effect. She said, "Whoops I'm getting dizzy." And she proceeded to sit on his lap. But simultaneously he had enough and he rose . . . she ended up on the floor. He dashed over to me and said politely, "I'll have to be excused. I have a headache. Will you please explain to Mr. Chaplin." He had seen this all and couldn't have cared less when he left. He said, "It was very amusing." Here were two comedians who didn't find the same things amusing.

Mr. Chaplin had games and all sorts of things to entertain his guests. Among them he had a large iron wheel. He could stand up in this and roll down his slanting lawn head over heels. A tall chap, a husband of one of the card players, tried the feat. But he forgot to hold his head down inside . . . and so it extended outside the wheel. Down the lawn he went banging his head horrible blows. When the thing finally came to a stop with him sprawled out on the grass, he was shaken and in great pain.

Mr. Chaplin and I rushed to his aid and hurriedly told his wife who was playing bridge. She never missed a trick! Others watching showed little concern and quickly resumed their play-acting. Mr. Chaplin directed his chauffeur to drive him home. The man left pale and sick. He was barely able to whisper, "No thank you, I'll be alright. You are very kind." I had offered to go with him and he seemed touched by this touch of kindness. As he limped down the stairs alone, I thought, "Hollywood is a strange cold world. The parties all seem like masquerades with everyone wearing false faces . . . some beautiful, but always false."

These same people gushed over Mr. Chaplin and he gushed over them. He surrounded himself with this type. When all had gone he said, "What a delightful evening and what charming folks." He loved this kind of man and woman. He said "I wish you were more like the girls who were here this evening, so outgoing and friendly." I told him frankly, "I have seen girls I should like to emulate . . . those with nice qualities and characters, but they were not here to-night. However one nice thing, you have always a lot of girls to choose from . . . you have no problem."

He was filled with pent up thoughts and mercilessly continued to chide me, "You're very old-fashioned in many of your ways and thoughts and require a great deal of patience. For instance the girls here do not insist upon marriage . . . for one thing. They know their place and they know this is the century when things are changing." I told him, "You seem to dislike the very ideals your pictures and stories put in my head. The clay doesn't please the potter . . . you don't care for what you've made. My ideals are in your way."

Then he went off on his main theme, "Women are lovely and I envy them at times. They have that one creative ability . . . that of having children. That is their one purpose . . . and it's enough." I agreed, "After marriage, if it unfolds for a couple to have children, it's beautiful . . . wonderful. But I do think women can contribute many other values as well."

He asked in a belittling manner, "Name any woman who has been great in a creative art form?" We had been through this before . . . I knew he would always be of this opinion. He was intent on finishing the evening in an argument. Like an ugly puppet with Hollywood pulling the strings, he talked on and on . . . thus ended this revolting night.

31

But Charlie the sweet one would reappear in response to some lovely people who would happen into his life. Those who wanted nothing from him and adored him solely as the great comic. He would feel their loving, honest thoughts, and would respond. He'd be himself. That true self who Shakespeare said "cannot be false to any man." How pleasant life became.

H. G. Wells[1] introduced two such good people to Charlie—Ivor Montagu[2] and Hell[3] his wife. They were beautiful and such fun, and they were from England. Charlie, almost at a glance felt the warmth of these dear ones. Charlie loved to entertain friends from his home country.

Ivor had many pictures and stories of old familiar places. This brought back Charlie's youth. It was thrilling to see his old homestead and exchange experiences. But he said one night to Ivor, "I'd never exchange one foot of my place here for all of England. I love it here. I love California, its climate, and I admire the American people." Ivor answered, "The United

[1] Herbert George Wells (b. 21 September. 1866; d.13 August 1946).

[2] Ivor Goldsmid Samuel Montagu (b. 23 April 1904, London; d. 5 November 1984, Watford, England) was enabled by a privileged background to indulge his two lifelong passions—the cinema and Left-wing politics. After accompanying Eisenstein on his ill-fated sojourn in Mexico in 1931, he returned to England and collaborated in several of Hitchcock's films: *The Man Who Knew Too Much* (1934), *Thirty-Nine Steps* (1935), *The Secret Agent* (1936). He later became the first film critic of *The Observer* (London) and *The New Statesman*.

[3] Eileen Hellstern (b. 14 May 1904, London; d. 2 October 1984, Watford, England) married Montagu on 10 January 1927.

States has opened its arms wide to you, loved you and enriched you. No wonder you feel the way you do."

We had wonderful days together while they were his house guests. They would discuss at length Charlie's great pictures, his sympathy with the downtrodden and his inspiring message. We became very close, almost like one family. They understood the relationship between Charlie and me . . . why it had extended over so many years . . . even before and after his marriages. Ivor wondered though, why we were not married . . . Some big psychologist had told Ivor in England, "When seeing *The Gold Rush* I could discern that Charlie Chaplin was truly in love with the girl. Perhaps he doesn't even realize this, but this is true." Ivor in turn watched and studied us to see if he could concur with him. He did. So Ivor could not refrain from asking, "Charlie, tell me why have you two not married? I feel for sure you are in love . . . with Georgia."

Charlie answered hesitatingly, "I met a fortune-teller[1] at a party recently and I asked her that same question. She warned me, 'Don't do it. I see trouble. This . . . this marriage would turn out badly, just as your two others have . . . no, do not spoil this lovely relationship.'" Charlie said, "You see Ivor, I've been through so much of this unpleasantness . . . I believed her. I think I'm a little bitter."

Just then Hell and I came up from the pool dripping wet. Charlie grabbed me, turned me about and led me back for another swim. When we reached the pool and were alone, he took me in his arms and held me close for ever so long. He said tenderly, "God was very generous to you, wasn't he? You're perfect from the tip of your curly head down to your feet. I regard you so highly, Georgia. I want you to know how precious you are to me. Please don't ever leave me. I'm sure something

[1] After Chaplin's estrangement from Paulette Goddard, Ivor Montagu sent him a telegram: "Now that the gipsys warning is over go ahead and marry Georgia she's the only one who ever really cared for you or indeed anyone but herself—If she'll have you now of course" (IM to CC, Knowle, Buckinghamshire, c1943: MP).

good will unfold for us." I didn't understand why he said all this . . . but it warmed me. I told him, "I feel so rewarded, so enriched by just knowing you. You've already changed me from an unhappy person into an inspired soul." He had heard this a hundred times before.

As we swam up and down the pool, we went over our meeting and every event in our days and years together. We often did this, it was such fun. He said again, "It's a Narcissus complex alright. I do see myself so much in you." I reminded him, "Remember Mr. Schulberg[1] of Paramount Studios and many others have often remarked that we look alike . . . that our smile and expressions are identical?" He said, "Yes . . . I guess people grow alike when they're together so long." As I thought of nothing else . . . I must have grown like him. I was commencing to realize that my teacher was becoming more my idol. This was not good!

Charlie jokingly challenged me, "I'll race you to the end of the 'Derby.'" That's what he called his pool. It was made in the shape of the famous hat. He beat me! I retaliated by saying, "If you had a tennis court I'd beat you. I'd make it a love set and in my favor. If only you had a court we could have a nice game."

Well, I never realized the chord I had struck, I never expected such a response! He turned into a happy inquiring child, "Oh Georgia, do you suppose I could ever learn to play tennis? Where . . . where could we build it?" He put his hands to his heart and said, "That's a game I've always wanted to try. Where could we put it?" I pointed to a large area right down from the pool and said "Right down there . . . there is the ideal spot." Like a small boy asking his mother, he inquired rather timidly, "After a second thought, do you think I should? Do you think it's too big an undertaking?"

Douglas Fairbanks once said to me, "You're just like a mother to Charlie. It's real nice and I like you for it." And so

[1] Benjamin Percival Schulberg (b. 19 January 1892, Bridgeport, Connecticut.; d. 1957) produced *Man of the Forest*, one of the three films Georgia made for Famous Players-Lasky.

I was. I assured Charlie by saying, "Why not do it?" You deserve the best. After all the joy you have given others, why do you hesitate? You should accept a little happiness for yourself especially when it is so wholesome and good for you." Continuing like a radiant child anticipating getting a certain toy for which he had longed . . . he clapped his hands together and shouted for joy saying, "O.K. We'll start our tennis court at once!" He took me by the hand and raced to the house to tell the great news to Ivor and Hell.

32

Among Charlie's dear friends in those days was Alexander P. Moore.[1] He was our ambassador to Spain and later to a country in South America. He had been the devoted husband of the famous actress and beauty Lillian Russell. He frequented the parties at Charlies' and at one time was his house guest.

One day we were chatting in the sun-garden patio, beside the pool. There he poured out his heart's deep love for his precious wife. He wanted to release his pent up feelings. He told me, "She was not only acclaimed the most beautiful woman in the world, but more important as the most loveable. I, who knew her so well, can only say 'Amen' to all her praises. Georgia, she was an angel."

Then he told me something I cherished. He explained what had helped make her so angelic. He told me in great detail of her scientific religion, her Christian faith, and how it had blessed her beyond measure. I did not remember all he said nor did I understand, but I felt uplifted for days. Later, as I grew in understanding and spirituality thanks to my heavenly association with Charlie, I was able to understand and accept this very religion.

Mr. Moore bought an unusually pretty pair of ear-rings in Peru when he was ambassador. He took them out of his pocket and handed them to me saying, "I want you to have

1 Alexander Pollock Moore (1867-1930), a newspaper editor and publisher, was appointed ambassador to Spain in 1923 by President Harding. He later served as ambassador to Peru. Moore married Lillian Russell in June 1912; she died in 1921.

these. I like you very much and you have been so attentive. I feel warmed by your kindness. Please accept this small token of appreciation?" I was so happy and I still treasure this precious gift to-day.

But life's experience is full of contrasts. Mr. Moore was no exception. Mr. Moore had a different type of lady friend now, who attended many of these functions with him. She was a wealthy woman and had more jewelry than I had ever seen outside of a store. She had square-cut, pear shaped, tear-drop diamonds, rubies and emeralds, which ranged in size from two to twenty-five carats and over. Besides this she had lots of pearls.

One night on the way to a party she accidentally broke her bracelet. She recovered everything but a small pearl. Charlie and Mr. Moore helped her search in the car for it. When we arrived at the house at her insistence, we all left her alone in the car. There she continued her search for the pearl. A good half hour later she came into the gathering, disheveled, peevish and worn out. She said sadly, "I've been on my hands and knees hunting in every inch of that car and I cannot find my pearl. My evening is ruined!"

Charlie said later, "Wouldn't you think with all her jewels she would have been generous and said, "Georgia, I hope you find it and if you do, I want you to keep it." Charlie added, "You see the more things we treasure, the more limitation we hoard. But not so with ideas, they multiply and enrich us. Ideas are pearls and we can all have them and use, any place and any time. They never wear out but we must search for them."

The following week he asked, "Will you accept a little gift from me? It's a lovely diamond bracelet. I would have bought it on the spot but I was afraid I'd better ask you first. Please let me give you something nice. It's not too awfully expensive. Please?"

At his insistence we journeyed downtown to the jewelry store and I saw the exquisite diamond bracelet and watch I was so dazzled by its beauty. But I said, "it's far too expensive and

I simply cannot accept it." However he could see that I loved it. He walked away and thought for awhile and came back with an arrangement. He said sweetly, "You know what I'm going to do? I'm going to take it home with me, and at our house parties I want you to wear this. It will make any dress look more tantalizing."

This seemed alright to me and I was so happy it was going to be close so I could see it anyway. He knew this arrangement wouldn't last long and it didn't. I fell in love with my bracelet and one night I forgot and wore it home. It was mine! I still have it and everytime I wear it I hear "What a gorgeous piece of jewelry . . . where did you get it? Aren't you afraid to wear it?" I'll always love it.

33

Mr. Chaplin counted his illustrious friends as gems. He valued them more highly than any earthly thing. He loved to exchange ideas with them and thrilled at the thought of such meetings.

Mr. George Bernard Shaw[1] was one of the great ones to Mr. Chaplin. He held him in the highest of esteem. Mr. Shaw was to call on Charlie, and he was awed by the thought of it. The occasion took on mammoth proportions to Charlie. He wanted so, to say and do just the perfect thing. Charlie had worked so hard to improve himself. He was a self-educated man. He studied constantly to correct his speech, grammar and manners. He wasted no time on self-pity over his past but enjoyed trying, persisting, sweating at his endeavors to become a cultured man.

For this particular encounter with George Bernard Shaw—he braced himself and gave deep thought to many brilliant things to say and subjects to discuss. Well, the important day arrived and so did Mr. Shaw. This was the big moment when Charlie expected all his preparation to pay off with large dividends.

Charlie threw out his chest and cleared his throat as he acted it all out for me saying, "I wanted to be so impressive. I

[1] George Bernard Shaw (b. 1856, Dublin; d. 1950) was an early admirer of Chaplin. He accompanied him to the London premiere of *City Lights* in February 1931. In the course of a world tour, Shaw visited Hollywood in March 1933 as the guest of W.R. Hearst, for whose syndicated newspapers he had written. He met Chaplin again in Honolulu in February 1936.

strutted up to him, hand extended and said, 'It's so nice to see you. My . . . aren't we . . . having . . . nice . . . weather?' " He put his hand to his brow and groaned, "Of all the inane things to say . . . of all the obvious trite banalities . . ." It was so comical to me the way he acted it out but he was in dispair [*sic*]. However, for only a moment or two. He soon joined me laughing. He added, "Mr. Shaw never answered and he shouldn't have . . . he just brought up a vital current subject and started discussing it as only he could do." Just as I had seen him do so many other times under similar circumstances . . . he rubbed his hands together and said, "I'm determined to do better next time . . ."

34

George Bernard Shaw wasn't the only great to visit Charlie Chaplin. There was a string of them. Among his most treasured friends was Ralph Barton,[1] the famous cartoonist. He was a rare and brilliant gem, for he was a true and warm friend. Neither Charlie nor Ralph wanted anything from the other, they just wanted to share. How refreshing and touching was this association.

Ralph Barton was a house guest at Charlie's home. What a retiring, sweet and humble one. There was an unreality about his presence. It was only when I was looking directly at him . . . I was sure he was still with us. He had one foot off this earth. Charlie knew of the dark hours Ralph had waded through in the past and his deep wish to be free, to escape it all. He was a complex soul.

Mr. Barton was always pleasant and content when the three of us were alone. When in a crowd he seemed to be marking time. He was a sad and moody man, who had lived life to its full and found it wanting, empty. He was surfeited and he wanted out, it seemed to me.

He was a sweet but bitter one, an iconoclast. He spent many hours of the day writing. He said, "My ideals have been swept away. My idols one by one have been shattered. I want to write a book, a word-cartoon, and reveal what some of the

[1] Ralph Barton (b. 14 August 1891, Kansas City; d. 20 May 1931), an artist and caricaturist, defended Chaplin against divorce publicity in an essay published in *The New Yorker* in January 1927. Invited to accompany Chaplin on his visit to Europe in February 1931, he returned to New York in March. Shortly afterwards he committed suicide.

world heroes are truly like. They then will stop holding these 'golden calves' so high and cease worshipping them." George Washington was one of his targets. However this ugly task he had set for himself didn't seem to come easy to him. He was so gentle and kind. Charlie and I would leave him alone and go play tennis or take a long walk, so he could write. When we'd return the page would still be blank . . . But in spite of his sorrowful outlook, the beauty of this man shone forth in his lovely drawings and illustrations, as seen in the works of Balzac.

One evening he arrived with a large package under his arm. It was artistically wrapped. Ralph timidly offered his gift to Charlie saying, "Will you accept this as a token of my appreciation for your friendship and hospitality?"

Ralph had quietly gone to Beverly Hills that morning and had his precious gift wrapped with special care. It was a present of love. Charlie quickly opened the pretty package. He gasped when he saw two original drawings of Ralph's. He fondled the works as if he had never received anything before as precious. He whispered with emotion, "Thank you Ralph. How . . . how can I put into words what I feel? They are exquisite! I'll forever be indebted to you."

These were the words Ralph was longing to hear. He became like a happy child who had made a loved one joyous. He knew he had pleased Charlie and he was delighted and warmed. If only he could have maintained this state of mind and not returned to being an adult.

These drawings were in different shades of grey, with a tiny accent of bright red. Charlie placed them in a prominent place in his living room for all to enjoy. He gave many parties in Ralph's honor.

At these gatherings he would withdraw into a corner near the door . . . as if getting ready to steal away. It was not very long before he did just that. He left us for good. This was a tragedy to Charlie who said, "He was too sensitive for this world. Life was too abrasive for him. I feel sad. I wish I could have helped him." Charlie mourned for Ralph Barton.

35

Weeks and weeks of joyous anticipation came to an end. The tennis court was finished . . . all was ready. But Charlie. . . he was not! Of course he had bought himself the most expensive racket he could purchase in Beverly Hills. However, he didn't know the racket from the ball . . . This did not deter him. He said confidently, "All it takes is a good eye and power . . . these I've got." Of course I had played tennis for years[1] and asked, "Would you like a few pointers?" He quickly assured me, "I'm alright, just tell me where to stand and keep score. I'll do the rest. I'll beat you. Want to bet? Remember how I beat you at swimming?" I thought to myself, "With that kind of confidence . . . who knows? He's so sure of himself, he just might pick it up in a minute." But I did have the temerity to say, "I have played this game for a long time." He held up his hand in protest and muttered, "Tut tut."

He looked like a little captain standing on the deck of his new ship, just setting sail to conquer the world. There he stood opposite me, Italian racket in hand and alongside him a box of luscious white spanking-new tennis balls. He gracefully picked up a ball and said like an old-timer, "Let's warm up." He threw the ball in the air, batted at it so hard . . . he twisted his legs and sat down. He gave me a silly grin, picked himself up smartly and slammed at another ball. He connected with this one and sent it sailing high above the fifteen-foot fence into the "yonder green." Up to now I had not even touched a ball . . . he had

[1] Several newspaper clippings from the beauty contest coverage make reference to Georgia's skill at tennis.

them all on his side . . . guarded by him. So I said cautiously, "Perhaps, if I lob you a few you can practice returning them?"

This he consented to—for a few times, but he ran so ferociously at the ball . . . only the net stopped him from coming over on my side. After almost breaking the net down and himself too . . . he said, "We'll continue in a few minutes but first I'll hit a few against the wall." Fiercely, he started hitting the balls against the wall. They came back to him like bullets . . . would hit his racket, fly over the fence and disappear. He was determined to lick the game that very day. The perspiration was dripping off the end of his nose. He went down to his last ball. He picked it up and banged it with all his might against the wall and it came right back and banged him right in the face. The air became blue with his rage . . . and that was the curtain for me. I left. Then I heard a plaintive call, "Georgia, please come back? I'm all ready now."

When I returned he had found only three of the balls. I said, "I'll hit them easy and you do the same. Just keep them low and don't try for power . . . remember we only have three balls left." I sent one over and again he started running around like a little jumping jack . . . still cock sure of himself and waving his racket hard. He was so wild . . . we finally got down to our last ball and this accidentally hit his racket and down the hill it went.

We both rushed down the hill to retrieve our last ball. We knew exactly where it had gone and Charlie raced ahead of me to get it. And he did. He plunged his hand down through a big bush and brought up the head of a huge snake! He threw his racket to the winds and we both ran for our lives. When we reached the green lawn, we flopped down . . . exhausted and bewildered. But his expression and the remembrance of the whole day sent me into the giggles. I laughed until the mascara ran down my cheeks. He couldn't see the joke, which made me laugh the more. He said, "I don't think it was so funny." But it was . . . from the start to the finish.

Charlie's new toy may have been rough for him to conquer, but he loved his tennis court. He couldn't wait to invite his famous friends to see and play on his new court. Among his first guests was Myron Selznick[1] and his wife, Marjorie Daw.[2] She had been a close friend of Tilden[3] the tennis great. Myron and Marjorie were tennis enthusiasts. Myron sitting on the edge of his seat was eager to try out the new court. He said, "I challenge anyone to a set of singles." Nobody accepted his invitation. He repeated his words and still no reply. So I spoke up and said, "I'll accept it."

Charlie started to smile and said to Myron, "She's kidding." Then Mr. Chaplin motioned for me to be quiet. Myron said very politely, "Thank you very much, but I feel like a hard set and we know even a good girl-player can't do that for a fellow." But no one else came forward to play against Myron. So he just sat waiting and hoping.

Charlie managed to take me aside and said, "Honey he wants a good game and you couldn't even connect with the ball the other day . . . please don't embarrass me. Don't ever offer again to play. Promise!" But I didn't promise . . . anything.

After a little while, right in front of God and man I dared to say, "I know I'm only a girl, but now I challenge you to a singles set. Myron, are you game?" He answered, graciously, "Why not?" Charlie was furious and put his hand over his

[1] Myron Selznick (b. 5 October 1898, Pittsburgh; d. 1944), a keen tennis player and organizer of Hollywood's annual tournament, was at this time head of the film colony's principal talent agency. The brother of David Selznick, then personal aide to B.P. Schulberg, he married Marjorie Daw in 1929.

[2] Marjorie Daw (b. 1902, Colorado Springs, Colorado.) had been a leading lady in Hollywood silents. A frequent screen partner and love interest of Douglas Fairbanks, she was for a time married to Chaplin's assistant director on *A Woman of Paris*, Eddie Sutherland. The Selznick's divorced 24 March 1942.

[3] William Tatem Tilden (1893-1953), known as "Big Bill," was U.S. tennis champion from 1920-1925, then again in 1929. His six consecutive championships were a record. Tilden was Professional Champion in 1931.

eyes. The rest of the crowd started talking and turning away. But when the playing continued for some time, Marjorie, Myron's wife called out, "What's the score?" Myron answered softly, "it's six-all." Everyone's head turned directly to the game and not another word was spoken. Charlie's mouth fell open and he stood up to watch the finish.

At the beginning of the seventh game I could see that Myron was getting tired. He evidently had been smoking too many cigarettes or whatever . . . I did know this, that he didn't like me to run up to the net after my serve and kill his returns. But I did just that and won the seventh game. Now it was his game to serve . . . it was no longer like a bullet. I had a chance to break his serve and win the set. Everyone was sitting on the end of their chairs. The game went to . . . my add . . . and I slammed his last serve down close to his alley and he couldn't get it. I won!

Everyone burst into applause . . . as Myron and I shook hands. All the women were delighted that the weaker sex had won over the stronger. All were happy but Marjorie. She said, teasing Myron, "I'll never forgive you letting a girl beat you." "But dear." Myron who was always so nice said, "Charlie, you could learn a great deal from this one."

Charlie who had watched with great trepidation was bewildered by the outcome. He said hesitatingly, "Georgia, I had no idea you could play so well. Why didn't you play like this with me the other day? Why didn't you give me a few pointers?" I just smiled. He quickly said, "Never mind, you don't have to tell me . . . I know . . . I wouldn't have listened." He grabbed me and hugged me and said, "I'm so proud of you." Myron was such a good sport about it. He came over, sat close to me and said, "You gave me an excellent game. I can't think of a nicer person I could have lost to."

Myron Selznick was one of the real lovely characters of Hollywood. Out of the crowds that played day after day at Charlie's, he was the only one who ever remembered to bring nice fresh boxes of tennis balls. It was a small gesture but it made an impression on Charlie, who was so sensitive to kindness and thoughtfulness expressed by others. He appreciated the spiritual side of Myron. Myron was a noble one. He disliked the callousness and selfishness he saw everywhere in movieland and he was a crusader for change and honesty. He was a prince.

would be reiterated, "Why aren't you like the other actresses . . . etc?" I'd answer naively, "I am just trying to be like the girls in your stories. They all had high ideals and so . . . do . . . you." I was foolish. Most of the time I knew him and was supposed to be his girl, as he called me. He had one of those actresses in the background of his life. I never knew this until I read about it recently in a book.

Finally, the whirlwind life of Hollywood parties began to bore him. He had been idle too long. He was always deluged with invitations from his world-wide admirers to come to Europe and return their visits. So he decided to take a short trip to the continent. Yet, he wondered if his decision was wise. I told him, "I think a trip to England would be wonderful. You haven't been home for years." He didn't agree. He quickly assured me, "This is my home and never forget it. If I go, I shall return . . . and soon."

As the time came closer to depart the less he felt like going. The day arrived. He said sadly, "Don't see me to the train. I don't want any tears . . . I feel sad enough now." So, he had Count Berlanger,[1] a dear friend of both of us, take me to the station and there we said, "Good-bye."

When he arrived in New York he phoned, almost in tears. He asked, "Why did I leave?" I comforted him saying, "It will do you good, it's a nice change." But he begged, "Please join me in New York and I'll call the whole trip off. I love the U.S., Beverly Hills and my home . . . what am I doing here?" He continued, "To tell the truth Georgia, I have a weird feeling that I won't get back . . . I'll be so lonesome for you . . . but believe me I'll be back very soon, in a few weeks."

He stayed one year. He never wrote one word. I had felt and seen this before . . . this callousness and coldness to those

[1] Count Berlanger is a rather mysterious figure, whom Ivor Montagu describes as "a young man-about-Hollywood of perfect exterior and elegant manners—here designated as Count B." *With Eisenstein in Hollywood*, p. 88.

for whom he proclaimed deep affection. Mr. Chaplin's so-called love was as whimsical, imaginary and unreal as was the Hollywood affection his flattering friends showered on him. He could turn this . . . thing . . . off or on with the bat of an eye. And he did. There was no manliness in him . . . no unselfishness, no support, no carrying through. Those qualities one associates with manhood, were not. But he expected all from a woman. He criticized, but could not or would not see himself.

How unlike the tenderness Charlie the little genius displayed in his pictures. But this all forced me to rethink, re-evaluate . . . Dr. Einstein's remark, "To me, God is a Supreme Intelligence" kept recurring to my thoughts. It expanded. I asked myself, "Are you worshipping Mr. Chaplin? Are you confusing this personality with Charlie, the little artist?" Then I thought further, "Even the courage, industry, unselfishness and ideals the little comic expresses are from this supreme intelligence. If, so . . . then I can appreciate and admire these virtues wherever expressed." None of these lovely qualities could be found in Mr. Chaplin . . . only their opposites. It was easy to separate this attractive but offensive Mr. Chaplin from Charlie.

At long last I was waking up. Anyway I found myself freer and happier. I soon got busy making a series of pictures[1] with George Brent.[2] Between pictures I played a lot of tennis. Mr. Chaplin had given me the run of his estate while he was in Europe and I made constant use of it. George Brent played tennis with me at Charlie's and so did many other good players.

[1] *The Lightning Warrior*, a Mascot Master Serial of twelve episodes, was considered its best. It was the star Rin Tin Tin's second serial, and last film for Mascot.

[2] George Brent (b. George Brendan Nolan, 15 March 1904; d. 1979), originally a stage actor, made his film debut in *Under Suspicion* (1931). He was later a successful contract player at Warner's.

I was happy enough. Still I found that when any man became fond of me, I would foolishly compare him to the little actor and the lovely qualities I saw in Charlie would be missing. When one became serious with me the answer had to be, "No." Of course I thought I was completely free. But was I?

I sought love and affection from my family. My sisters had married but visited us frequently. Father, mother and I were a close little family. I made a good audience for their differences and joys. They would have been closer and far happier without me as their audience. I wasn't wise enough then to know this. I let them convince me otherwise.

The beauties and perfect weather of California and particularly Los Angeles, continued to thrill my parents. In contrast to the cold winds and snow of Chicago, it seemed like paradise to them. They appeared younger each day. Thank goodness . . . that Charlie had seen *The Salvation Hunters* and then helped me . . . for then I was able to supply a beautiful home and pay all those annoying little bills for mother. Her back had straightened . . . relieved of this load and even Dad's head had gone higher.

During this long year that Mr. Chaplin sojourned in Europe, my sister Frances always inquired about Mr. Chaplin. I never had anything to report. This day she asked as usual, "Whenever . . . is Mr. Chaplin returning . . . from his extended stay abroad?" I tried to avoid this subject by changing to another topic, but back she would return to it. All my life she had known how to get me. This time I concealed my emotions and answered happily, "I can't say . . . but I hope he stays as long as he wants to . . ." I thought I had her fooled . . . for she smiled at me.

She abruptly snapped her purse open and pulled out a long news clipping . . . She laughed and waved it in my face and said, "Take a look and read it but don't weep . . . it shows him lying on some Riviera beach with a Parisian beauty.[1] It seems he . . . wants . . . to stay alright. Look, isn't she a beauty?"

My face was strained and my voice tense as I replied, "Thank you for bringing me the clipping. I might not have seen it . . . I'll take it into my room and read it." I ran into my room before the tears could start. I really didn't know which was hurting most . . . the news? . . . or her attitude? I asked myself, "Why does she delight in saying cutting things? Her life is so full, she cannot be jealous of mine. Why did she bring me that . . . news?" I couldn't answer . . . I couldn't.

I heard a loud bang on my door. It made my heart stop. It was Frances saying happily, "I'm sorry, I've got to leave. Hubby's at the door and wants me to join him. He can't get along without me by his side. See you soon." I managed to say, "So-long."

It wasn't a moment when I heard a soft tap at my door. Of course it was Melissa. She said tenderly, "Come out honey, and have tea with mother and me." They knew that my heart was sad and they knew the right medicine. My hurt feelings melted away under the warmth and love Melissa and mother showered upon me . . . Love does heal, while thoughtlessness and unkindness do bruise. I was famished for affection. Who isn't? The seed of doubt had been planted. I wondered if Mr. Chaplin ever would return to the United States or Hollywood? But most of all I wondered, "If he does come back, will he call me?"

I didn't have to wait long, for the very next day splashed in large head lines was the announcement, "Charles Chaplin returns to U.S." All the reporters and loads of celebrities in

[1] Chaplin's companion at this time was May Reeves, whose account of his temperament and behaviour confirms those of Georgia and Lita Grey. To all the three he appeared very changeable and undependable. "Unhappily," she writes, "Charlie's good humour did not last long. It shifted like a weathercock. Sometimes he overflowed with tenderness, sometimes he was hard and inflexible. Only tears could calm him . . ." *Charles Chaplin Intime*, edited by Claire Goll (Paris: Gaillard, 1935), p. 119.

New York turned out to greet him. He looked radiant, relaxed and tanned in his photographs. In contrast I had let foolish people and bad thoughts steal away my joy. But it really didn't matter what I looked like because I knew he wasn't going to call . . . not after all this time. I really didn't care . . .

But the moment he reached Hollywood he immediately got in touch with me. Though he had not written me one word in one year, he greeted me as if he had been in close contact every day. At his insistence we went to his house. He said joyously, "I've got a big surprise for you." He had brought back two large valises filled with gifts for me. He continued, "I knew these . . . things would make you happy."

He said, "I had lots of fun buying these presents and things. It's such a joy seeing the delight of these simple people when you make a lot of purchases." I replied, "It's nice . . . you thought of their happiness. But it's not only things that make people happy." He never heard me. He went on . . . "They evoked so much love. I couldn't do enough. After leaving Paris, I remembered a little girl I had met there and I sent her a little doll." I said, "Well, I'm glad you . . . remembered . . . her. It took you one year to remember me." He wasn't listening. He added, "And the Parisian women, they are so beautiful . . . so smartly dressed too." I interjected, "I'm wearing a new dress . . . I bought it for this night . . . the night of your return . . . of course I've had it sometime . . . since I didn't know . . ." He slowly looked me up and down and said, "I wish you could see the dazzling outfits of the women of Paris. Sit down and I'll try to describe them to you." I sat down but I was commencing to boil inside.

Finally he saw me as we sat directly opposite of each other. It was as if I had just entered. He said, "Well now, how has my simple little Georgia been?" My patience was gone. I asked, "Do you really care?" He just shook his head and said, "I can't help comparing you with all the other women of the world . . . the smart, in-the-know women I've just been with. It's a shame . . . with your looks . . . it's a pity . . . such a waste."

I slammed my hand on the table and said, "I'm never going to be anyone but myself . . . not Parisian . . . not anyone . . . but me . . . American me . . . that's all." He said rather high and mighty, "Well let's not raise our voice . . . after all I can't help comparing you with those I've just been around . . . too bad that head of yours is so full of puritanical ideas. Seems more than ever to me old-fashioned and bourgeois . . ."

I arose in haste from the table and answered, "That head full of ideals was filled by you. You, it was who filled me full, up to my neck with honorable thoughts and noble notions. And now the potter doesn't like the form his clay has taken. It's your doing . . ." He said coldly, "So I didn't write to you for a year. You'll forget all about that when you see the pretty things I got you. Let's forget all this and open the trunks." Now I wasn't hearing him. I continued, "No, it wasn't you who filled my head with ideals. It was your opposite, Charlie."

I walked quickly out of the room to the hall where my coat was. He followed saying, "I didn't mean to compare you . . . I'm sorry. There was no one in Europe I cared about." But I wasn't listening. With tears in my eyes, hysterically I said, "I don't want things . . . you haven't explained your silence . . . you haven't said one loving thing." I opened the door and started out. He protested asking, "What is there to say?" I answered, "Nothing, not anything. It's all very clear to me and you've already said too much."

I bounded out onto the porch. He grabbed his coat and came out with me. I stopped him and asked, "Will you please let the chauffeur take me? I want to go home alone and please don't call me anymore." We met for this one ugly encounter after one year apart.

Top left, left to right: *St. Joseph, Missouri, c. 1901; Helen, Eugenia, and Georgia Hale.* Top right: *Georgia, c. 1908.* Bottom, left to right: *First winter in Chicago, c. 1903; Georgia, Eugenia (Gene) and Helen. (Editor's Collection)*

Top left: *Graduation photo from Englewood High School, June 1918.* Top right: *Georgia on right as Ralph Rackstraw in* H.M.S. Pinafore. *Bottom: A modelling assignment. (Editor's Collection)*

Top: *A little like Bebe Daniels.* Bottom: *The inscription on the back of the photo reads: "Dearest Mother, This was taken at exposition [Goldwyn]. The little dolls represent the names [Conrad Nagel and Eileen Pringle]. Do you like them? Love, Dixie."* *(Editor's Collection)*

From The Salvation Hunters, *1925* . From left to right: *George K. Arthur, Nellie Bly Baker, Georgia, Otto Matiesen, and seated on the running board, Bruce Guerin. Courtesy of the Academy of Motion Picture Arts and Sciences.*

Publicity stills c. 1925. Top: *Photograph by Paralta.* Bottom: *Photograph by Melbourne Spurr. (Editor's Collection)*

"My first shots were to be scenes outside his cabin."

Chaplin directing Georgia and Malcolm Waite (Jack Cameron).

Chaplin and Georgia between takes.

Chaplin relaxing on the set with the "girls."

Georgia and Chaplin enjoying an intimate moment during a break.

"To Georgia Hale with sincere good wishes from your friend Mack Swain."
(Editor's Collection)

Top: *Publicity still. Photograph by Paralta. (Editor's Collection)* Bottom: *Georgia's last scenes with Chaplin on board* The Lark, *April 1925.*

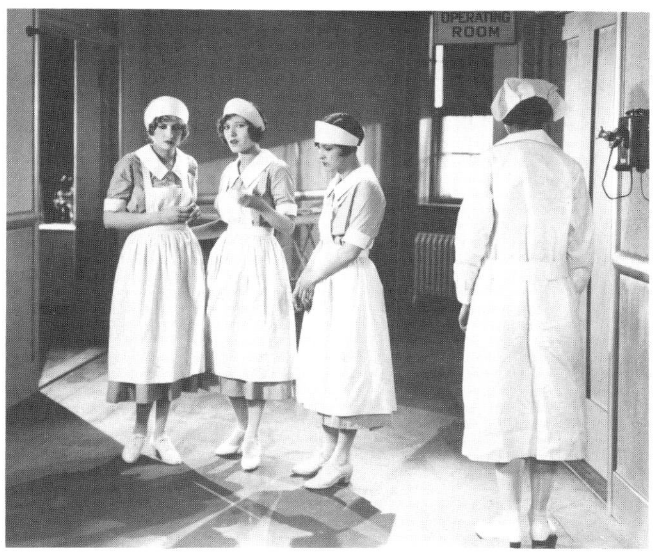

Top: *Georgia and Josef von Sternberg during the making of* Wheels of Destiny, *1927.* Bottom: *Georgia as Nurse Wendell in* The Rainmaker, *1926. (Editor's Collection)*

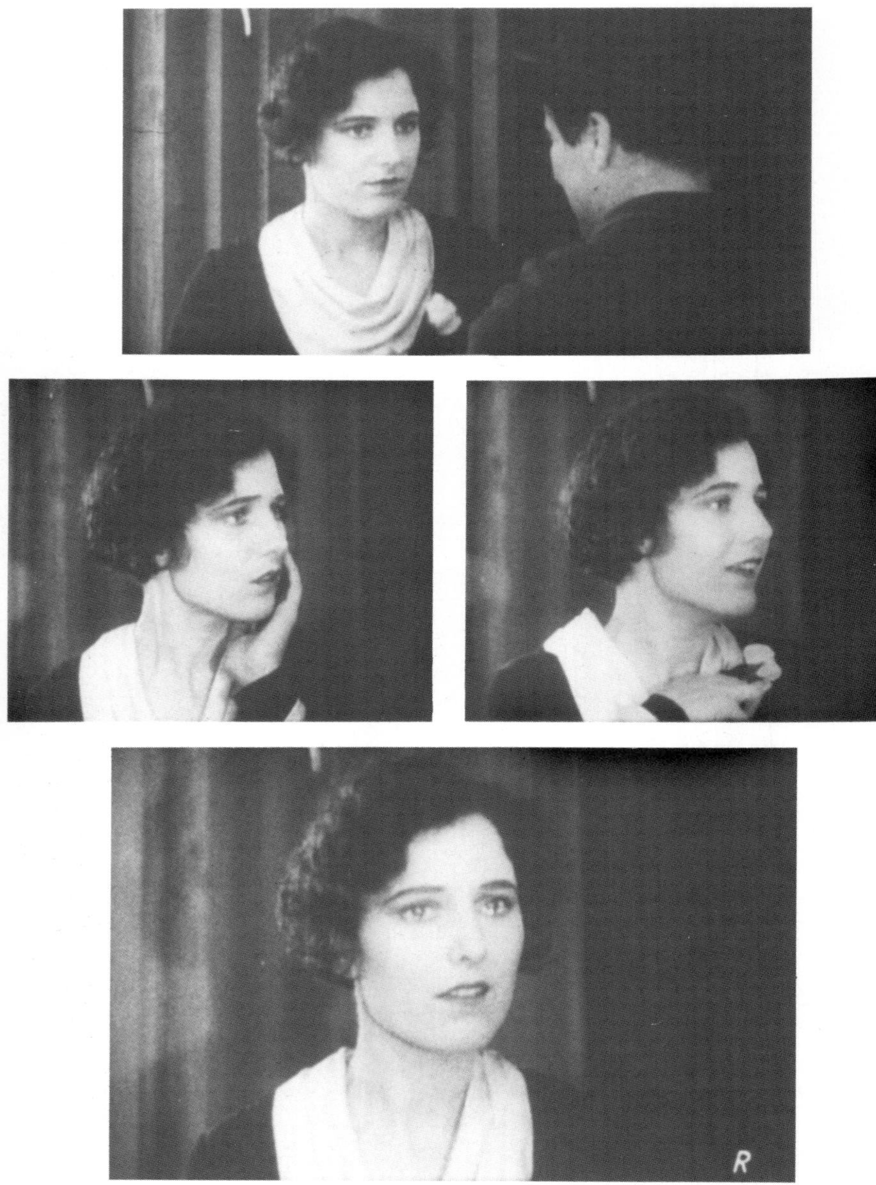

Chaplin coaching Georgia's screen-test for City Lights, *1929*.

Top left: *Ivor and "Hell" Montagu.* Top right, left to right: *Georgia, Ivor, Eisenstein, Eduard Tisse and Chaplin.* Bottom, left to right: *Eduard Tisse, Chaplin, Georgia and Eisenstein. (Editor's Collection)*

Top: *Georgia as a blond. A publicity still for* The Lightning Warrior, *1931.*
Bottom: *Georgia , c. 1943. Photograph by Melbourne Spurr. (Editor's Collection)*

38

Thereafter Mr. Chaplin made *Modern Times* with Paulette Goddard.[1] Finally this whole episode came to a resounding end. Another chapter of his Hollywood life banged to a close.

I didn't see the picture for a long time after its release.[2] Unconsciously I had been avoiding it. Then one day I was drawn to see it. There was such pathos in this film to me. It was a story of a man pitted against the dire effects of his own knowledge . . . the machine. The rapid, tiring work—work he was forced to do by his employer, to match that of the machine, was comical but pathetic. It was a hopeless task. After days of this grind, the poor little fellow would end up with the "jerks" which he couldn't turn off.

It reminded me again of his past. Charlie had shown me many times how he tried to beat the machine even then. He made those little cork boats and objects when he was a mere child. He made them by the hundreds just like a machine and then sold them to help his mother pay the bills. He repeated this story to me many times. He loved to recall how happy his mother was when she'd see his pockets stuffed full of change. His reward was that big kiss and hug from his mam. I never tired of hearing this heart-touching tale of his youth.

1 Paulette Goddard (b. Marion Levy, 3 June 1905, Great Neck, Long Island; d. 23 April 1990) had been a "Goldwyn Girl" in *The Kid from Spain*. She met Chaplin shortly after his return to the U.S. from Europe in 1932. Though never married, they were close companions, until they parted permanently in December 1941.

2 *Modern Times* had its premiere at the Rivoli Theatre, New York, on 5 February 1936.

Modern Times inspired me once again. I felt the same glow and uplift his every picture always gave me. And I was not the only one, thousands felt the same. A little woman next to me couldn't contain herself. She leaned over close and said, "We come to the movies to be entertained and forget our worries, to see something worthwhile, something with a message. His pictures give me something. I feel I can go out and laugh at my troubles." She smiled happily and asked, "Why aren't there more Charlie Chaplin's?" I answered, "Yes, his pictures are so darn wholesome. Aren't they? I, too, always feel better after I've seen one of his movies." She giggled and said, "My children wish he was their teacher at school. They say, 'He'd entertain us and instruct us at the same time.'" Then she added with a twinkle in her eye, "He is cute, isn't he?"

How many men, women and children he made happy! How they enjoyed seeing something artistic as well as funny. I realized that day too, how important it is to enrich our consciousness constantly with such beauty, in order to counteract the miserable stuff we continually have thrust upon us. The news, entertainment world, and just the everyday scenes around us . . . all the filth our senses are heir to . . . swamp us.

I couldn't forget the picture. The devotion and sweet love he had for the girl was so touching. The ending was so happy. I could still see the two, walking off into the sunlight, hand and hand. I know comparisons are "odious" as the great poet said, but the men I had met and gone around with were such a letdown. How could they be otherwise, after I had known Charlie. It was like being in heaven and then having to return to earth for me. After seeing the show, I wanted to see him, to talk to him, to feel him close. But, of course, I had told him, "Never call me again." Now I longed to hear from him.

Unbeknown to me, at the same time Charlie had been seeing me in *The Gold Rush*. He had been re-running it. He enjoyed anew my performance. He studied my expressions and movements. He wanted to see me, to talk to me and feel me close. But he could hear my words, "Never call me again."

However, he was so thrilled with the picture and wanted me to be with him to enjoy it together. He wanted to tell me all over again how he loved me in that part. He decided then and there to re-do the picture. And he decided I'd have to take part in this undertaking. So . . .

My phone rang. A voice . . . familiar . . . was asking, "May I speak to Georgia?" I just said, "Charlie!" This time . . . I wasn't dreaming. It was real! He said tenderly, "Georgia, How are you? I've missed seeing you . . . what are you doing? When may I see you?" He spoke rapidly and animatedly, as if he was eager to come right over and pick me up. I answered just as quickly and as inspired, "I'm fine right now . . . now I'm fine. It is so good to hear your voice. I'm not doing anything . . . and I can see you . . . now." He laughed like a boy and said, "I'll be right over."

I hardly had time to doll up before he was at the front door. But I didn't care! I ran and opened the door. We both frantically reached out for the other . . . There we stood for five minutes without saying a word. Then he asked "Would you like to go to the Cocoanut [*sic*] Grove? I thought there we could talk . . . and dine and dance. It's been a long time since we've danced . . . too long." I asked excitedly, "Do I look all right?" He said generously, "You're beautiful."

I didn't care how I looked or appeared to others . . . just so he thought I was beautiful. That's all that counted to me. During the evening he said, "I've wanted to be with you all along. No one else has taken your place, not for a moment." Now I could be and breathe easier . . . it was as if I was back home after a long absence. I told him, "I've felt so lost for so long and now I feel that I've been found . . . and by the right one." He whispered while we were dancing, "I find you so different . . . no matter what I have said or say I never really want you to change. You know I am not religious but I don't like a materially-minded girl for very long. I've just finished with that kind and you're like a breath of fresh air."

Then the incredible happened. I thought the evening was already complete. But when we returned to the table he asked timidly, "How would you like to sign a new contract with me? I'm going to re-do *The Gold Rush.* I answered joyously, "I don't have to say a word. You know my answer of course, of course I'd love it." This contract was to last until he was forced to close his studio in the United States.

Charlie changed *The Gold Rush.* He re-edited it, narrated it and scored the music. He would hum the melodies and I'd pick them out on the piano and write them down.

While working he smoked incessantly. He noticed of course, that I didn't smoke. He said, "You still don't smoke and yet you never seem to get nervous or feel the need of a cigarette." "I don't like to see a girl smoke," I answered. "Really, I don't care about seeing a man smoke either." He said with a finality, "I'm stopping here and now." Then he proceeded to throw all his packages of cigarettes into the waste-paper basket. This scene and dialogue were repeated many times during our companionship.

One day thereafter, for a little "breather," we took a trip to Catalina Island. We sailed on the big boat "The Avalon." The fresh breezes were so delightful we went up on the top deck to sniff some of the fresh air. We had just inhaled about two exhilarating breaths, when a man came up and sat down directly in front of us. He was puffing a cigarette and blowing clouds of smoke in the clean ocean atmosphere. The wind carried it right back into our faces.

Charlie started to gasp and fume with anger. He proceeded to expound to me on the evils of smoking. "Smoking is truly an evil. It's not only dangerous . . . it dulls your senses . . . you can't enjoy life as keenly as you can without them. Believe me, it's enslaving . . . it's no good." I answered, "Yes, Charlie, I believe you." Then he proclaimed a little louder, "I just can't understand people who smoke. How selfish . . . how utterly inconsiderate is anyone who smokes." His voice filled the deck . . . "There's no excuse filling others' lungs with that foul stuff . . . and without their consent."

About this time everyone's eyes were on the man. He arose and silent stole away . . . as he flipped his cigarette into the sea. Charlie smiled to me triumphantly. I had to laugh to myself at him. He was so much like a child. The moment he quit smoking, it was as if he had never committed the offense. It was as if he had never indulged and he had no tolerance for anyone who hadn't seen the light the moment he did.

39

Charlie, a highly keyed intuitive person, was also very sensitive. One time during our musical sessions, he played his organ into the small hours. He would improvise and find lovely melodies, while I would read and enjoy the Bible and other great books.

I had progressed to the point, at last, where I worshipped the ideas expressed by the brilliant men of the past and present. I no long associated them exclusively with Charlie. I had my books stashed away in his library with his complete approval. Although my books were all religious, he'd say with that beatific smile, "I like to have you religious. It keeps you good." But he'd shy away if I ever tried to read anything out of these books. He would laughingly say, "I don't need it. I'm too good already." Then he'd grin and show those big white teeth like a naughty child. I stopped trying to convert him or read to him.

On his seven-acre estate he felt free to play the organ as late as he pleased, knowing for certain that he could not disturb his far away neighbors. He said one night, "I'm going to work late to-night. I feel so inspired. Thank goodness, nobody can hear me. That's the joy of having a large estate . . . the marvelous privacy."

The following day I didn't see him until noon, for I knew he must have worked far into the night on his music. I came bounding in, eager to hear his new numbers. But something seemed to be troubling him. All the inspiration of the night before was gone. He said in a very subdued tone, "Let's go for a walk in the garden. We strolled along silently. He had such a sad expression, I was afraid to start the conversation. But finally I asked, "What's bothering you? Couldn't you work out any new melodies last night?" He frowned at that . . .

We strolled down one side of the hill and then back up . . . all the while he was mute. There was no song in his heart now. What a night had made! What a contrast from the humming, singing and playing musician of the night before. I started down the other side. He stopped abruptly and said, "I don't want to go down there!" I asked, "Why not? I thought it might be nice to enjoy the flowers."

He pointed down to the garden and said wistfully, "I went for a walk to see our prize dahlias this morning." I laughed and remarked, "I'm so delighted you remembered the name of the flowers . . . good for you." He dearly loved the flowers and plants in his garden but he never knew the name of one of them. Flowers and arrangements had been taught to me early by my mother. I would ask him the name of a flower, just to tease him. He'd always reply with the same question timidly, "Is it a geranium?" Now he had added dahlias, and I was pleased with my pupil.

But he wasn't happy about anything this day, I could plainly see. I said, "Please, tell me . . . what happened this morning?" He hesitatingly answered, "Well . . . when I went down to the garden this morning, I heard a voice calling 'Charlie, Charlie.' I looked up, and there stood Georgie Jessel[1] across the road on his estate. He waved his hand at me and shouted, 'Thank you for the concert last night. I can't tell you how much I enjoyed it.' "

I couldn't believe it and interjected, "He could hear you at that distance?" But he continued with a sheepish look in his eyes, "I tried hard to conceal my embarrassment . . . and stammered, 'I'm very happy . . . happy . . . you liked it.' Then I waved a foolish 'farewell' and beat it up the hill," he added disgustedly.

1 George Jessel (b. 3 April 1893, New York; d. 24 May 1981) was a vaudeville comedian, singer, songwriter and producer.

I quickly turned my face away for I couldn't keep from smiling. If the Empire State building had fallen on him, —he couldn't have looked more crushed. He said, "Please don't smile . . ." I could see there was no talking him out of this or getting him to laugh it off. This left a deep impression on Charlie. I begged him to play the organ but he wouldn't go near it.

However soon this void was filled. We were out shopping for a pretty set of dishes for my sister's wedding one day, when quite accidentally his eyes fell on a sparkling new accordion. He had missed playing his organ. He just could not resist this instrument. It was like a toy and he was like a boy. He bought it there and then. When he returned to my house, he walked around my place trying to play it, while I changed my clothes for the evening. He had never touched an accordion before. By the time I was ready, he was playing that instrument like a trouper.

He was so delighted with himself, that he started dancing a tap routine to his rhythms. He told me, "These are the steps and patterns I used in the Folies Bergère in Paris years ago." I never knew he could tap-dance. I was an enthusiastic audience. He laid aside his new toy and asked me, "Would you like me to teach you a little routine?" I hesitated thinking I couldn't learn his hard steps, but sure enough he could teach tap as readily as he could teach acting. He was such fun!

I exclaimed, "They must have loved you in Paris?" But he answered, "Really, Georgia, this is the country that I owe everything to . . . it has showered blessings on me. There is no place in the world that is comparable. The United States can do anything it puts its mind to, and overnight. Look what it did in the Second World War under the leadership of Franklin Roosevelt . . . It's white saviour. Overnight, it was a standing arsenal and this from a dead start. It has proven its greatness. Hasn't it? This is where I want to live my life." It had indeed piled Charlie's lap high with rare gifts, but to live his life here . . . was not to be one of them.

Charlie, the genius, had a feeling of great concern for the underdog. He breathed this tender solicitude for the poor, the underprivileged, the forgotten, the ignorant . . . throughout his pictures. Mr. Chaplin was cold, sometimes cruel. He was a snob. Although he went through the motions of caring, his philosophy was conservative. No one enjoyed more being at the top of the heap, looking down. He loved high society and he loved wealth, which he never shared, unless forced to do so. Charlie and Mr. Chaplin were opposites.

40

One evening we were invited to a party at Mr. and Mrs. Jascha Heifetz[1]—the former Mrs. Florence Vidor.[2] It was a fun evening. They had waxed a big slab of cement, where we could all dance in the open, just a few feet from the ocean.

At the peak of the evening all the guests crowded around Mr. Heifetz and begged him to play. I shall always remember his answer, "But I'm so out of practice." Then we learned that he had not practiced his full eight hours or more that day. I could hear Charlie saying, "Genius isn't just inspiration, it's mostly perspiration."

But Jascha Heifetz was so gracious. He smiled happily, and asked after playing a big number, "What would you like to hear now?" A chorus of voices requested, "Estrellita?" This was the tune on everyone's lips at that time. It was a little bit of heaven come down to earth, to be in the presence of such an artist and hear so close at hand his melodious playing.

That evening Charlie stole over to me and whispered, "I feel like letting go . . . a little . . . to-night. Is it alright if I take a few cocktails?" This was unusual for him. Charlie never felt the need for a drink for inspiration. He asked like a tiny boy and I replied like his mother, "You'll have to make that decision

[1] In an interview given in Decemeber 1920, Chaplin, a self-taught violinist, claimed to have played "a bit of Bach" for the virtuoso Jascha Heifetz (b. 2 February 1901, Vilna; d. 10 March 1987, Los Angeles) when the latter dined at his home.

[2] The actress Florence Vidor (b. Florence Cobb, 23 July 1895, Houston, Texas; d. 1977) married King Vidor in 1915. She divorced him in 1925 and married Heifetz in 1928.

Charlie . . . it's up to you." Charlie disappeared and I was deserted for quite some time.

All the guests were called onto the dance floor and told to join hands. It was a "mixer." I was happy for I had been alone and felt strange. It made everyone relax, get together and change partners. The ladies were told to go to their left . . . then a call came to stop and dance with the new partner. My new one turned out to be Ronald Colman.[1]

This was the first time I had met Mr. Colman. He was delighted with my dancing and said, "My, you are so smooth and follow so easily." I thanked him for being so encouraging. He said, "I can't lead very well. I'd like to be selfish and keep you for my partner." I smiled and said happily, "I don't think anyone would mind a bit." Charlie, by chance, walked by and saw us laughing and dancing. He smiled and waved and went merrily on his way.

After the dance Mr. Colman asked me, "Will you join me for a drink of fruit punch?" Charlie had completely disappeared again so I answered, "Yes, I'd be delighted." We sat and talked. He said, "I asked to be introduced to you in the beginning of the evening. With the blond hair . . . you resembled a Lady . . . I knew from England. I was surprised when you told me your name. Weren't you a brunette in *The Gold Rush*?" I told him, "I bleached my hair just for a lark. Yes, I'm truly a dark-haired girl."

He knew more about me than I had thought for he said, "I hear you are an excellent tennis player. Would you give me the pleasure of playing tennis with me?" I said laughingly, "You can't believe all that you hear, but I'd be delighted to play with you." I felt the eyes of someone staring at me. I looked

[1] Before agreeing to make Samuel Goldwyn a partner in United Artists in October 1927, Fairbanks and Pickford stipulated that under the contract he would have to deliver six pictures starring the celebrated English actor Ronald Colman (b. 9 February 1891, Richmond, England; d. 1958), and the actress Vilma Banky, Goldwyn's leading stars.

up and across the room, quite a distance away, I could see Charlie beckoning to me. I immediately excused myself from Ronald Colman and hurried back to Charlie. He said rather abruptly, "Let's go."

On the way home, Charlie wasn't a bit the gay and high one he had been at the party. On the contrary, he seemed quiet and a little depressed. I said, "As a rule you are hilarious after a party. You said that you wanted to 'let go' to-night and have a few cocktails. Did you have the drinks? Did you 'let go' and have a good time?" He wouldn't talk. I was commencing to worry. I thought perhaps the drinking had made him ill. I ventured one more question, "Are you alright?"

He remained silent. We were approaching near to my home. "Why won't he speak?" I asked myself. Finally, he asked softly, "What were you and Ronald Colman talking about . . . and for so long?" I answered, pleased that he had spoken, "Oh, he just wants to play tennis with me." He quickly turned to me and asked, "Are you? You're not going to . . . are you?" I smiled to myself because now I knew, now I understood why he was depressed. I immediately reassured him, "No, not if you don't want me to."

That is all he needed to be perfectly content and happy again. He nimbly put his feet under him and turned squarely to me. He said adoringly (as if he had not neglected me for the entire evening), "You were beautiful tonight as a blonde. I know I didn't want you to bleach your hair, but I must admit you were a hit." He snuggled close to me and said, "Let's go to my place and raid the refrigerator?" This we loved to do, it was a little like stealing our own food from the servants . . . of course Charlie had paid for the whole deal. Sometimes it even felt like the servants were the bosses, owned the place and we were intruding.

His Japanese servants, ten of them, had a huge refrigerator of their own. It was filled with strange food . . . that is to us . . . dried fish, roes of different colors and designs, long black eels and many peculiar looking edibles that we couldn't name.

Charlie's was stuffed with . . . chicken, beef, cold-cuts, imported delicacies, cheeses, caviar, pâté de foie gras and . . . always jello in different shapes and colors. After carefully scanning all these choice dishes, he would invariably—settle for a bowl of cereal and cream. It was always cream and not milk. He confessed, "I never had cream or butter as a child. It was too expensive, so to this day I dearly love them. I can't get enough of either." He would place this dish of plain cereal and cream before him and would proceed to eat, as a king would a sumptuous feast.

He would gracefully partake of every crumb, making each flake seem delectable and "yummie." Just as he made his old shoe seem an enviable repast to Mack Swain[1] . . . the hungry miner in *The Gold Rush*. Even though I had made up my mind to resist eating anything fattening, I'd be just as taken in as Mack Swain was . . . I'd pull myself up to the table, pile my bowl high with cereal, then drown it in deep rich cream. I could resist anything but temptation!

[1] Mack Swain (b. 16 February 1876, Salt Lake City, Utah; d. 1935) entered pictures as a member of the Keystone Company in 1913, supporting Chaplin in many of his early shorts. Rescued from oblivion by him in the early 1920s, Swain appeared in *The Pilgrim* (1922) and as Big Jim McKay in *The Gold Rush*.

41

One night when we returned rather late to his place, I decided to go upstairs and doll up a little. Charlie went on his way into the living room, where I was to join him. We had planned as usual, to steal into the servants' quarters and have a late-late snack.

In a short time I heard him coming up the staircase. I couldn't understand . . . I thought, "Perhaps he's tired of waiting and is hungry." I hurriedly ran down the steps and met him halfway up. I said, "Let's go down into the kitchen, I'm starving too." He put his fingers to his lips and whispered, "Sh . . . sh. I just did the worst thing!" Then he stamped his foot and exclaimed, "Oh darn, what a fool I am."

He took me by the hand and led me back upstairs saying "I don't want anything to eat. My appetite is gone. I don't want to go back down there." I couldn't understand and asked, "What's the matter? A few moments ago, you were so happy and so famished." He put his hand on his stomach and said, "I couldn't eat, now."

Then he scratched his head and with a deep scowl he said wistfully, "You know we were going to steal into the servants' quarters. Well instead, one of the servants stole into our quarters, into the living room. Naturally, at this hour, he was sure I was in bed sound asleep. Of course he felt he was safe and free to live it up a bit. There he stood before the fireplace, rocking back and forth on his feet and looking up to the ceiling, happily dreaming and enjoying the heat and solitude."

Charlie banged his hand on his forehead and said reproachfully, "But no . . . no I had to shock him and spoil his few moments of pleasure! I had to walk smack in on him and frighten him." Then Charlie went into his pantomime . . . he jumped and bowed to the floor . . . just as the servant had done. Then he continued as the servant, "Oh, I so sorry, please forgive? I never did this be . . . I . . . I'm just so sorry, Mester Chaplin." Charlie said stammering, "Don't mind me . . ." They both scurried out of the room at the same time. Charlie said foolishly, "We almost bumped into each other."

It had been so well acted and he looked so forlorn . . . I just couldn't help smiling. Charlie glanced at me and saw the smile and his face lightened. Then I giggled. He joined me and we both burst into laughter. "What a sweet sensitive little fellow you are," I said. His appetite returned and we crept down the stairs, peeked into the kitchen . . . the coast was clear . . . we had our snack.

It was fun roaming over his large estate day or night. I was never afraid with Charlie around, because he was never afraid. I caught his feeling. Physically he feared no one. He was a bit of a hypochondriac though. His medicine chest was filled with assorted medicines, and at the mention of a disease he'd hasten to get it, like a new-cut garment. But being the artist he was . . . ideas would crowd out these disturbing thoughts and he'd be inspired and well again.

Charlie didn't seem to live in a world of danger. For such a wealthy man he moved about and lived fearlessly. Someone gave him a gun to have for protection but he didn't want it and he soon gave it away. One thing he was unconscious of—what clothes he wore. He never sported expensive coats or suits, jewelry—nor did he carry large sums of money. However he did love and wear funny little cloth-topped button shoes. But no one would steal them or even be seen wearing them . . . but Charlie. He was so cute!

In contrast Josef von Sternberg dressed expensively and always had with him big amounts of money. He lived in a swanky building with an underground garage, one of the very first apartment buildings in Hollywood with that luxury. But one night when he drove into it . . . some gangsters were waiting for him. They got in and ordered, "Back up and keep your mouth shut. Just drive!" Well, with a gun in his ribs he had no choice. He begged, "Please take everything I've got but spare me." That's exactly what they did. They relieved him of his bills and exquisite camel's hair coat, then shoved him out of his gorgeous Packard and told him "Walk!" he did . . . for miles!

Charlie was so different. He would reach into his closet and pull out some thread-bare coat, which he wouldn't part with, and joyfully put it on. In fact Kono would have delivered several handsome coats and place them casually around the living room. Then he'd come to me and plead, "Please, if you possibly can, get Mester Chaplin to point out which one he likes?" Then very discreetly I'd ask Charlie, "Which one of these do you think . . . is nice?" I'd pretend I was only half interested in the coats or his opinion. He'd glance over the lot and after a moment's thought he'd wave at one and say, "That one . . . is alright."

I'd run to Kono with the word and that would be Charlie's new coat. Which, by the way, he'd thoroughly enjoy. Kono would throw out the old coat and place the new one in its place. Unconsciously Charlie would put on the new one. He'd say, "I like the feel of this material. Nice, isn't it?" Then he wouldn't part with this one . . . for years.

How I loved Charlie's place and those heavenly days we spent together. We liked the same things. Each day revealed more of his affectionate nature. The little tramp the world saw on the screen was the real Charlie, and my admiration grew more and more. The better I knew him, the closer we became.

He seemed to cloak the flowers, animals and beautiful hills around his home with his great love. They must have felt it as I did. Charlie appreciated others who loved animals as he did. He said, "I admire William Randolph Hearst[1] so much. On his big ranch in San Simeon, he has put signs everywhere,

[1] Chaplin had been on familiar terms with William Randolph Hearst (b. 29 April 1863, San Francisco; d. 1951) since 1923, and had been a frequent guest at San Simeon.

'Animals have the right of way' . . . Just think, this place is a castle filled with priceless treasures from all over the world and yet he remembers the small living things. Isn't that a kind gesture?"

One day on Charlie's hilly place, a little kitten fell down an old well-shaft. He told me, "I heard the cry of a tiny kitten. I followed it . . . to the old well. When I looked down and saw the baby crying to me for help, I vowed I'd move heaven and earth to save it. I had forgotten to have that old well filled and my heart was filled with self-condemnation.

Immediately I got in touch with my pal Douglas Fairbanks, and together we started to descend. But when we reached the bottom we were becoming overcome by fumes. Douglas said, 'My God, I feel dizzy . . . I smell fumes. We'd better get out in a hurry . . . if we can make it.' I started coughing but I grabbed the cat and held him tight. However, I needed two hands to ascend. It was laborious, but Doug got behind me and pushed me up with his strong arms. He became almost exhausted as we neared the top. One deep breath of fresh air gave me all the strength I needed to lift Doug up and out of the well. When we finally reached the fresh air and warm earth we both laid down flat and thanked goodness . . . we'd made it. The little kitten said 'Meow.' That was our reward. Our mission was a success," Charlie exclaimed.

This was only one adventure. Those hills were roamed by small and sometimes large animals . . . and creeping things. But it made the place enchanting and exciting. It was a world apart and yet so close to everyone and everything. We'd find big feet marks . . . perhaps those of deer or even mountain lions . . . they play in those hills. But one day a low moving little creature hopped his way into Charlie's house. He was sitting on the couch quietly dreaming, when he looked up and saw this strange animal stealthily cross the hallway. He said, "I sprung to my feet as if I'd been fired at. I frantically called for help, but no one could hear me. I was afraid to move. There I sat cringing."

Finally Kono[1] came in and asked nonchalantly, "Did you call Mester Chaplin? I wasn't sure, I thought I heard your voice." Charlie answered, "Indeed I did call . . . I yelled. Come with me and help me hunt for some peculiar thing that just came in here through that door!"

They hunted. At last, Charlie happened to look into his bathroom. He leaned over and peeked into his tub. He let out one big scream . . . for sitting helplessly in his bathtub was a little skunk. He had good manners, for there was no bad odor. He was far more frightened than Charlie and his heart melted when the little creature looked up at Charlie with appealing eyes. He became our dear little pet. He inherited a nice cage and was fed the best of delicacies. But alas, one day, he disappeared for more adventurous parts.

Charlie's encounter with each new creature would make his hair stand on end, for he was not a man of the great outdoors. But he loved it all, passionately. Charlie liked a poem I wrote to our little pet mouse. He lived securely at the bottom of the hill but he too disappeared— one day . . .

A City Mouse

In a sweet green meadow lived our little mouse
And a hole in the ground was his little house.
A nice big leaf so soft and brown
In a wind tumbled down
And hid the little door
So you couldn't see it anymore.

[1] Kono left Chaplin's employment in 1936, and was given a six months' contract at the United Artists offices in Tokyo. His option was not renewed, and he returned to the U.S. His whereabouts after 1940 are unknown, but in a letter to the Montagu's, Georgia wrote: "Remember Kono, the Jap servant? You know he turned out to be a spy for Japan. Of course Frank, the Jap under Kono, was taken away with his other ten servants to concentration camps." (KP: May 1943).

This little mouse once lived in town
And he'd received full many a frown
From the cats that roamed about
(He was safer here, no doubt)
But his little heart was sad
When it should have been so glad.

Things were very quiet here
Not a sound that he could hear
Reminded him of any city noise
Bark of dogs or shout of boys
So the peace began to pall
He was lonesome that was all.

Then one bright and sunny day
(Maybe Sunday, who can say)
A big car stops right by his tree.
(Picnic party, gay and free)
And when they sit down to dine
Mousey says this chance is mine.

Was he thankful for a crumb
A feast for many days to come
No sir, not a bit was he
Freedom was all that he could see
From behind a pile or rocks
He slips himself into a box.

Hidden in a corner he
Still as any mouse could be
And he hears them laugh and play
Many hours, oh, he should say
Then at last with shake and jar
Starts the motor of the car.

And they go for many a mile
While Mousey sits so still the while
With his little eyes shut tite
He is getting quite a fright.
Thru a hole he peeks around
Lots of lights, joy, noise and sound.

Then they come to a quick stop
At command of motor cop
And his eyes just bulge with joy
What cares he for cat or boy
Each familiar sound and sight
Fills him with a new delight

In the darkness, drops he in
Into all noise and din
Now his life will be at stake
Every moment, asleep, awake.
He must steal his every bite
Sleep in days, roam out at night.

And he scampered quick away
Where he went no one shall say
But his heart was light with glee
A city Mouse once more was he
Constant dangers, never sure,
But the world—there lay the lure.

Charlie was more like a child than an adult and that's why he was so much fun.

42

Then . . . there was Mr. Chaplin. When there was no inspiration for making a picture or writing a story, the dear little tramp seemed to fade away. Mr. Chaplin would appear. He would go to one party after another, where he would be the toast of the crowd, the center of attraction. He'd coax me to go with him. I would dutifully go, but they were for the most part very boring and I could not conceal this.

He would be disgusted and angry with me and say, "I don't understand your attitude. Why don't you find these affairs delightful? Most girls in Hollywood would . . . and they'd be happy to go with me." I could only answer again, " I know very well the girls adore you and would be proud to be seen with you. But somehow I can't find pleasure in these parties." This would call forth the familiar theme (that of trying to change me). He'd entreat, "Why don't you wake up ! Join my chic friends and relax, before it's too late." But even threats couldn't change my feelings.

This gulf was wide and grew wider between Mr. Chaplin and me. We really never had anything in common. We didn't like the same things. His whole character and philosophy was so material, so unlike Charlie's. He loved the unlovely. Mr. Chaplin loved the coarse and common. He felt he was bestride Hollywood and he was enjoying the ride. He could be very secretive about some of his friends and some of his deeds. He never wanted this part of his private life brought into the light. He wanted no publicity on this part of his life. I was kept in ignorance of it and his close friend.

However Charlie was open and wanted the light of publicity on his great works. Mr. Chaplin was not the abundant Charlie. He thought in dribbles . . . He was very selfish and afraid. He would say, "Why didn't you turn off the electricity, when you left that room?" Then he would rush past me and snap the switch off. He'd many times say, "I have a great fear of being poor again."

Whereas, Charlie the artist, loaned Samuel Goldwyn[1] a large sum of money to finish a picture. Charlie said, "He has exhausted other sources and I must come to his aid." This whole deal turned out good for all concerned. The picture was a success and Charlie was repaid, in money and gratitude. But Charlie, the little genius, had taken a chance for a friend. He gave wisely and unstintingly to those who deserved it.

Mr. Chaplin's so-called friends were like him . . . exactly. I really never wanted to become acquainted with them, and he found it convenient for him to carry on friendships and affairs with those I didn't know. I was naive. I never realized what went on in his life away from me. In a cruel way Mr. Chaplin tried to change me and of course I tried to change him . . . but we never budged an inch. Mr. Chaplin continued this whirl and it became harder for me to feel the real presence of Charlie at all. This little tramp, my spiritual guide . . . I kept asking myself, "Where has he gone? Where?"

[1] Samuel Goldwyn (b. Shmuel Gelbfisz, 27 August 1882, Warsaw; d. 1974) had become an independent producer by 1925, releasing his films in association with United Artists. He later became a partner, though was unsuccessful in his attempt to take over in 1937.

43

Then one evening . . . he . . . he called. His voice was subdued and hesitant. It was Mr. Chaplin, but it sounded like the little tramp . . . I thought. He asked to see me . . . and we met at my place. I was then living in a small apartment in Hollywood.[1]

I had decided to live alone, away from my parents. This was what I should have done years before. I had, unknowingly, acted as a wedge between my parents. Each one had used me as an audience to complain to about the other. Now they had no one separating them . . . they moved closer together. Why had I not understood this years before? "The things that we would . . . that we do not" . . . oh dear!

Fortunately, now I had a place where Charlie and I could talk and be alone. This night had a sombre tone, sad and sweet. He held me tightly in his arms, as if not wanting to let me go for a moment. We discussed our life together from the day we met. We often did this, but something was different about it this time.

He asked, "We'll always be together . . . won't we?" Then with a note of deep remorse he added, almost like making a summation of the years, "You know your philosophy and ideals have often shut me out and forced me away from you to others, but I have never really cared for nor been attracted to anyone but you."

Then pleadingly, and with a strange urgency he said, "You must listen this time. Please Georgia, don't ask me, 'Why' . . .

[1] At this time Georgia lived at 1665 North Sycamore Street in Hollywood.

Just trust me this time, this once. Please go away with me, far away, this night . . . immediately?" I thought earnestly for some time, and then I had to say, "Yes, yes I will . . . if everything is alright and correct. Yes, I will . . . but I must have a day to get a few things together."

He seemed distracted and said, "No, let's leave now, at once." I smiled with joy, but I didn't understand his words. He held me closer and whispered, "Get your things. Let's go." I answered again happily, "To-morrow." Then I insisted that he must leave . . . it was so late . . . it was almost getting light. He pleaded once again at the door and my answer was "to-morrow."

He said, softly, "Good-bye." It was strange and different. His voice was sad. I wanted to run after him and say, "Alright . . . yes, let's run away . . . now." But he had entered the elevator. He was gone! I felt a peculiar, unfamiliar feeling. But then I knew it only meant a day and we'd be together . . . I was ecstatically happy . . .[1]

It was a radiant California day, a gentle breeze was blowing. The air was whirling, tossing the fragrance of sweet scented flowers. Into this beauty I started on a lazy stroll. Everyone had planted and watered and that Supreme Intelligence had given the increase. What else could have formed the myriad outlines and blazoned the earth with such rich greens and brilliant colors. I found myself identifying the human with the divine. I had come a long way from having no God. "The little comic has brought me to the threshold of a new world," I told myself.

Around the corner, into my world of loveliness, came a chap moving towards me in a wheel-chair. I didn't recognize him. He greeted me saying, "Hello, Georgia! Don't you know

[1] Georgia repeated this story in a letter written many years later—"You know the night before he married Oona he came to my house and begged me to leave the country with him. But I knew it wasn't right not with him in his situation. So at three in the morning he left and how sad it all was—" (MP: 6 January, 1978).

me?" It took a few seconds for me to realize who it was. Quickly I stammered, "But of course . . . Fred. It's . . . so nice to see you." He saw my surprise and dismay . . . and my reluctance to say more. He said simply and succinctly, "The doctors have given me just a couple of more months . . . and that will be it."

My heart throbbed with sorrow. He had been such a strong, husky and happy fellow. I tried hard to say some comforting words. They all sounded so empty, so impotent. I wanted to help this man. But I couldn't do or say anything meaningful.

Charlie's loving philosophy had taken me a long way up the mountain path out of a dismal valley . . . but I had nothing to give to this fellow. Confronted by this tragedy I felt so inadequate, so incapable. I felt sad. I found myself returning to the days of my youth asking the same old questions all over again, "Why? Why did this befall this good man? Why can I not help?" I wanted more knowledge. I felt I was treading water. I wanted to go forward—but how? I prayed . . . I actually prayed!

This time I didn't turn to Charlie . . . but to that Supreme Intelligence Dr. Einstein had spoken of. I prayed to that "One," who had made the pretty flowers whose perfume was caressing my senses. I said, "Please, give me wisdom, so that I may say a word in season . . . that I may be able to help my fellow man?" This man in the wheel-chair . . . what a discordant note . . . into an otherwise perfect day! "Yet, it caused me to pray," I thought. And it seemed it was the first time I'd ever prayed aright. Anyway, it made me feel better.

As I continued my foot steps homeward and looked into the brilliant faces of my little flower-friends, my heart grew light again. The pansies nodded to me, the roses and the petunias showered me with the most costly perfume. Nothing could really take my joy from me . . . for I had Charlie. My own world was full! I sang joyously, as I bounded up my steps.

My song was interrupted by the shrill voice of a neighbour yelling, "Did you hear the news? Your boss Mr. Chaplin got married to-day in Santa Barbara."[1] Everything stopped . . . my song . . . my joy . . . my being. My whole world ceased to be! I was mute. I couldn't answer. I stepped forward in a trance. I found myself inside the house . . . somehow. I closed my bedroom door. The warm breeze had turned cold. I felt chilled. I wept until I could cry no more . . . I shuddered. I was freezing . . . then I touched my forehead, it was ablaze, as on fire . . . I couldn't remember anything . . . where was I? I felt deliriously alone . . . so utterly deserted . . . so . . . I . . .

[1] Chaplin married Oona O'Neill at Carpenteria, Santa Barbara, California, 16 June 1943.

44

A soft knock . . . knock . . . knock . . . on my door . . . then . . . it slowly opened.[1] *There . . . stood . . . Charlie. He whispered indistinctly, "Hurry . . . let's leave immediately. Are . . . you . . . ready?" I answered, "Oh, yes . . . I've been expecting you . . . I've been waiting." I grabbed my things and we ran down the hall, out the door, and into the waiting car. We sped along a tree-lined avenue, out into the lush fields. Waving farewell to California, we boarded our plane. Our destination was . . . far away Greece. But it had always been near to our hearts and its laws, dear.*

Miles and miles rolled away under us, as we sailed and sailed through kindly skies of blue and lacy clowds and star-spangled nights. Finally we arrived. All the smiling faces and happy hearts that had been with us, seemed to rush past us and go directly to a waiting old motor coach. The last, a chubby faced little man, turned to us and said warmly, "Come along." Charlie looked at me . . . we both burst into laughter as we agreed, "Why not?"

We skipped along with the others and crowded into the bus. Whither—we knew not, nor did we care. With every mile, the scenery became more heavenly. The whole landscape was pregnant with flowering trees and shrubs. The earth was bursting. We traveled many miles out into the country, and then suddenly from behind a slope, a quaint little village came into view.

Charlie was so excited, he could hardly wait to touch his feet to the ground of this enchanting place. He lifted me off the steps and whirled me around in the air. It was fresh and exhilarating.

[1] The following two chapters, 44 and 45, interrupt Georgia's narrative, and therefore have been italicized. See Editor's Introduction, p. xx.

He exclaimed as he took a deep breath, "The air sparkles with cleanness. Look, it's filled with diamonds. I wonder . . . do people live forever here? It's like drinking in life itself, with every breath."

Hand in hand we danced along, as we did the town . . . a small cafe, a few shops and some buildings. But down at the end of the town was a rather large structure. That was where all our new friends of the trip were heading. So we followed. Why not? As we came closer, we saw a little cross on the top. It was their church.

We arrived at their place of worship. It was such a big church for such a small community. Maybe their faith was in this proportion. Charlie stopped and looked up at the grand building. He took me lovingly in his arms and said, "This is what I wanted to find here. Will you marry me? . . . now . . . to-day?" My expression gave my answer, but I quickly whispered, "Yes . . . yes."

Gently but firmly, he took me by the hand and started to walk, our pace increased, then we started to run. When we reached the church, they all greeted us, as if expecting us . . . Charlie shyly reached into his pocket and pulled out dark glasses and put them on. Although no one seemed to recognize him. They just accepted us with warm friendship and child-like joy. There was no "nation-consciousness" here . . . just people.

Charlie, timidly, whispered something to the minister. He answered with a broad smile, "Certainly, it will add to our day of happiness. You're just in time. After our feast, we will all go into the fields and pick flowers. At this time of the year, they beckon us to come and pick them. They want to brighten the hearts and homes of those who are unable to come out and get them. This is a holy day, our holiday. With a wave of his hand, the music stopped and then he announced, "Gather close folks and hear the good news. Our festivities are complete, for we are going to have a wedding."

A sacred silence stole over the crowd. Charlie studied all around . . . every face was beautiful with a sweet expression of approval. He slipped his dark glasses off, and into his pocket. Now I could see the light in his dark blue eyes. They were fearless and mellowed by their friendship . . . The minister read from the Bible, spoke our names and listened to the words, "I do." The reverent expression on each face never changed. The ceremony ended. They passed a large golden goblet from which each one drank. Charlie asked, "And what may this be?" The minister answered softly, with a gentle smile on his lips, "It's a potion of love." Every face simultaneously broke into a broad smile. They all surrounded us and insisted that we stay for the feast. We couldn't have slipped away . . . We really didn't want to leave these dear people.

We stayed with them the entire day. We went with them into the lush fields and slopes of their enchanting village. We picked flowers and roamed the meadows with these wonderful folks until we dropped exhausted on a soft bed of yellow wild flowers. The earth was warm, our bodies were hot. The chilly air awakened us. The long shadow told us that our first lovely day was coming to a close. Charlie tenderly reminded me, "We'd better rush and find a place to live."

We rose and hurried back through the meadows and hills. With every step and breath, Charlie seemed to grow more virile. He would leap upon a ledge and reach down and pull me up, as if I had no weight. It was like being born again into a world's new spring. We returned to the church to pick up our things. Just to the left of the church, almost hidden by trees, we saw a big circular plaza or village center. It was almost completely surrounded by colorful two-story buildings. In the middle of this brick plaza was a fountain, where we found two villagers sitting. Charlie inquired about lodgings. They both pointed to a red house saying, "Go to Mr. Petros. He will be glad to see you and help you."

A little boy of about seven answered the door and in a stammering voice said, "I'm Nnnnn . . . ic Ppppetros. I'll call my father." Mr. Petros appeared. He filled the doorway. He was a tall, dark and powerful man but kindly. He was unusually nice to Charlie and me. He seemed to want us to have the best. He gave us the house right next to his and it had the very best view of the "Center." Little Nic took us to our door and like a little gentleman unlocked our door, turned on the lights and then bowed to the floor saying, "M..m..m..uch happiness."

Charlie and I stood for a moment watching our little friend depart. The child had made us feel so welcome. Charlie exclaimed, "What a wistful, loving expression in that boy's eyes. He warmed my heart." Then we literally bounded into the house. We couldn't wait to explore our new—our first home. They must have known we were coming. The fire-place was glowing, the ice-box was filled with food and fruits of bright colors. It was all too good to be untrue. We climbed the stairs to our bedroom . . . and to the stars for we could have reached out our window and touched the heavens. The night had fallen but the darkness and the light seemed both alike here. There was something magic about our new-found home.

From our bed we could see a slice of silvery moon. As we laid there so close, staring at the moon, no sound could be heard but the racing of our hearts. When we spoke, our words had very little meaning. He said, still gazing at the heavens, "Honey . . . moon." I hardly took note of the words, the silence was so powerful. My being was waiting for the touch of his hand on my heart. I simply asked, not really wanting a reply, "I wonder . . . what . . . honey . . . moon means?" He touched me. His hands caressed me all over. The silence of the room was filled with the pounding of our emotion, our passion. Finally he answered with a question, "What . . . what means?" He kissed me tenderly. I couldn't remember my question. He grabbed me fiercely and held me close. Now we were silent . . . silently conversing. Rapidly he was declaring, "I love you . . . I love you . . ." And I was murmuring, "I love you too . . . I love you. The stillness continued, yet we were telling and hearing . . . all. At long last we were understanding . . . knowing each other. The silence continued until we had said everything. We had no secrets . . . we were one. Our breathlessness had yielded to a sweet calm.

Our love was so complete. It filled our home, but that was not the boundary. It was unselfish and extended out to every one of the villagers. Charlie delighted in studying the people. He wanted to know what made them so wonderful. He searched their thoughts and took notes of their deeds. He said, "Here are worthy souls."

He looked and found real talent in everyone. He would happily say, "There is genius in all of you." And they seemed to respond to his words. Industriously he'd spend his days trying to bring these gifts and talents to the surface. He was enriching their whole lives. He became their counsellor. In fact, they started speaking of him as their teacher. At last, they endearingly named him "Teacher." Later they called him just "Teach."

I would watch Charlie from my window which looked down onto the "Center." There I could see him teaching little Nic Petros how to make tiny boats and other toys. Nic's interesting display showed real artistry and attracted many buyers, including Charlie. This gave Nic confidence and manliness.

But this day . . . he kneeled down at Charlie's feet and tearfully pleaded, "Pl . . . pl . . . pl . . . ease . . . h..h..help me to speak, as other b..b..boys?" This cry for help touched a responsive chord in Charlie's heart and his great desire became to rid this child of this affliction. I could hear him say to Nic, "Don't be afraid! I will help you . . . I will!" I could see a soft smile steal over the face of Nic. He relaxed. He believed.

Thereafter, Charlie devoted his time and strength to this child. He not only gave him assurance in selling and management, he tutored him in his speech. The little fellow would imitate Charlie and gradually, although it seemed quite suddenly, Nic spoke out clearly and with certainty. Love had melted away fear, for Nic loved his teacher and Charlie loved his pupil. It was Nic who started everyone calling Charlie "Teach."

So Charlie became the village professor alright. He showed the man in the street a quicker way to clean the fountain and drain it. The children and adults gathered around him to learn. He taught them new dances and songs. Some became proficient in tap routines.

But the dramatic group was the most appreciated by the community and by the actors themselves. The whole town turned out for the play. It was staged at the corner of the Plaza. The pantomime was superb and the few lines were excellent. It was like a ballet. Charlie had chosen the most fascinating and handsome chap to play the leading role, that of an artist. This painter was in quest of the perfect model for his masterpiece.

The stage, in the opening scene, was filled with the loveliest maids of the town. All were dressed up in dainty dresses and their looks were adorned with bright ribbons and shiny curls. They were looking their smartest. The discriminating painter strutted like a great ballet dancer from one applicant to another, carefully looking over each one. Each beautiful girl did an enchanting bit of acting and dancing in her own enticing individual way. But . . . no one would do. He pleads with open arms, "Is there no one else?" The manager steps forward and again points to his pretty girls.

The artist despondently starts to leave . . . the strut is gone, his head is bowed. But he stops abruptly, his shoulders slowly straighten. He has noticed a shy young girl standing in the rear, off to the side. Her plain soft dress clings softly to her body, no bows or curls adorn her head. There is no self-assurance flashing from her eyes. Why has he stopped? Her sensitive, unearthy expression has caught his eye.

The princely artist whirls himself about and comes close to her. He beckons to her. But she is still. He says in a low tone, "Come here child." Only her eyes move to the side, then to the other. She cannot believe he means her. But he extends his graceful strong hand to her and steps directly toward her.

She is immobile. But he gently leads her to the front of the stage and lifts her easily and gracefully onto a high pedestal, near his easel. He steps back to study her. The other girls start laughing softly, but he waves them away. They all steal from the stage one by one . . . silently. The laughter has gone.

Alone now with the girl, he moves her head about to let the light play upon her features. She appears very plain. The audience at this point is surely saying, "Why has he chosen her? The others were prettier. Her hair is pinned back too tightly and her ears are a little prominent." She has kept her eyes downcast since coming forward. She has no expression. The villagers are of one accord and we hear off-stage, "She has never been thought of . . . as even pretty."

But the artist placed her head and her body in a graceful position, she became more womanly. His lighting brought out the perfect symmetry of her features. Then he reached up and deftly took a pin from her hair. Her dark tresses fell loosely around her face and shoulders. Gently he removed her waist and draped her bare shoulders with an orchid scarf. She was quite beautiful. The artist took her delicate hand, and just before he placed a flower in it, he raised her fingertips to his lips.

He tenderly kissed her hand and placed it artistically near her face. She became alive. His kiss had awakened her. She looked up . . . her wondrous eyes opened wide. He handed her a mirror. She slowly turned and hesitatingly glanced into it. Quickly she turned full face to the audience. Now we could see her realize what the audience had already discovered.

Her face shone with radiant joy. She looked into the mirror again and breathed, "I'm . . . you have made me . . . lovely . . . I'm beautiful!" "Hold it," shouted the artist as he backed away to his easel. He picked up his brush hurriedly, looked deep into the enchanting eyes of his precious model and stood still . . . the ballet was ended. The curtains closed on this masterpiece of beauty.

After a few moments of complete silence . . . the audience burst into applause. The curtains opened . . . the still picture slowly came to life. The artist extended his arms to his model. He leaned toward her and lifted her high above his head. Slowly she descended on his body until their lips met . . . When the applause subsided, they parted and strolled hand in hand up stage . . . and made their exit.

But the applause continued. The crowds started yelling, "Bravo . . . Teach . . . Teach." Finally Charlie appeared in the center of the stage and came directly forward. The people went crazy. All the cast joined him and formed a line on either side. One by one they drifted off and again Charlie was alone. This time the people jumped up on the stage and cheered. The last I could see of Charlie was his big smile, he was so hidden by his admirers.

That evening while we were watching our "honey-moon" arise in the sky, he said, "I hope nothing ever enters 'Our Garden.' I have found happiness where I least expected. Not in a career or fame but in loving and being loved. Our love has such great grace, it overflows in my heart and includes even the least of our town-folks . . . yes . . . the whole world." He spoke with emotion . . . more like a boy . . . than an adult. Each day he appeared younger to me. His love . . . his caresses were stronger . . . yet always gentle. He kissed the hairs of my head . . . he closed my eyes with his lips. He loved me from the tip of my head down to my toes. Charlie was an artist at loving. He understood a woman. I felt so desired and so desirous . . .

Yet his love was so spiritual and pure. It left no regrets. He was so unselfish, unearthy. Still this did not weaken our romance . . . it strengthened it. It was always new . . . renewed. I understood then how enduring and satisfying is a true and honest feeling and how fleeting and unfulfilling is selfishness and deceit. What a cheat is anything that dopes our senses and steals from us the keen enjoyment of each other. Smoking, drinking and narcotics . . . how pitiful are their promises. These sweet people had not been taken in by their lies. Charlie whispered, "We've found the truth in 'Our Garden' and it's fun . . . real fun."

45

Bright and early, the town-folks were busy gathering flowers and decorating the Plaza. We were sure it was some important day for a celebration. We didn't know what or why . . . we just joined in the fun as usual . . .

We gathered flowers, made garlands and helped beautify the large wooden table which was placed almost under our windows. Soon the table was piled high with fruits and food. It looked like the feasts of olden days. Musicians were seated around the fountain. All came to attention. A horn sounded and from every direction the villagers started streaming in from the fields and from their houses to take their places. They all stepped and moved in time to the soft-playing music.

A gesture and the melody stopped. Mr. Petros raised his son little Nic up and put him on top of the table. Charlie and I were delighted. He whispered happily, "The celebration is for my little Nic . . . how nice." Charlie's little student said in a clear unhesitating manner, "We are attempting, in a small way today, to show our gratitude to one in our midst who has made each one of us feel . . . necessary . . . needed and loved. He has taught us to use our talents . . . that we knew not of. He has inspired us, encouraged us to add to these talents. Today we want to pay our tribute to him. You all know who it is.

He jumped down from the table without saying another word and rushed over to Charlie. We were so surprised! Nic stood on his tip-toes and whispered into Charlie's ear, "Will you please close your eyes . . . real tight . . . for a moment?" Then he turned to me and said sweetly, "And you too . . . please." We both did as we were coaxed to do.

Then in one big chorus, the whole township yelled, "Surprise . . . surprise!" I saw Charlie open one eye and peek . . . then he opened both eyes . . . wide. His mouth dropped open when he saw a huge rope strung from top to bottom with flowers and gifts, drop from our upstairs window, down onto the table in front of him.

Nic jumped upon the table again and spoke for the congregation. "To-night we want you . . . Charlie . . . to pull this rope up into your home. On it is tied a small gift of gratitude from every member of this community. May it bring joy to you and yours, for you will be pulling at the heart-strings of our love . . . all hail." All shouted, "To our Teach . . . our beloved Teach." It grew louder and louder . . . "Teach . . . Teach . . ."

They lifted Charlie high onto their shoulders and started circling around the table in time with the animated music. Charlie was excited and radiantly happy. He waved kisses to each one as he was whirled along, faster and faster. The music grew in intensity. Even the dogs joined in and barked loudly and darted around quickly under foot. My head was bursting with excitement and joy for Charlie. I backed away. I wanted to drink in the whole scene of smiling faces.

But I was stopped abruptly by strange voices. I turned quickly and saw two unfamiliar men. One was very tall and slender, he appeared to be a business man. The other fellow was short and stout. He was a coarse-appearing man. Both of their faces were stern. What a contrast with those around them.

As they spoke to the villagers, I could see their smiles leave. My heart chilled. "Who are these men? What could they be saying?" I asked myself. The town folks didn't seem to know these men, nor would they answer their questions. They just shrugged their shoulders and stared.

This infuriated the men. They spoke with animation to each other and they shouted to the crowd. They shook their fists at the people and threatened them. But each person slowly moved his head side to side and said softly, "No." The music slowed . . . then ceased. The laughter and singing stopped.

Now I could hear their harsh words to the villagers, "You'd better tell us . . . if Charlie Chaplin lives here . . . or you'll be in deep trouble!" They waited . . . then screamed, "You stupid things . . . I don't think you've ever heard of him or who he is." I was as bewildered as my friends. I was choking with emotion. One question followed another, "Do these dear ones know Charlie as the famous actor . . . Charlie Chaplin? Or are they pretending?"

Mr. Petros stood tall above the others in all ways. He was aware of more than anyone ever realized. His slightest glance was an order to the locals. The men approached Petros. Almost at the same time, two lines of humanity formed solidly on either side of him. Charlie could not be seen.

The men now started questioning Mr. Petros, but they lowered their voices in his presence. "Do you know the famous comedian, Charlie Chaplin? . . . Could you tell us . . . if he . . . is living here?" they inquired politely. Calmly Mr. Petros repeated, "Mr. Chap..p..lin? No . . . there is no one here called Mr. Cha..p..lin." He nodded to his left . . . then to the right. With one accord . . . they all silently confirmed his words.

Mr. Petros quickly dismissed the whole thing and asked, with a big smile, "Will you please join us in our feast? You must be hungry." But just as quickly the taller man spoke out, "No . . . no . . . we're here for one thing . . . Mr. Charles Chaplin . . . not to eat and drink." He took a badge and shoved it under Mr. Petros' nose, but he seemed unimpressed.

The short fellow turned to his companion and said, "I don't think we'll get any place with this man." The tall one answered in a stern voice, "Go get her!" At that command, he whirled around and came directly over to me and said roughly, "You'd better come with me!" Thoughts of fear and confusion gripped me. I followed the bully as if I'd been suddenly hypnotized. I wanted to yell out but I couldn't.

When we reached the tall man, I could hear a low rumbling noise start and spread rapidly throughout the crowd. The two men grew tense and so did their hold on me. I wanted to scream, "... Charlie ..." but I dare not. The tall one said caustically, "Hurry your step." The three of us started walking towards the street that leads through the town to the bus stop. The thunder of the crowd had flashed to a roar at our backs.

At this point, the tall man gave a nod to his friend. He stopped. Swiftly he turned on the crowd and covered them with a gun. Then he grimly shouted, "You all stay ... stay where you are ... not one more step ... and you'd better believe me!" Mr. Petros, topping his command shrieked, as if to the house-tops, "They're ... taking ... Georgia away." Everyone joined in roaring, "GEORGIA ... GEORGIA ..."

Charlie broke through the crowds and came running to me. Soberly he demanded, "take your hands off her." The men quickly released my arms and grabbed Charlie. But he broke from them and threw his arms around me, and held me to him saying, "I won't let them take you ... I won't." Then he turned and faced the town people and said tenderly, pleadingly, "Dear ones, go back! I implore you. I beg you, don't endanger yourselves. Stay where you are ... please? ... please?"

Holding me tightly, he pleaded passionately, "Dearest, do this for me ... please go back with these people ... then I'll know you are safe." The men pulled at his arm saying, "Hurry it up!" I cried out, "Charlie I won't ... I can't leave you. I want to go with you ... I must ... I must." He took me tenderly and held me far away from him. The tears rushed into my eyes. Charlie said, "Georgia honey, don't cry ... it hurts me so. You know nothing can keep us apart. Where is your faith dear?" I managed to whisper, "I'll try ... but what is it? What do they want?"

He just shrugged his shoulders helplessly and answered, "Who knows ... who knows ..." He smiled bravely and waved a kiss ... his lips were moving ... but I could not hear him. As they took him away, I became hysterical. He was gone! I cried out, "Charlie ... Charlie." It became like a nightmare. I couldn't bear it. I called, "Charlie . . . Charlie." The crowds were mute . . . they had vanished . . . only a dog barked sharply, savagely, fiercely. I yelled louder. I screamed. I shrieked . . . so loudly . . . I woke . . . I woke myself up . . .

It had been a dream! It had all been a dream . . . a dream! All of it had been a dream!

46

My mother and sisters were standing over me as I lay limp in my bed. Tears of gratitude were pouring down their faces. I knew they were tears of joy for they were smiling. "Why are . . . they smiling?" I asked myself. As if from a great distance I could hear mother say, "Thank goodness, she is . . . at last . . . awake!"

I could hear a dog barking . . . loudly. Slowly, I raised my hands over my ears. My sister quickly went to the window and I heard her say, "Whitie, stop barking . . . Georgia is awake . . . she's awake . . . thank heavens . . . and thank you Whitie . . . thank you . . . you are a precious doggie."

The noise stopped. Everyone stood over me . . . gazing. I could discern their radiant faces . . . or was I still dreaming? My mother hummed a familiar tune as she rushed from the room to get some food for me. I could hear them saying, "Now, maybe she'll eat. Custard . . . and milk . . . what else can we get her? It's a miracle! . . . that's what it is! She was in such a long . . . long coma."

My great experience . . . my wonderful dream had been so vivid, so real. Now this awakening . . . this whole thing seemed far more like a dream. The aura of my precious trip hovered about me. I felt enriched. I had lived a lifetime of complete fulfillment. Now, nothing mattered. I had a secret. My folks didn't know. They would never know.

During the following days I returned to my dream again and again. I lived it over many, many times. No one knew. It was child-like I know . . . that is, keeping it a secret . . . but I didn't want to share this experience with anyone . . . until now.

It was my secret, my retreat, where I could find romance and beauty. I found fulfillment in "my garden."

After a period of love and care, I timidly went forth. I tried to join the world once again. Friends lovingly invited me to their parties. But I still seemed so apart. Gradually, I became accustomed to it all. I met many attractive men . . . attractive men? They were all fashioned after the Hollywood "Mr. Chaplin." However this attractive personality . . . no longer appealed to me. I had been cured. My experience with him had been enough. I no longer wanted that type near me. The years of one long nightmare with him was enough.

But that wonderful dream with Charlie I wanted to repeat. I watched for a "Charlie" to appear. But I could not find him. I tried . . . I tried . . . but I could not adjust. My sojourn into that ideal dream world was too fresh in my memory. I retreated back into a shell. I couldn't buy anything that had been offered me. Everything seemed tarnished. I wasn't seeing correctly, but . . . through a glass darkly. My world was grey . . . no black . . . even the light . . . it was cold and chilling. I stayed alone for days, weeks, months. Then one day I fearfully, haltingly ventured out for a short walk. My past was like a fog, heavy with lead. I trudged forth into my future as though through deep sand.

Through my hazy vision . . . I vaguely noticed a man . . . walking briskly toward me. I cast my eyes down and turned my head away. The footsteps stopped suddenly and I heard a voice saying, "Hi . . . Hello, Georgia." Then a question, "Is that you Georgia?" I looked up . . . it was Fred . . . Fred, the man in the wheelchair who had been given only a few months to live . . . My mouth dropped open!

He spoke again softly, "Georgia, I hardly knew you. You look so delicate. Are you alright?" I regained my voice and said, "Fred . . . Fred, are you alright? What about you? The last time we met I hardly knew you. You were in a wheelchair . . . I'm alright . . . but . . . tell me . . . what about you . . . I can't believe my eyes . . . please, please, tell me everything?"

He seemed to sense a deep need, a yearning to hear of something good. He answered lovingly, "Come, sit down. I know this old brick fence isn't too comfortable, but what I'm about to tell is . . ." I was so eager to hear what he had to say. I couldn't quite understand my keen anticipation. He said joyously, "I'm not the same man you last saw. I'm a new man, completely whole . . . I was healed." I asked, "Did the physician say so?" He answered, "Yes, the Great Physician said so." "Please explain! I do not follow you," I implored. He continued, "You know I was never religious. I could never love a God who sent all these calamities on his creation. One day in my darkest hour, a friend, . . . a true friend introduced me to the real God whose name is Love. That's how he put it . . . 'Fred meet the true God who is infinitely loving and loves you and is bestowing health and all good into your consciousness and being.' Georgia he went on like this for an hour and suddenly I felt strong and well. My limbs strengthened and I stood upright. It was a miracle, a marvel. I didn't understand then but I've since tried hard to make it my own. A knowledge of God that is a science and Christian . . . Christian Science."

He talked at length . . . for over an hour. His voice was beautiful, it was like music to me. I took his hand and thanked him again and again. When I arose to leave I felt light as feather. I walked home, as if skating on ice. His glorious experience filled me with a new desire. Although I couldn't quote one sentence he had said I felt filled with a message. I had a purpose now.

When I reached home, I had no desire to crawl back into that shell I'd been in. I wanted to greet my neighbors . . . I wanted to share my joy. Even my dear mother who was out in the yard remarked, "Georgia, where have you been? The walk has done you good. You are radiant and appear stronger." I laughed and said, "Isn't that funny? I was about to say that I've never seen you look so well." We threw our arms around each other and then she said a strange thing, "You know, you seem so enriched by this whole experience." She smiled and added,

"You're your old self again." But I knew as the days passed, I wasn't being my "old self" as mother said. I felt new, a new self. I was more friendly. I felt what Will Rogers must have experienced when he said, "I've never met a man I couldn't like."

Then I recalled how Charlie, the beloved "Teacher," saw in each one of those villagers, an individual with talent and grace. What was more, they responded to his vision of them and performed. But this was part of my secret, my precious dream. This became . . . sort of a pattern for me. I forgot that old self and thought of others. As so many others have experienced, it was like being born again. I felt beautiful and young inside.

When I went to parties now . . . I found more of "Charlie" in men and less of "Mr. Chaplin." The fellows I met seemed to respond to my vision of them . . . full of honor and gentle qualities. I now realized if I was going to meet nice people it had to begin with me. It wasn't long before it happened. It follows as the night the day . . . I found charming and nice companions.

The other evening, one of these attractive gentlemen took me dining and dancing. A group of twelve were seated near us. As my friend and I were enjoying our dinner and dancing, my companion said, "Have you noticed how that group keep staring at you?" I answered, "No, I haven't noticed anyone but you. I'm having so much fun dancing with you. You must have been a professional."

Then he said seriously, "I wish it were not just my dancing that pleased you about me. I wish that you cared for me in every way . . . then maybe you'd say 'Yes' . . . Georgia." I was silent. He continued, "How many suitors must have said these same words and how many times . . . have you said 'No'? Tell me?" He came to the point and asked, "Why have you never married?" I thought, "I have been married . . . but it was only a dream . . . that's true." I had to be truthful so I answered as if I were telling him a secret, "I met my ideal and . . . but . . ." He inquired, "Yes . . . but what? Where is he?" I laughed and pointed to my heart.

When we got up to leave, one from the group of twelve came over and asked in front of my friend, "Georgia Hale?" I answered, "Yes." He asked, "May I have your autograph?" He was quickly joined by his companions who all asked, "May we have your signature? We all loved you so much with Charlie Chaplin in *The Gold Rush*." My friend stood silent, looking inquiringly at me. I busily signed my name for each one of the twelve. This was not new for me. It happens frequently and always whenever I attend a showing of *The Gold Rush*.

But for my friend this was something new. He said "Georgia . . . Hale! You couldn't have been in that picture . . . with Chaplin. You are so young." I smiled and said, "You're very kind to say that." He insisted, "I'm not being kind but truthful." I couldn't help but smile at his . . . bewilderment? How flimsy is this thing called human love! His expression was comical. It made me laugh out loud. He stammered, "Georgia, darling, I don't care about your past . . . nor anything pertaining to it . . ."

I had to interrupt him. I said clearly, "But I do care about my past and everything pertaining to it. I love it! I love that moment a beam of light flooded my dark world . . . and it never left. It's with me right now. I don't want to forget it, nor the man who turned on that light . . . Charlie Chaplin."

* * * * * * * * * *

Filmography

Note: Georgia's earliest screen appearences went uncredited.

THE ENEMIES OF WOMEN

Cosmopolitan Productions. *Dist* Goldwyn Distributing Corp. ca 15 Apr 1923. Si; b&w. 35 mm. 11 reels, 10,501 ft.

Dir Alan Crosland. *Scen* John Lynch. *Photog* Ira Morgan. *Sets* Joseph Urban *Prod Mgr* John Lynch. *Cost* Gretl Urban.

Cast: Lionel Barrymore (*Prince Lubimoff*), Alma Rubens (*Alicia*), Pedro De Cordoba (*Atilio Castro*), Gareth Hughes (*Spadoni*), Gladys Hulette (*Vittoria*), William Thompson (*Colonel Marcos*), William Collier Jr. (*Gaston*), Mario Majeroni (*Duke de Delille*), Betty Boulton (*Alicia's maid*), Madame Jean Brindeau (*Madame Spadoni*), Ivan Linow (*terrorist*), Paul Panzer (*Cossack*).

THE TEMPLE OF VENUS

Fox Film Corp. 29 Oct 1923. Si; b&w. 35 mm. 7 reels, 6,695 ft.

Pres by William Fox. *Dir* Henry Otto. *Story-Scen* Henry Otto, Catherine Carr. *Photog* Joe August.

Cast: William Walling (*Denis Dean*), Mary Philbin (*Moira*), Mickey McBan (*Mickey*), Alice Day (*Peggy*), David Butler (*Nat*

Harper), William Boyd (*Stanley Dale*), Phyllis Haver (*Constance Lane*), Leon Barry (*Phil Greyson*), Celeste Lee (*Venus*), Señorita Consuella (*Thetis*), Robert Klein (*Neptune*), Marilyn Boyd (*Juno*), Frank Keller (*Jupiter*), Lorraine Eason (*Echo*), Helen Vigil (*Diana*).

RENO

Goldwyn Pictures. *Dist* Goldwyn-Cosmopolitan Distributing Corp. 1 Dec 1923. Si; b&w. 35 mm. 7 reels, 6,612 ft.

Dir-Writ Rupert Hughes. *Photog* John J. Mescall.

Cast: Helene Chadwick (*Mrs. Emily Dysart Tappan*), Lew Cody (*Roy Tappan*), George Walsh (*Walter Heath*), Carmel Myers (*Mrs. Dora Carson Tappan*), Dale Fuller (*Aunt Alida Kane*), Hedda Hopper (*Mrs. Kate Norton Tappan*), Kathleen Key (*Yvette, the governess*), Rush Hughes (*Jerry Dysart, Emily's brother*), Marjorie Bonner (*Marjory Towne*), Richard Wayne (*Arthur Clayton*).

Note: Working title: *Law Against Law.*

NO MORE WOMEN

Associated Authors. *Dist* Allied Producers and Distributors. 18 Jan 1924. Si; b&w. 35 mm. 6 reels, 6,186 ft.

Pres by Frank Woods, Thompson Buchanan, Elmer Harris, Clark W. Thomas. *Prod-Writ* Elmer Harris. *Dir* Lloyd Igraham. *Mus Synop* James C. Bradford. *Casting Dir* Horace Williams.

Cast: Matt Moore (*Peter Maddox*), Madge Bellamy (*Peggy Van Dyke*), Kathleen Clifford (*Daisy Crenshaw*), Clarence Burton (*"Beef" Hogan*), George Cooper (*Tex*), H. Reeves-Smith (*Howard Van Dyke*), Stanhope Wheatcroft (*Randolph Parker*), Don (*herself, a dog*).

BY DIVINE RIGHT

Grand-Asher Distributing Corp. *Dist* Film Booking Offices of America. 17 Feb 1924 . Si; b&w. 35mm. 7 reels, 6,885 ft.

Pres by Harry Asher. *Dir* R.William Neill. *Scen* Josef von Sternberg. *Adapt* Florence Hein. *Photog* Ray June.

Cast: Mildred Harris (*The Girl*), Anders Randolf (*Trent, "The Boss"*), Elliott Dexter (*Austin Farrol, "The Prince"*), Sidney Bracey (*The Hireling*), Jeanne Carpenter (*The Trent baby*), Grace Carlyle (*Mrs. Trent*), De Witt Jennings (*"Tug" Wilson*).

Note: Reviewed in late 1923 as *The Way Men Love*, in 7451 ft.

FOR SALE

Associated First National Pictures. 15 June 1924. Si; b&w. 35 mm. 8 reels, 7,840 ft.

Pers Supv-Story Earl Hudson. *Dir* George Archainbaud. *Ed Dir* Marion Fairfax *Scen* Fred Stanley. *Photog* T.D. McCord. *Architecture* Milton Menasco. *Film Ed* George McGuire.

Cast: Claire Windsor (*Eleanor Bates*), Adolphe Menjou (*Joseph Hudley*), Robert Ellis (*Allan Penfield*), Mary Carr (*Mrs. Harrison Bates*), Tully Marshall (*Harrison Bates*), John Patrick (*Cabot Stanton*), Vera Reynolds (*Betty Twombly-Smith*), Jule

Power (*Mrs. Twombly-Smith*), Lou Payne (*Mr. Twombly-Smith*).

A SELF-MADE FAILURE

J.K.McDonald Productions. *Dist* Associated First National Pictures. 29 Jun 1924. Si; b&w. 35 mm. 8 reels, 7345 ft.

Pres. by J.K. McDonald. *Dir* William Beaudine. *Scen* Violet Clark, Lex Neal, John Grey. *Adapt* Tamar Lane. *Story* J.K. McDonald. *Photog* Ray June, Barney McGill. *Film Ed* H.P. Bretherton, Beth Matz.

Cast: Ben Alexander (*Sonny*), Lloyd Hamilton (*Breezy*), Matt Moore (*John Steele*), Patsy Ruth Miller (*Alice Neal*), Mary Carr (*Grandma Neal*), Sam De Grasse (*Cyrus Cruikshank*), Chuck Reisner (*Spike Malone*), Victor Potel (*Pokey Jones*), Alta Allen (*Mrs. Spike Malone*), Joel McCrea (*Verman*).

Note: Working title: *The Goof.*

THE TOMBOY

Chadwick Pictures. 26 Dec 1924. Si; b&w. 35 mm. 6 reels.

Dir David Kirkland. *Story* Frank Dazey. *Photog* Milton Moore.

Cast: Herbert Rawlinson (*Aldon Farwell*), Dorothy Devore (*Tommy Smith*), James Barrows (*Henry Smith*), Lee Moran (*Hiram, the sheriff*), Helen Lynch (*Sweetie Higgins*), Lottie Williams (*Mrs. Higgins*), Harry Gribbon (*Rugby Blood*), Virginia True Boardman (*Mrs. Smith*).

Note: The Standard Casting Directory for 1924 lists as one of Georgia's screen credits the *Tom Boy Series*, a somewhat misleading title, as no such series was made. The only known feature made during 1924 by an independent studio is the one listed above. It seems unlikely that having appeared as an ingenue in several other features that year, she would have returned to making shorts.

THE SALVATION HUNTERS

Academy Photoplays. *Dist* United Artists. ca7 Feb 1925. Si; b&w. 3mm. 6 reels, 5,930 ft.

Dir-Story-Scen Josef von Sternberg. *Photog* Edward Gheller. *Prod Asst* George Ruric, Robert Chapman.

Cast: George K. Arthur (*The Boy*), Georgia Hale (*The Girl*), Bruce Guerin (*The Child*), Otto Matieson (*The Man*), Nellie Bly Baker (*The Woman*), Olaf Hytten (*The Brute*), Stuart Holmes (*The Gentleman*).

THE GOLD RUSH

Charles Chaplin Productions. *Dist* United Artists. 16 Aug 1925. Si; b&w. 35 mm. 9reels, 8,555ft.

Prod-Dir-Writ Charlie Chaplin. *Photog* Roland H. Totheroh. *Camera* Jack Wilson. *Tech Dir* Charles D. Hall. *Ass Dir* Charles F. Reisner, Harry d'Abbadie d'Arrast. *Prod Mgr* Alfred Reeves.

Cast: Charlie Chaplin (*The Lone Prospector*), Mack Swain (*Big Jim McKay*), Tom Murray (*Black Larsen*), Georgia Hale (*The Girl*), Betty Morrissey (*The Girl's Friend*), Malcolm Waite (*Jack Cameron*), Henry Bergman (*Hank Curtis*).

THE RAINMAKER

Famous Players-Lasky. *Dist* Paramount Pictures. 10 May 1926. Si; b&w. 35mm. 7 reels, 6,055 ft.

Pres by Adolph Zukor, Jesse L. Lasky. *Dir* Clarence Badger. *Scen* Hope Loring, Louis Duryea Lighton. *Photog* H. Kinley Martin.

Cast: William Collier, Jr. (*Bobby Robertson*), Georgia Hale (*Nell Wendell*), Ernest Torrence (*Mike*), Brandon Hurst (*Doyle*), Joseph Dowling (*Father Murphy*), Tom Wilson (*Chocolate*), Martha Maddox (*head nurse*), Charles K. French (*hospital doctor*), Jack Richardson (*western doctor*), Melbourne MacDowell (*Benson*).

THE GREAT GATSBY

Famous Players-Lasky. *Dist* Paramount Pictures. 8 Nov 1926. Si; b&w. 35mm. 8 reels, 7296 ft.

Pres by Adolph Zukor, Jesse L. Lasky. *Dir* Herbert Brenon. *Screenplay* Becky Gardiner. *Adapt* Elizabeth Meehan. *Photog* Leo Tover. *Asst Dir* Ray Lissner.

Cast: Warner Baxter (*Jay Gatsby*), Lois Wilson (*Daisy Buchanan*), Neil Hamilton (*Nick Carraway*), Georgia Hale (*Myrtle Wilson*), William Powell (*George Wilson*), Hale Hamilton (*Tom Buchanan*), George Nash (*Charles Wolf*), Carmelita Geraghty (*Jordon Baker*), Eric Blore (*Lord Digby*), "Gunboat" Smith (*Bert*), Claire Whitney (*Catherine*).

MAN OF THE FOREST

Famous Players-Lasky. *Dist* Paramount Pictures. 27 Dec 1926. Si; b&w. 35mm. 6 reels, 5,187 ft.

Pres by Adolph Zukor, Jesse L. Lasky. *Assoc Prod* B.P. Schulberg. *Dir* John Waters. *Screenplay* Fred Myton. *Adapt* Max Marcin *Photog* C. Edgar Schoenbaum.

Cast: Jack Holt (*Mike Dale*), Georgia Hale (*Nancy Raynor*), El Brendel (*Horace Pipp*), Warner Oland (*Clint Beasley*), Tom Kennedy (*sheriff*), George Fawcett (*Nancy's uncle*), Ivan Christie (*Snake Anson*), Bruce Gordon (*Jim Wilson*), Vester Pegg (*Moses*), Willard Cooley (*deputy sheriff*), Guy Oliver (*first deputy*), Walter Ackerman (*second deputy*), Duke R. Lee (*Martin Mulvery*).

HILLS OF PERIL

Fox Film Corp. 1 May 1927. Si; b&w. 35mm. 5 reels, 4,983 ft.

Pres by William Fox. *Dir* Lambert Hillyer. *Scen* Jack Jungmeyer. *Photog* Reginald Lyons. *Ass Dir* Ted Brooks.

Cast: Buck Jones (*Laramie*), Georgia Hale (*Ellen*), Albert J. Smith (*Rand*), Buck Black (*Grimes's boy*), William Welch (*Grimes*), Marjorie Beebe (*Sophia*), Duke Green (*Jake*), Charles Athloff (*Ezra*), Robert Kortman (*Red*).

Note: Working title: *Holy Terror.*

THE WHEEL OF DESTINY

Duke Worne Productions. *Dist* Rayart Pictures. Oct 1927. Si; b&w. 35mm. 6 reels, 5,746 or 5,869 ft.

Dir Duke Worne. *Scen* George W. Pyper. *Photog* Walter Griffen.

Cast: Forrest Stanley, Georgia Hale, Percy Challenger, Miss Du Pont, Ernest Hilliard, Sammy Blum, B. Hyman, Jack Herrick.

THE FLOATING COLLEGE (1928) 6 reels. b&w

Dir George J. Crone. *Writ* Stuart Anthony. *Titl* Paul Perez. *Photog* Harry Jackson. *Edit* Desmond O'Brien.

Cast: Sally O'Neil (*Pat Bixby*), William Collier, Jr. (*George Dewey*), Georgia Hale (*Frances Bixby*), Harvey Clark (*The Dean*), Georgie Harris (*Snug*), E.J. Ratcliffe (*Nathan Bixby*), Virginia Sale (*Miss Cobbs*).

A WOMAN AGAINST THE WORLD

Tiffany-Stahl Productions. 1 Jan 1928. Si; b&w. 35 mm. 6 reels, 5,283 ft.

Dir George Archainbaud. *Cont* Gertrude Orr. *Titl* Frederic Hatton, Fanny Hatton. *Story* Albert Shelby Le Vino. *Photog* Chester Lyons. *Set Dsgn* Burgess Beall. *Film Ed* Desmond O'Brien.

Cast: Harrison Ford (*Schulyer Van Loan*), Georgia Hale (*Carol Hill*), Lee Moran (*Bob Yates*), Harvey Clark (*city editor*), Walter Hiers (*reporter*), Gertrude Olmstead (*Bernice Crane, bride*), William Tooker (*bride's father*), Ida Darling (*bride's mother, Mrs. Crane*), Wade Boteler (*Jim Barnes, chauffeur*), Charles Clary (*warden*), Sally Rand (*Maysie Bell*), Rosemary Theby (*housekeeper*), Jim Farley (*detective*).

THE RAWHIDE KID

Universal Pictures. 29 Jan 1928. Si; b&w. 35 mm. 6 reels, 5,383 ft.

Pres by Carl Laemmle. *Dir* Del Andrews. *Cont* Arthur Statter. *Titl* Tom Reed. *Adapt* Isadore Bernstein. *Story* Peter B. Kyne. *Photog* Harry Neumann. *Art Dir* David S. Garber. *Film Ed* Rodney Hickok.

Cast: Hoot Gibson (*Dennis O'Hara*), Georgia Hale (*Jessica Silverberg*), Frank Hagney (*J. Francis Jackson*), William H. Strauss (*Simon Silverberg*), Harry Todd (*Comic*), Tom Lingham (*deputy*).

THE LAST MOMENT

Samuel Freedman— Edward M. Spitz. *Dist* Zakoro Film Corp. 15 Feb 1928. Si; b&w. 35 mm. 6 reels, 5,600 ft.

Dir-Writ Paul Fejos. *Photog* Leon Shamroy. *Film Ed* Paul Fejos.

Cast: Otto Matiesen (*The Man*), Julius Molnar, Jr. (*The Man as a Child*), Lucille La Verne (*The Innkeeper*), Anielka Elter (*A Woman*), Georgia Hale (*His Second Wife*), Isabelle Lamore (*His First Wife*), Vivian Winston (*A Woman*).

A TRICK OF HEARTS (Universal Jewel)

Universal Pictures. 18 Mar 1928. Si; b&w. 35 mm. 6 reels, 5,495 ft.

Dir Reeves Eason. *Cont* Arthur Statter. *Titl* Tom Reed. *Story* Irving Dodge. *Photog* Harry Neumann. *Film Ed* M.C. Dewar.

Cast: Hoot Gibson (*Ben Tully*), Georgia Hale (*The Girl*), Heinie Conklin (*The Crook*).

Note: Working titles: *The Horse Trader*; *Western Suffragettes.*

GYPSY OF THE NORTH

Trem Carr Productions. *Dist* Rayart Pictures. Mar or Apr 1928. Si: b&w. 6 reels, 5,813 or 5,976 ft.

Dir Scott Pembroke. *Scen* Arthur Hoerl. *Story* Howard Emmett Rogers. *Photog* Hap Depew. *Film Ed* Charles A. Post.

Cast: Georgia Hale (*Alice Culhane*), Huntley Gordon (*Steve Farrell*), Jack Dougherty (*Chappie Evans*), William Quinn (*Baptiste*), Hugh Saxon (*Davey*), Henry Roquemore (*theatre manager*), Erin La Bissoniere (*Jane*).

THE LIGHTNING WARRIOR

Mascot b&w 12 Chapters

Dir Armand Schaefer, Benjamin Kline. *Prod* Nat Levine. *Scen* Wyndham Gittens, Ford Beebe, Colbert Clark c Ernest Miller, William C. Nobles, Tom Galligan.

Cast: Rin Tin Tin, Frankie Darro, George Brent, Georgia Hale, Yakima Canutt, Kermit Maynard, Bob Kortman, Frank Brownlee.

Acknowledgments

During the year or more that I have spent shepherding Georgia Hale's memoirs from manuscript to printed page, I have been impressed by the benevolent cooperation of innumerable people to whom I have applied for information, and those on whom I have depended for support and encouragement.

My deepest appreciation must go to Herman and Helen Bessler for having entrusted to me Georgia Hale's personal papers.

To Shoji Masuzawa I should like to acknowledge a special debt of gratitude. His patience and skill helped to transform my ideas on design and layout, and without whose assistance, this book could never have been completed.

In particular, I am deeply grateful to Pam Paumier for her kindness in allowing me to select and include photographs from the Chaplin archive. These are the copyright and property of Roy Export Company Establishment.

My thanks also to Kevin Brownlow who first fired my interest in Georgia by allowing me to glimpse his copy of the typescript.

A special note of appreciation is due to Richard Gordon and the Estate of the late Raymond Rohauer for kindly giving me permission to reproduce frame enlargements of Georgia's screen-test for *City Lights*; these are from The Rohauer Collection.

In thanking those who were so generous with their time, I must acknowledge the invaluable contributions of Stephen Stearns, Alice Artzt, Bruce Lawton, Stan Tafell, and Rowna Barnett.

I also wish to acknowledge the assistance I have received from officials and staff of the following: Janet Moat, Special Collections, British Film Institute; Sam Gill and Howard Prouty, Margaret Herrick Library; Jay Katzman, Englewood Academy; Nick Posegay, Chicago Public Schools; Shari Ebert, Chicago Musical College, Roosevelt University; Betty Reid and George Matthews, CPGB Archives, London; Lindsay Henderson, IMS Trust; Scottish Borders Enterprise; Ned Comstock, Doheny Library; the staff of the Lincoln Center Library for the Performing Arts (Billy Rose Collection).

Finally, I am especially grateful to my husband, Victor, for his invaluable advice and constant support.

The work on this volume would not have been possible without these people and institutions; any faults in the volume are mine and mine alone.

Index

Page references in **bold** indicate a biographical note.

A

B

C

D

E

F

G

H

I

J

K

L

M

N

O

P

R

S

T

U

V

W

Z

About the Editor

Born in Canada, Heather Kiernan was educated at Toronto and Cambridge, England. A cultural historian and British Council recipient, Ms. Kiernan won a Scottish Film Council Award for her documentary treatment, *Chaplin: A Comedian Sees the World*. She has been a free-lance editor for the Canadian journal, *Queen's Quarterly*. Ms. Kiernan is currently at work on a study of Chaplin for a series on American Radicals.